# THE FIRST REPUBLICAN ARMY

A NATION DIVIDED:
STUDIES IN THE CIVIL WAR ERA

Orville Vernon Burton and Elizabeth R. Varon, *Editors*

# THE FIRST REPUBLICAN ARMY

## THE ARMY OF VIRGINIA AND THE RADICALIZATION OF THE CIVIL WAR

JOHN H. MATSUI

UNIVERSITY OF VIRGINIA PRESS
*Charlottesville & London*

For my father

University of Virginia Press

Printed in the United States of America on acid-free paper

*First published 2016*

9 8 7 6 5 4 3 2 1

Library of Congress Cataloging-in-Publication Data

Names: Matsui, John H., 1981– author.
Title: The first Republican army : the Army of Virginia and the radicalization of the Civil War / John H. Matsui.
Description: Charlottesville : University of Virginia Press, 2016. | Series: A nation divided: studies in the civil war era | Includes bibliographical references and index.
Identifiers: LCCN 2016012002 | ISBN 9780813939278 (cloth : alk. paper) | ISBN 9780813939285 (e-book)
Subjects: LCSH: United States. Army of Virginia. | United States—Politics and government—1861–1865. | Politics and war—United States—History—19th century. | Republican Party (U.S. : 1854– )—History—19th century. | Bull Run, 2nd Battle of, Va., 1862. | Pope, John, 1822–1892.
Classification: LCC E470.2 .M38 2016 | DDC 973.7/455—dc23
*LC record available at* http://lccn.loc.gov/2016012002

# Contents

# Illustrations

# Acknowledgments

THE GENESIS FOR this book was my undergraduate senior thesis, or namely the many conversations I had with my advisor about John Pope. James McPherson heard and read far too many attempts by a callow youth to rehabilitate General Pope. Research began while I was writing my dissertation. Thanks to funding from the William L. Clements Library I was able to turn to the library's Civil War holdings when I exhausted the archives' collections of abolitionist correspondence. My eternal gratitude goes to Brian Dunnigan, then acting director of the Clements, for permitting the slight detour.

Vernon Burton and Dick Holway believed in and began campaigning for this book's inclusion in the University of Virginia Press's A Nation Divided series while I was still a graduate student. Without them this book would not have found itself between these two covers. Sheila McMillen, Kenny Marotta, and my colleague Timothy Dowling helped me wrestle the manuscript into a readable form. Anna Kariel has been incredibly helpful in the manuscript preparation process.

My father accompanied me on one of the grand research adventures that led to this book. He flew from California to Pennsylvania to enable me to conduct research in rural Pennsylvania. We met at Swarthmore outside Philadelphia and then drove out to Carlisle and Harrisburg. I do not know what he learned while I sat in the Pennsylvania State Archives and U.S. Army Military History Institute, but we both enjoyed visiting Amish Country in Lancaster. Little did I know at that time that he was helping to acclimate me to life in rural America. This book is dedicated to him, with love.

As solitary as this project seemed in its initial research stages, historians always have good company in the archivists who preserve the manuscripts we delve through. My heartfelt thanks goes to the archivists at the Chicago Historical Society, Historical Society of Pennsylvania, Indiana Historical Society, Library of Congress, Massachusetts Historical Society, Pennsylvania State Archives, New-York Historical Society, Ohio Historical Society, Wisconsin Historical Society, and the U.S. Army Military History Institute. My gratitude also goes to the archivists at Duke University, Princeton University, Stanford University, University of California at Berkeley, and the William L. Clements Library at the University of Michigan.

The final challenge has been tracking down illustrations to enliven these pages. Anna Kariel has gone beyond the call of duty in advising a publishing tenderfoot in the ways of illustration selection. Lisa McCown of the Leyburn Library at Washington and Lee University helped me find and scan a crucial copy of *Harper's Weekly.*

# THE FIRST REPUBLICAN ARMY

# Introduction

Politics shaped military operations during the American Civil War, not least because the citizen-soldiers who fought on both sides were politically enfranchised, literate, and vocal. "Confusion to Generals who instead of winning the applause and love of a nation by daring deeds" on the battlefield pursued fame "by delay, political intrigue," and pandering to Democratic Party newspapers, a general complained from the Army of the Potomac in July 1862.[1] David Bell Birney was the son of an anti-slavery politician and expressed himself disgusted with the limited war policies of an army dominated by conservative, Democratic-leaning West Point graduates. Nowhere did politics intervene more visibly in military affairs than in Virginia, the site of—or neighbor to—both warring capitals. Centerpiece of the rival war efforts' martial manpower as well as domestic and foreign press attention, Virginia witnessed the baptism by fire of two ideologically charged Union armies in 1862, George Brinton McClellan's Democratic Army of the Potomac and the Republican Army of Virginia. At the heart of this story of political warfare and wartime politics was the Army of Virginia. During its brief existence (June–September 1862), this army's Republican generals, officers, and enlisted men pushed the Lincoln administration to destroy the Confederacy's armies, punish its civilians, and free its slaves. These goals warred with northern Democrats' desire to preserve the status quo antebellum.

*The First Republican Army* demonstrates the increasing discontent of Union citizen-soldiers and their elected officers with the intransigent white population of Virginia. Radical Republicans in Congress joined northern troops and a cadre of anti-slavery generals in the view that harsher occupation policies were needed than the limited war policies governing civil-military relations set forth by West Point–trained generals like McClellan. These Republican constituencies united in the efforts of western general John Pope and the new Army of Virginia to punish disloyal civilians and protect self-emancipated slaves in an attempt to wrest control of the war effort from conservative Democrats and moderate Republicans alike.

Northern politicians and generals could not shape war policy separately from the opinions and actions of common fighting men and their elected officers. By June 1862, many Union volunteer company and field-grade officers and enlisted men serving in Virginia disagreed with the policy of West Point–trained generals who sought to respect the property of civilians who aided Confederate forces and scorned the federal government. Contributing to the spread of this ideology was the practice of electing officers. Initially, many regimental commanders were appointed by their state governors to recruit the regiments. Those colonels in turn chose company commanders to recruit the men to fill each regiment's ten companies. These commanders' replacements, however—following resignations and death from illness or wounds—and the majority of other officers were chosen by election; as of January 22, 1861, field-grade officers were elected by their fellow officers and company-grade officers by enlisted men.[2] A significant part of the property these officers were tasked with protecting consisted of 500,000 slaves, and northern soldiers—many encountering slavery for the first time—were appalled by slavery while failing to see slaves as even potential citizens.[3] These volunteer officers—as Republican Party voters—pressed their generals and soldiers to wage war in a Republican fashion.

The democratic process by which volunteer officers were chosen to lead Civil War armies lends credence to a new kind of army study, one focusing on the political motivations and cliques of military commanders as they interacted with their internal and external foes, enlisted men, civilians, and the enslaved. Previous generations of military historians have focused on the ideological differences of the civil and military leaders of opposing nation-states. With the New Military History's emphasis on cultural, racial, and gender analysis, scholars have begun to study the conflicts within armies at war, as well as the internal divisions of wartime societies, encompassing political conflict as well as civil-military relations in occupied territories.[4]

Sharing this emphasis, this book, unlike many unit histories, does not focus on battles or even a major campaign.[5] Instead, it studies the shifting ideologies both of military and political elites and of volunteer officers and soldiers. Considering the political composition of the Army of Virginia reveals how the political ideology of volunteer officers inspired them to wage a Republican war against southern Democratic partisans-turned-rebels. This school of thought—the impact of political and racial matters on military operations—shines through in recent texts.[6]

Students of the American Civil War are familiar with the Army of Northern Virginia, the most militarily effective of the Confederacy's armies, yet the Union Army of Virginia remains largely unknown. Although a growing historiography covers the major Union and Confederate armies—their composition and battlefield performance—not a single modern work deals with this force.[7] The army is particularly understudied when compared to George McClellan's Army of the Potomac, which preceded and later assimilated its constituent parts. Not one of the Army of Virginia's three corps was commemorated with a unit history by its surviving veterans or subsequent historians, unlike the II, V, and VI corps of McClellan's army.[8] And a series of monographs on major Civil War campaigns bypasses the Army of Virginia's participation in the Second Manassas campaign.[9] Yet the Army of Virginia, small and ephemeral though it was—existing for less than three months before being merged with the Army of the Potomac and vanquished in the one major battle in its only major campaign—provides a vantage point for the study of the Republican Party's changing ideology and the ramifications of that shift for civil-military relations.[10]

The Union Army of Virginia was assembled in June 1862 from three units occupying northern Virginia and guarding Washington. Those units were organized into three corps, commanded by Franz Sigel, Nathaniel Banks, and Irvin McDowell, with John Pope overseeing the new organization of roughly fifty thousand men. The three units that became the Army of Virginia were tasked with: (1) threatening Richmond on the direct overland route from Washington; (2) safeguarding the Shenandoah Valley, an agricultural breadbasket and invasion route into Maryland and Pennsylvania; and (3) protecting the federal capital. The army's size and its defense-oriented tasks—tied to the protection of Washington—prevented its aggressive commander from taking the war to the Confederacy. Despite participating in the Second Battle of Bull Run and the Battle of Cedar Mountain, Pope's force was an army of occupation, better placed to oppress Confederate civilians than to suppress rebel field armies—and oppress them it did, led by Republican generals and with the approval of Republican politicians.

This book's contention is that the Army of Virginia was the first Republican-led army, the harbinger and, after absorption into McClellan's army, the vanguard of the pro-emancipation and punitive turn of the overall Union war effort. A majority of the army's constituents—

from commander John Pope to the lowest private—identified with the antebellum ideology of the Republican Party and radically opposed both slavery and pro-Confederate white civilians. Unlike the Army of the Potomac, the Army of Virginia was demonstrably anti-slavery from top to bottom.[11] Until the Emancipation Proclamation went into effect and African Americans formally joined the Union war effort, the Army of Virginia constituted the Republican Party-in-arms.

President Abraham Lincoln frustrated abolitionists and anti-slavery politicians by dilatory or retrograde policies regarding slavery in the first year of the war.[12] But three politically astute generals pushed Lincoln to acknowledge the relation of slavery to military efforts to preserve the Union: Benjamin F. Butler, David Hunter, and John Frémont. They had little success in 1861.

Butler, a Democratic political general from Massachusetts, designated the fugitive slaves who sought freedom within his army in May 1861 as "contraband of war." Butler officially confiscated them as useful to the enemy and worth denying to the Confederacy.[13] Although most white northerners agreed that pro- and anti-slavery politics had dragged the nation into civil war, they were not prepared to allow African Americans—even those born free—to fight for their country in 1861. They contended that it was a white man's war, just as they claimed in the antebellum decades that theirs was a white man's country. The movement of thousands of self-emancipated "contrabands" toward Union lines represented the willful action of African Americans to compel white combatants to accept their humanity and desire for freedom as factors in the war.

Lincoln accepted Butler's reasoning in the case of "contrabands" but acted decisively against the preemptive actions of other Union generals. Late in 1861, Frémont and Hunter declared the slaves of rebel masters free in Missouri, Georgia, South Carolina, and Florida.[14] Lincoln objected to emancipation on a military rather than a civil basis and rescinded the generals' decrees, to the consternation of abolitionists.[15] Convinced that slavery was the root cause of southern secession and a key bulwark to the Confederate war effort (an opinion shared by an increasing proportion of white northerners as the war dragged on), abolitionists wondered why Lincoln dithered.

By the summer of 1862, Union political and military elites waged an increasingly organized and centrally controlled campaign to coerce the rebellious states to recognize the authority of the federal government. It was as part of this campaign that John Pope was brought east after demonstrating aggressiveness in battle at Corinth, Mississippi, and achieving the nearly bloodless capture of a rebel force at Island Number Ten on the Mississippi.[16] If Lincoln and his generals sought to minimize the friction of multiple small commands by coordinating their efforts, however, they reckoned without the jealousies of existing commanders—especially McClellan, who waged a political campaign against his new rival.

A "war [raged] within the Union high command" during the summer of 1862.[17] In a broad sense, the divide was between Republicans, represented by Pope's army of Unionists, who desired the abolition of slavery and the southern way of life, and Democrats, McClellan's Unionists, who fought for a return to the status quo antebellum.[18] The stark differences between anti-slavery generals in the Army of Virginia and those in the Army of the Potomac appears most bluntly in numerical terms. Of thirty-eight army, corps, division, and brigade commanders in the three corps of the Army of Virginia in August 1862, eleven were publicly anti-slavery, including two of three corps commanders. They were John Pope, Nathaniel Banks, and Franz Sigel (corps commanders); Rufus King, Robert Schenck, and Carl Schurz (division commanders); and Henry Bohlen, Wladimir Krzyzanowski, Nathaniel McLean, Robert Milroy, and Abram Piatt (brigade commanders). The majority—Sigel, Schenck, Schurz, Bohlen, Krzyzanowski, McLean, and Milroy—were in the heavily German American I Corps. Another two I Corps brigade commanders—Julius Stahel and Alexander Schimmelfennig—might be credited as anti-slavery on the basis of their participation in the 1848 revolutions in Germany and Hungary.[19] The fifty commanders in McClellan's five corps included only two anti-slavery generals—Samuel Heintzelman and David Bell Birney (son of Kentucky-born abolitionist and former slaveholder James Birney)—both in III Corps, where only three of eight generals were West Point graduates. The other abolitionist general in McClellan's army, Oliver Howard, was recuperating from the loss of an arm at Seven Pines.

The pinnacle of the Potomac army's command was conservative. George McClellan's Democratic leanings were well known by the spring of 1862, when a Democratic member of the Joint Committee on the Conduct of the War visited McClellan's headquarters and found it swarming with politicians of the "Peace Democrat" stripe.[20] His chief-of-staff, Randolph Marcy, was—besides being McClellan's father-in-law—an avowed Democratic partisan. Marcy wrote McClellan's future wife of his wish that presidential candidate James Buchanan would "defeat the miserable set of abolitionists" headed by Republican John Frémont in 1856, "as they are most contemptible and their success would be a serious calamity" for the nation.[21]

No fewer than twenty-two of McClellan's forty-four general officers were Democrats (versus three Republicans), compared to eleven Republicans out of thirty-three generals in the Army of Virginia (opposed to three Democrats). Most of the remaining generals were apolitical West Point professionals—for instance Edwin Sumner (commander of McClellan's II Corps), a relative of Massachusetts Republican Charles Sumner—who had no known political affiliation.[22] McClellan preferred West Point alumni to political appointees; thirty-three of the Potomac army's forty-four generals present for duty on June 26 were military academy graduates, compared to fifteen of Pope's thirty-three. That less than half of Pope's generals attended West Point stood in contrast to the three-quarters predominance of academy graduates in McClellan's army.

The nearly unanimous conservatism of McClellan's generals on slavery and the conduct of the war confirmed radical suspicions. Even moderate Republicans like President Lincoln were hardly surprised at the strong Democratic showing among West Point alumni. Lincoln confessed to General Carl Schurz—responding to Schurz's complaint that too few anti-slavery Republicans were appointed general officers—that "very few of our [political] friends had a military education or were of the profession of arms." Lincoln similarly told the brother of New York's Democratic governor-elect that he "had appointed most of the officers from among Democrats because most of the West Point men were Democrats . . . and because antislavery men, being generally much akin to peace, had never interested themselves in military matters and in getting up companies, as Democrats had."[23] Indiana Republican George W. Julian estimated that four-fifths of the brigadier and major generals in the Union armies voted Democratic in 1860.[24] Loyalty to Democratic ideology extended from the top down in McClellan's army, from generals to regimental and company officers to the common soldier.

The conflict within the Union Army's high command could also be viewed as a struggle between West Point alumni and those outside of that martial circle. A more accurate way of viewing the factions might be that Democratic-leaning West Point graduates opposed an alliance of "political generals"—military amateurs but politically influential in civilian life and appointed on that basis—and Republican West Point alumni. As for political differences between the soldiers in the Army of Virginia and those of McClellan's organization, demographic origin provides a key explanation.

Both armies contained regiments from the anti-slavery strongholds of New England, upstate New York, and the northern Midwest, but a third of Pope's army was German American, concentrated in I Corps and led by German refugees from the 1848 revolutions.[25] The Army of the Potomac had a greater share of Irish immigrants in its ranks, in line with the large immigrant population in the northeastern states. A third of Pope's infantry regiments by contrast hailed from beyond the mid-Atlantic and New England regions; 90 percent of McClellan's army was composed of regiments from these Atlantic seaboard states. The men of the Army of Virginia were more representative of the population of the loyal states than any other army, and as this book shows, shared other demographic traits that accounted for that army's ideological stance. As for the antebellum regular army officers (most of them West Point graduates) who led many Union brigades, divisions, and army corps, historian William B. Skelton has demonstrated that they hailed disproportionately from elite social and religious circles.[26]

The politics of enlisted men as well as officers is evident in their writings, upon which this book draws. The voices of common soldiers preserved in letters and diary entries are a significant development in telling the history of this conflict. In addition, journalists and correspondents pervaded all levels and ranks of the Union armies. While reporters for nationally prominent papers found a way to fit in with an army, often by gaining a place at army headquarters, private soldiers wrote home—frequently using pen names—to their local papers. Journalism did not get much more democratic than this, as enlisted men and volunteer officers wrote for their home audiences with a focus on local boys and their experiences of the war.[27] Part of the lasting fascination with the American Civil War stems from the fact that, probably for the first time, a majority of the soldiers involved in a war were functionally literate. Readers of Civil War history need not rely on the word of generals and politicians for accounts of events ranging from the epic to the quotidian, essential to this study of the shifting political ideology of enlisted men and officers. Of course the spelling and grammar of many soldiers and even some officers leave much to be desired for historians seeking to decipher their letters, and thousands of soldiers were in fact illiterate. A journalist was asked by a soldier to write a letter for him on the day of the Battle of Cedar Mountain. "My dear Mary, we are going into action soon," the soldier declared, "and I send you my love. Kiss baby, and if I am not killed I will write to you after the fight." The reporter mailed the letter for the soldier but soon read the private's name on the list of those killed in action at Cedar Mountain.[28]

In addition to my selection of twenty-five general officers who served in the Army of Virginia for detailed analysis, 250 volunteer officers and soldiers were chosen to form a source base for this study. They were selected to present a demographically representative sample of the men in an army that was itself more representative of the population of white northern men who voted for Abraham Lincoln in 1860 than McClellan's Army of the Potomac. These citizen-soldiers and elected officers were picked on the basis that their manuscript letters or diaries had been deposited in a dozen major archives in Midwestern, border South, and northeastern states. The contemporary nature of their writings provide insights into their thoughts while serving with Pope, rather than being limited to reflections penned decades after the fact.

A final word about structure is warranted. The book consists of this introduction, seven chapters, and an epilogue. The first chapter establishes the political context in which the Army of Virginia was created. The second chapter presents the background, appointment, and initial policy reforms of John Pope. The third chapter deals with the challenges to cohesiveness within the army as well as its military failure and dissolution. The fourth defines the particular significance of politics in the experience of the army's generals, volunteer officers, and enlisted men. The fifth chapter demonstrates the influence of demography and the experience of occupation on the political choices of the members of Pope's army. The penultimate chapter illustrates the mix of political and other motives expressed in harsh treatment of rebellious citizens, both sanctioned and illicit, highlighting the challenges faced by the sort of revolutionary force the Army of Virginia had become. The final chapter shows how the experiences of corps brought as late reinforcements to the Army of Virginia illustrate the changing political climate.

# 1 The Origins of the Army of Virginia

THE COMMONWEALTH OF Virginia, the namesake and witness to the birth and violent death of the Army of Virginia, was the focus of domestic and international attention during the war years. If the American Civil War was won and lost west of the Appalachians, an inordinate amount of resources and manpower was expended by the U.S. and Confederate governments to conquer or defend Virginia, and understandably so. Influential members of the British and French empires debating recognition of the Confederacy looked at the struggle between North and South as largely one between Washington and Richmond over one hundred miles of Virginian land. Virginia was the most populous—in terms of black and white southerners—the most industrialized, and the most politically important Confederate state, beyond eventually playing host to the rebel capital.[1] A third of Virginians were enslaved—and another 58,000 African Americans were free—a significant potential source of labor and information to Union and Confederate armies.[2]

If in 1861 few white Americans believed that a civil war would result in death and destruction visited on civilians, lonely prophetic voices warned of devastation to come for all who supported secession, not just rebel combatants. "I judge now that large bodies of soldiers are being marshaled and encamped near you," Pennsylvanian Samuel Halsey wrote his brother. By the outbreak of civil war, Joseph Halsey had practiced law in Culpeper, Virginia, for decades. Despite his northern birth, Joseph should not expect that his "property & effects" were not "liable to the dreadful ravages incident to a cruel war."[3] "You may think your people able to withstand all the forces the North can move against you," Samuel admonished. "The hordes and vandals will devastate your fair land and mar your happiness."[4]

The Union "vandals" who threatened to "devastate" fair Virginia were split into two major "hordes" in June 1862, the month that would see the formation of the Army of Virginia. Some fifty thousand troops occupied northern Virginia, spread in three clumps from the mountains of present-day West Virginia to the Shenandoah Valley to the northern bank of the Rappahannock River (midway between the warring capitals). The bulk of the Union forces were just east of the Confederate capital; troops in George McClellan's Army of the Potomac could hear Richmond's church bells. Despite outnumbering the defenders, McClellan's host assumed a defensive position against the Confederate Army of Northern Virginia.[5]

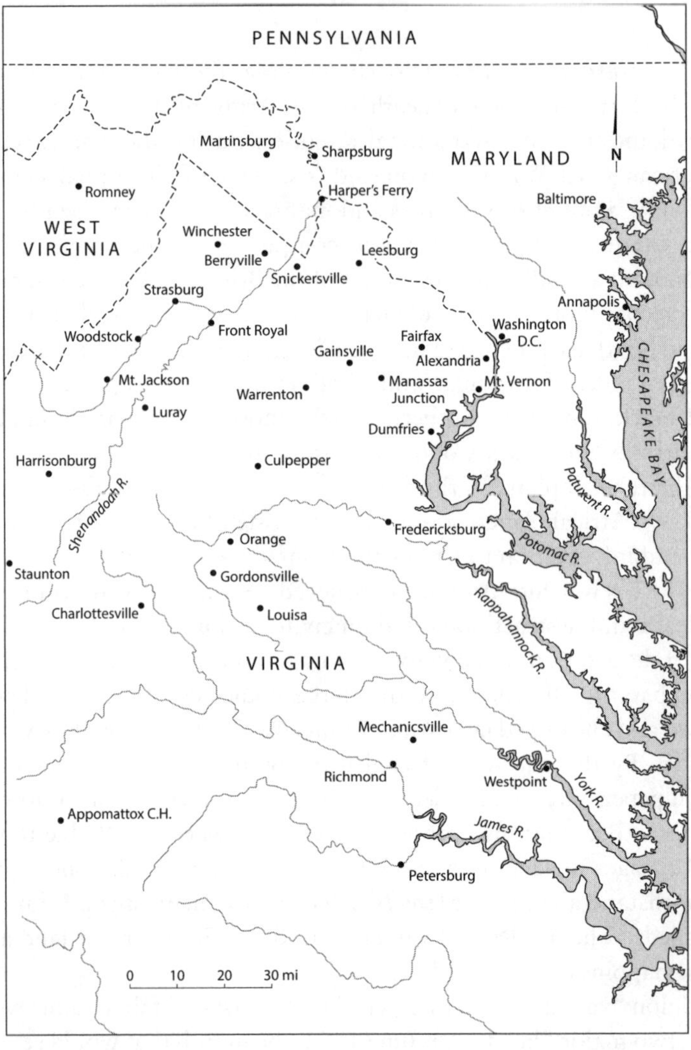


Northern Virginia, 1862. (Map by Bill Nelson)

The three corps that would form the Army of Virginia were separated by twenty miles or more from each other in June. The Mountain Department, led by John Frémont, defended the Unionists of western Virginia from Confederate vengeance. The second, originally V Corps of the Army of the Potomac, stood under Nathaniel Banks in the Shenandoah Valley to oppose Thomas "Stonewall" Jackson's rebel force and deny this key farmland to the Confederacy. The final force, I Corps of the Potomac army under Irvin McDowell, held the Rappahannock line, with headquarters at Fredericksburg.[6] These groups were riven with conflicts from top to bottom, from the frustrated ambitions of officers to the intra-army animosities, annoyance with rebellious civilians, and poor discipline of common soldiers.

The areas the corps defended were strategic backwaters. West Point generals found command of the forces defending Washington frustrating, particularly those seeking battlefield fame, higher rank, or a postwar political career. "It has become an adage here," wrote a cavalry trooper, "that if you want to break down a General send him to Western Virginia the neglected department, [as it] is used only as a *gulotine* for those whose energy is likely to gain them fame. A transfer [here] is an evidence of the displeasure or jealousy of certain politicians."[7]

Stonewall Jackson had already defeated elements of each of these three disparate forces, crushing their morale. A western general in Banks's force lamented the disheartening situation: "When I see three military departments divided and powerless, which if united might combine an irresistible force which could march to Richmond, I feel disgusted and heartsick. Such are the departments commanded by McDowell, Banks, and Fremont."[8] A junior officer from Massachusetts echoed this pessimism: "Matters do not look very encouraging for us but as though we were frittering away our strength by scattering our forces. The whole result of dividing Virginia into separate departments has been terribly disastrous and resulted in the wasting of our strength."[9] The units were, moreover, poorly disciplined. The forces in the Shenandoah Valley in particular had an unsavory reputation for plundering, and no part of these three corps was more vilified for its punitive, vengeful, or simply pragmatic actions than the large German American contingent.

Unionists in Virginia castigated the disproportionately German American division commanded by Louis Blenker for indiscipline and looting. The division, originally belonging to the II Corps of the Army of the Potomac and with perhaps 70 percent of its men European-born, had been sent to reinforce Frémont in western Virginia.[10] Blenker was a German revolutionary who left the Rhineland for the United States after the failure of the 1848 revolutions and, in 1861, organized the 8th New York Regiment.[11] The provost marshal of Harrisonburg noted that "Fremont's army was largely composed of German troops, and there were many stragglers who did more or less pillaging. I arrested a number of these and confined them in a guard house. Some of them had women's apparel; viz., bonnets and big hoopskirts. These I turned over to the town authorities."[12] He did not mention what local authorities made of them.

Blenker's men "might have belonged to the free bands of the Black Forest. They were the most lawless men in the Federal service, and what they did not steal they destroyed. Such volunteers were mercenaries, in every sense of the word," wrote a reporter from Philadelphia. "I have been told that they slaughtered sheep and cattle in pure wantonness. . . . The Germans, as a rule, lacked the dash of the Irish troops and the tact of the Americans. They thought and fought in masses, had little individuality, and were thick-skulled; but they were persevering and had their hearts in the cause."[13]

"Blencker's troops are all Germans, and as precious a pack of scoundrels as were ever brought together. The general himself is the greatest rascal in the pack. They have made the valley of Virginia feel the war and I must say for that I am not sorry," a New York general noted, demonstrating his Yankee prejudice against German immigrants *and* Virginians. "We treated all kindly, it did no good, now they will begin to understand what war is. . . . We can get along without Dutch generals or Dutch soldiers, and it is a great pity that any [volunteered]."[14]

Members of Blenker's division held a different point of view. They faced days of rain and muddy roads, and the army's commissary department failed to feed them. These conditions induced them to take from the one source readily available: civilians.[15] If the concentration of German American units in Blenker's division led to negative stereotyping of German soldiers, they had their reasons for joining homogenous regiments. "The German soldier, perhaps unconsciously, felt that at the same time he was fighting for preservation of the Union he was fighting for the honor of the German people," historian Ella Lonn argues, "which explains his desire to serve in a German unit."[16] They won few friends among proslavery Virginians, however, for their conviction was that slavery must be destroyed to preserve the Union, thus enabling Confederates to combine nativism with racism.[17]

Native-born Yankees were not the only soldiers operating in the

Shenandoah to criticize the behavior of Blenker's division. His command was "notorious for months on account of their thefts and dastardly insults to women and children in that part of the State under Federal domination," noted rebel general Richard Ewell.[18] He viewed them as "stupid, ignorant Dutch," guilty of "ill-treating the people, robbing and stealing and wantonly killing" livestock. "These people are committing more wanton injury than they did in the Mexican War," Ewell wrote, "and are as cowardly as villainous."[19]

Pro-Confederate civilians in Virginia were more directly affected by "Dutch" foraging than rebel soldiers. Citizens of Port Republic "could perceive but little difference between officers and privates" in Frémont's force; "they seemed all to be upon a regularly organized plundering expedition in the name of the government."[20] Reverend Cumberland George of Culpeper claimed the German soldiers were "about as cleanly and intellectual as the overgrown sows of '*der Vaterland*.'" But the pastor conceded that another group of Yankees might be worse than the supposed mercenaries from Germany: the "Puritans and psalm-singers of pious New England."[21]

Self-emancipated African Americans found refuge and employment in the disparate Union armies in the Shenandoah Valley, just as they did to a lesser extent with McClellan's army on the peninsula between the James and York Rivers. Men found work as teamsters, officers' servants, and cooks, while women washed clothes and cooked. They were not always welcomed by Union armies in early 1862, even if known to be the most loyal segment of the population of Virginia. "The darkies are all for the Union, and from actual observation I can say that their love for their masters is grossly exaggerated," a company clerk wrote in March. "They followed us in large numbers but as feeding them would entail privation on our own troops, an order was issued and carried out, to drive them away."[22]

Other fugitives were more fortunate. A cook employed by the Seventh Indiana of McDowell's corps fell into rebel hands on June 9 at Port Republic but escaped.[23] Soldiers of the 13th Massachusetts marching near Fredericksburg in May enticed a "darkey boy" to leave his master and join them. He "was highly delighted with the thought of being free, but said he could not leave behind a half dollar that he had earned and had up at [his master's] house," and after retrieving his fortune joined the New England regiment. He "stayed with us for a long time, being a good, faithful boy." The Bay Staters nicknamed him "Marvel."[24] When

Union forces abandoned Winchester and the valley in May, Union soldiers noted that "there were nearly as many Negroes on the Retrete as there were Soldiers[,] the Roads were Black with them."[25]

Northern soldiers marveled at the depth of the disloyalty of civilians in the Shenandoah Valley and northern Virginia while marching through or occupying the towns and farming villages of those regions. The three counties at the heart of the valley—Rockingham, Augusta, and Rockbridge—became solidly secessionist following the bombardment of Fort Sumter. "Secession was not what the voters in the Valley wanted, but they believed they had been given no other choice." For white denizens of the valley, "the time had come to unite with the Lower South and face the Republicans with a unified and common front."[26] The first observation made by Union soldiers was that white Virginian society was divided into two distinct classes: "Nearly all the wealthy people were owners of slaves, and the slaves did all the work, both in the house and out. Their owners did not, but rather looked down upon the class that had to work. As all the Yankees were men who had to earn their living, they considered themselves far above us," and taught their children likewise, noted a Maine cavalry trooper. "Then there was another class made up of poor whites completely under the control of the slave-owners. They did not have any education and in a great many respects, did not seem as intelligent as the slaves."[27] Yet the valley was largely Unionist prior to Sumter and contained far fewer slaves than the tidewater counties (where more than half of residents were enslaved) in which McClellan campaigned. It was telling that slaves—from regions where less than a quarter of the population was African American—would flock to Pope's camps in large numbers.[28]

The policy of conservative West Point generals to protect the property and rights of southern civilians, including the families of leading Confederates, was a growing annoyance to Union soldiers. McClellan and his generals fought to maintain the status quo antebellum, while Republican commanders increasingly favored revolutionary transformation of the Confederate states by punishing pro-secession civilians and freeing their slaves.[29] Left to their own devices, Union soldiers were looting abandoned property by late 1861. "There has been a great waste of property here," a Wisconsin soldier wrote from Arlington. "Thousands of negroes masters have run away and left the negroes to take care of the property. They don't take very good care of it." Soldiers could enter abandoned homes "and get a nice piano or a nice mirror to ornament their tent with. They ate from tables that cost not less than $50."[30]

During the spring of 1862, Union soldiers stationed in western Virginia, the Shenandoah Valley, and near Fredericksburg awaited the outcome of McClellan's offensive against Richmond. When news arrived of McClellan's defeat and subsequent retreat toward the Virginia coast, soldiers in northern Virginia responded with disbelief and anger. Despite the loss of "ten thousand more brave spirits yet the lenient course [is] pursued in dealing with treason." A Wisconsin lieutenant noted with outrage that after a long day's march, the men under his command reached a bivouac bereft of any fallen tree branches but with a rail fence conveniently nearby. The men "used only sufficient rails to cook with" but were nevertheless ordered to rebuild the fence. Adding insult to injury, the fence was on the property of the adjutant general of the rebel army. Such stringent orders "to protect Rebbles and their property" by conservative generals like McDowell impelled many Union soldiers "to swear" them to be "traitors."[31]

Union soldiers campaigning in the Shenandoah Valley in the spring and summer of 1862, whether from the cities of the northeastern seaboard or western farms, found Virginia a backward land in need of Yankee ingenuity. A New Yorker commented on dilapidated houses whose similarly ramshackle inhabitants "barely existed—did not live" in them, in a settlement near the Rapidan River. "One meets many just such dwellings and just such residents in the South; men who lie around loose rather than stand erect on God's footstool; men who seem to have no heritage of ideas or manly aspiration, but manage in a very desultory way to keep body and soul together," he continued. "Labor is degrading" to these people, "so of course the sons are idle; a slave or two become the scapegoats of their masters' idleness." These "poor white trash" were to this northerner's mind "the worst victims of slavery," and he struggled "with a feeling of contempt" for them as Americans trapped between "haughty" white slaveholders and black slaves.[32]

Officers joined enlisted men in seeing opportunities in a land bereft of initiative and enterprise. A brigadier general from Detroit in Banks's force found the few dwellings near Front Royal "very large, but [all] have a rundown air—very a la Virginia. It is not easy to account for, but this whole beautiful Valley with its productive soil presents very few indications of prosperity. Houses and appurtenances have an air of neglect and dilapidation," he wrote his daughter. "I think they are all in debt and spend yearly more than they raise."[33] "Front Royal is quite a pretty place though it is old," a soldier in the 13th Massachusetts wrote his daughter, and if the buildings "look bad they have nice gardens of flowers. Lettuce and some other kinds of greens are large enough to eat." At least some of his appraisal was due to an interest in supplementing his army rations by way of illicit forage.[34]

The women of northern Virginia behaved in an especially galling manner toward Union troops of all ranks: "When any of these rebels or rebel sympathizers had to go before the provost-marshall, and take the oath [of allegiance to the federal government] it was a bitter pill for them, especially for the women and the young ladies; as they were more incensed against us than the men. They gave us some terrible tongue lashings and some even spit in our faces. We had to watch them closely as there were many spies." The Maine trooper who penned these recollections had good grounds for these claims; Union cavalry in the Shenandoah Valley spent an inordinate amount of time chasing spies and guarding headquarters where loyalty oaths were taken. "They would taunt us by calling us 'mean Yankees' and say 'You-uns have no business down here among we-uns.' It was almost like being in a foreign country."[35]

Another trooper in the 1st Maine Cavalry sought to reason with the white women of Virginia but gained little ground. A woman in White Plains demanded to know "what possessed me that I should come way down there [from Maine] to make war upon my countrymen." She claimed southerners had endured northern insults for years, but now "the abolition spirit that had seized upon the North had at last driven them to madness and [they] were very reluctantly obliged to resort to self defense." She had three brothers serving in the rebel army and would remain loyal to the Confederacy if they faltered. "I bid her good-bye, saying that I hoped she would see the error of her ways," the abashed New Englander wrote, "and that before any of her brothers were killed, this strife would cease."[36]

"While we ware Camped at Warrenton a number of Ladys got together at a Large house in front of our Camp and hoisted a rebel Flag," a Wisconsin lieutenant wrote his wife. "It created the gratest excitement in the Camps and some two or three hundred rushed to the house and tore it down. The excitement was so grate that a Strong guard" had to be set "to protect the lives and Property of those that put up the flag." The officer of the day was just finishing the placement of his men when the women put up another rebel flag. The guard tore it down and the officer "told them that if they showed another they must protect themselves." The general commanding the Union camp raised the stakes by hoisting a U.S. flag, threatening the house's destruction if it were misused. The raconteur continued that the rebel women "use the old story of [their] being poor defenseless women and children and should be protected and be allowed to do as they like but that thing is pla[ye]d out I hope." While "there is no Northern Soldier that would insult a Lady whether she bee from the North or South union or Rebel as long as she is a Lady but when they make She Devils of themselves and abuse our men and do it on purpose the time is not far distant when for such things they won't be protected."[37]

In Virginia, echoes could be heard of the frustration of the Union occupation force in New Orleans—from Commandant Benjamin Butler on down—and of their temptation to downgrade refined "ladies" to prostitutes for their unladylike, politicized behavior.[38] If the women of Virginia were openly secessionist in sentiment, civilian men of military age in areas occupied by federal troops were suspected of being spies, saboteurs, or guerrillas. Fredericksburg "is filled with Rebel Soldiers that have Deserted or Pretend they have, others that have bin wounded and [come] home others that Dress in citizens clo[th]es and [return] home on a visit," wrote a worried officer charged with guarding the city's railroad bridge.[39] The defining moment for the Union force commanded by Banks—now the Army of Virginia's II Corps—regarding the loyalties of Virginian civilians came in the aftermath of the defeat at Winchester. Citizens of Winchester fired on them as they retreated through town. The visceral image of southern women killing Union soldiers was particularly damning.[40]

Many of the officers and men who looked down on southern culture and the denizens of Virginia voted for Abraham Lincoln and the Republican ticket in 1860. But even strongly Democratic officers could lose patience with southern civilians. "The ruffianly countenance of" Colonel John Geary discouraged one Virginia woman when she sought recompense for the shooting of her cattle and turkeys by his men. Geary "seemed annoyed at my report of the disorderly conduct of the soldiers on my place and gave most peremptory orders that any man found beyond the lines without a pass should be shot." While he approved orders to provide her with payment for her loss, she heard him tell his staff officer not to "bother me with any more such business," implying that his heart was not in rectifying civil-military disputes.[41]

The very next day this Virginian heard of a shocking incident involving Colonel Geary and three young women. When his forces entered the town of Middleburg, the colonel "took possession of the parlors and best bed rooms of the [Stephensons'] house confining the family to the attic and the cellar rooms. The day after his arrival Col. Geary missed his pistol off the table in the parlor where he had laid it. He became enraged instantly" and accused the family of the theft. "The three girls Josephine, Mittie and Nannie were in the passage. He drew his sword on them, called out" for the guards to arrest the ladies. Mrs. Stephenson was locked in the basement. Finally, Geary threatened the elderly Mr. Stephenson with destruction of his house "in ten minutes if the pistol was not instantly produced. Just as he got through with imprisoning the whole family his own son handed him the pistol which he had misplaced."[42]

Geary ordered the family's release without an apology, leaving a staff officer to make his excuses. Geary's staff and headquarters bodyguard of soldiers were not much better. Rather, they engaged in class warfare in the Stephensons' house. "To annoy the family they constantly have the servant women in their rooms drinking and eating cake and bonbons with them and [recently] while Mittie was in the kitchen one of them came in and put his arm around the cook and pinched her cheek." Geary's staff officers might be excused for misplaced attempts at gallantry toward single women, but common soldiers were another animal altogether. "The guards jump from behind the doors and *boo* at the girls as they pass."[43]

Geary had a habit of drawing his sword on unarmed southern women. Less than two months after the incident at the Stephensons' residence, the colonel's regiment was occupying the town of Warrenton. Geary designated the "house of Mr. Foster his Headquarters and while at dinner one day he remarked that the Confederate army was composed of the meanest, low bred silt of men that has ever come under his notice, Miss Kate Foster replied that mean men" served on "both sides." Geary "instantly arose and drew his sword on her—some of his officers interfered—he remarked he would not permit her to make such remarks in the presence of his men." The woman who recorded this incident was well aware of the earlier incident in Middleburg.[44] Southern civilians found it difficult to distinguish between Union officers and men when the former seemed to exhibit no more in the way of manners and restraint than their subordinates, even when the officers were prominent antebellum Democrats.

Geary's behavior was not countenanced on the peninsula in McClellan's discipline-obsessed army, but his frustrations and those of antislavery German immigrants-in-arms were understandable. Even as McClellan's army fell back from Richmond in the face of Robert E. Lee's June-to-July counteroffensive, the larger Union war effort was stalling. Western Union armies made little progress after capturing Corinth and spent the summer protecting their supply lines. Secretary of War Edwin

Stanton's April 3 decision (General Order 33) to close federal recruiting offices in favor of state efforts bore sour fruit three months later when new volunteers were required to replenish the depleted eastern armies. Governors attempted to fill the recruiting gap, with mixed success. On June 28, Lincoln called for 300,000 additional volunteers.[45] Until they stepped forward, equipped and trained, Lincoln expected the forces on occupation duty in northern Virginia and the Shenandoah Valley—demoralized and disorganized though they might be—to provide McClellan with the margin of victory.

In the midst of these conflicts, events on the ground and in Washington were leading to the creation of the Army of Virginia. While the Union forces in the Shenandoah Valley and the vicinity of Fredericksburg fought a series of sharp but unsuccessful engagements with Stonewall Jackson, the main Union Army in Virginia had launched a major campaign to take Richmond. George McClellan believed that a second overland advance from Manassas to Fredericksburg and then to Richmond was an inferior strategic option to the amphibious alternative.

By the dawn of 1862, McClellan was wedded to the idea of leaving a covering force behind in the vicinity of Washington—the three corps-sized units that would make up the Union Army of Virginia—and embarking the bulk of his army aboard ships to sail down the coast of Virginia. They would land on the peninsula formed by the York and James Rivers and thus face a much shorter, and purportedly undefended, route to the rebel capital. Here was an opportunity that epitomized McClellan's interest in the application of military science and strategy.

But the Peninsula Campaign failed. Brainchild of a Democratic general, the campaign provided Republican politicians and journalists with a convenient "object of political denigration," namely the supposedly sophisticated West Point preserve of "strategy."[46] Specialized, professional knowledge and sophisticated campaign plans had run into the brick wall of reality and Carl von Clausewitz's "fog of war."

The confidence of congressional radicals in McClellan—and in West Point graduates generally—had never been strong. Since the start of the war, the radical wing of congressional Republicans—politicians who sought the abolition of slavery and the application of severe measures in the suppression of the Confederate rebellion—had been seeking alliances with generals in the field. Their task was lightened by the appointment of dozens of "political generals," men with limited military experience chosen for positions of high military authority on the basis of their clout with the soldiers and voters at home.[47] Republicans found few recruits in the upper echelons of the Army of the Potomac, the major field army east of the Appalachians. Conservative West Point graduates, led by McClellan, dominated this force, leaning Democratic when at all partisan.[48] Congressional radicals were emboldened by the Second Confiscation and Militia Acts—both passed on July 17, 1862—to demand that Union armies confiscate rebel property and slaves, and employ slaves against their masters (potentially as soldiers), to bring the costs of war home to pro-Confederate civilians.[49] The question remained whether West Point alumni would enforce Republican laws.

West Point–trained officers were supposed to be professionals, beyond partisanship, although their appointments to the military academy as cadets depended on the personal selection of a congressman or the president.[50] This roadblock to military radicalization would be eased by the formation of the Army of Virginia. Many of the generals in the new army—cobbled together from units tasked with defending western Virginia, the Shenandoah Valley, and the nation's capital while the Army of the Potomac sought to capture Richmond—were political appointees.

Thousands of partisan northerners looked to Lincoln for elevation through the normal channel of patronage. Not only was he the first Republican president. Faced with a civil war and the task of recruiting unprecedented numbers of citizen-soldiers and dozens of general officers, Lincoln was required to distribute hundreds of civilian *and* military patronage posts.[51] He found it politically expedient—if not always efficient in outcome—to ensure that the loyal states' regional and ethno-cultural constituencies were represented in his military appointments. In appointing a mix of Democratic and Republican, German and Irish and Yankee generals—akin to the "team of rivals" in his cabinet—Lincoln united the loyal population behind the war effort and around regional politicos newly minted as generals.[52]

An anecdote illustrates the humorous—if dangerous—quality of Lincoln's efforts to placate various constituencies. Scanning a list of colonels eligible for promotion to brigadier general, Lincoln fixated on Alexander Schimmelfennig. He noted "there has got to be something done unquestionably in the interest of the Dutch, and to that end I want Schimmelfennig appointed." Secretary Stanton disagreed, arguing for better qualified colonels. "Mr. President, perhaps this Shimmel-what's-his-name is not as highly recommended as some other German officer." "No matter about that," Lincoln rejoined, "his name will make up for any difference there may be, and I'll take the risk of his coming out alright. *Schim-mel-fen-NIG* must be appointed."[53]

The popular affirmation of this policy and the pride of serving under a general of one's own ethnicity may be seen in the phrase of German American soldiers in I Corps of the Army of Virginia: "I fights mit Sigel." Once John Frémont resigned from the Army of Virginia, Franz Sigel replaced him at the head of the heavily German I Corps, and morale in the corps improved dramatically, as noted by German-language newspapers: "Since Sigel assumed command, a completely different spirit has settled over all of the corps, and the German troops in particular."[54] The conduct of Frémont's German units during the spring campaign in the Shenandoah had been heavily criticized. Frémont's "army" taken as a whole "is nothing more than a magnificent wreck, with plenty of good large pieces left to make something of," a staff officer noted. "Sigel is the man who keeps up the troops and every Regiment here would come under his command if [the matter was] left to them."[55]

Two of the Army of Virginia's three corps commanders were political generals with no West Point training whatsoever. Frémont, the initial chief of I Corps, was the darling of abolitionists and Radical Republicans alike. Frémont was not admitted to McClellan's clique for lack of West Point credentials, and his political activities further alienated professional soldiers. Frémont was, after all, the first Republican presidential candidate in 1856. In Missouri during 1861 in charge of the Department of the West, faced with grueling combat against thousands of guerillas, Frémont unilaterally ordered the emancipation of the state's slaves.[56]

Frémont's act, condemned and then overruled by Lincoln, was applauded by anti-slavery politicians. The president's subsequent removal of Frémont from command made him a martyr in the eyes of abolitionists and anti-slavery politicians. On March 11, 1862, the combined support of Republican newspapers and the Joint Committee on the Conduct of the War compelled the president to give Frémont a new command, the Mountain Department in western Virginia.[57]

Frémont established the headquarters of his new department in Wheeling. An English traveler touring the Union states in 1862 found Wheeling "a go-ahead place, in its way, for a Southern city, loyal to the Union. It will be the capital of the new State of Western Virginia, if it ever succeeds in establishing its independence; and it is the headquarters of the emancipation party in the state, probably because its German population is considerable."[58] The general had strong reasons to set up shop in Wheeling, a town filled with anti-slavery loyalists of German ethnicity simultaneously congenial to his personal political views and his largely German American command. The town was soon filled with the "foreign officers" habitually drawn to Frémont's headquarters as moths to a flame.

Conservative Unionists and secessionists in western Virginia complained of the excesses of Frémont's men—particularly Louis Blenker's Germans—in looting from civilians. A trooper in the 1st Virginia Cavalry noted rumors in Pennsylvania newspapers that "every man woman and child" in western Virginia's "Fayette Co was about to revolt unless Gen Freemont was immediately removed from this dept." While commenting that "this news comes from a source not altogether reliable," the trooper was not particularly reliable either. He held that Frémont had completely "driven Jackson from the Valley" by "rapid marches and vigorous attacks," when it was Stonewall Jackson who was responsible for the "rapid marches and vigorous attacks" in which Frémont was "driven" back.[59]

Frémont was looking increasingly attractive as an alternative and more authentically anti-slavery candidate than Lincoln would be in the 1864 presidential election. Several radical politicians defended him when Frémont was attacked by conservatives in Congress. "In my narrow quarters here I have yet had no opportunity and could make none—for either attack or defense," Frémont wrote radical Pennsylvania Representative Thaddeus Stevens.[60]

Frémont possessed "all the qualities of genius except ability," historian Archer Jones has commented.[61] At least a few of his soldiers thought otherwise. "Our General has as yet done nothing to lessen the confidence of the soldiers under him," but in the recent valley campaign "has strengthened that confidence," a cavalry trooper argued the week before Pope took command.[62] The assessment of Frémont's generalship by high-ranking officers accorded with Jones's. Robert Milroy, one of Frémont's brigade commanders and a fellow anti-slavery Republican, penned a fitting epitaph to Frémont's military career. "The world had been much deceived in that man," Milroy wrote his wife. "As a general he was a perfect failure."[63]

Unwilling to serve under a former subordinate from his tour of duty in Missouri, Frémont resigned upon hearing of Pope's ascendancy to army command over him, leaving the reins of I Corps in the hands of its senior division commander, General Robert Schenck of Ohio. The command "has come upon me very suddenly," Schenck confessed to his daughter, and the state in which Frémont left it did not help: "I find every thing in chaotic confusion, and more work, work, work than I can do."[64] Schenck soon learned, moreover, that Lincoln was appointing a general from Irvin McDowell's command in Frémont's place. After briefly mulling resignation, Schenck admitted his relief at returning to division command. "Such confusion and such disorder," Schenck noted in his postmortem assessment of Frémont's headquarters. "He had permitted all affairs to be principally in the hands of his Dutch, French, Italian, Hungarian etc etc aides—a perfect polyglot staff;—and they, a set of dunderheads, *knew* nothing, and could *do* that *and* nothing more!"[65]

Frémont's permanent replacement was the former German revolutionary Franz Sigel, an inspired choice on political if not military grounds.[66] Sigel was a political general, a significant figure among the millions of German Americans upon whose votes Abraham Lincoln would rely for reelection in 1864. St. Louis's most prominent immigrant, Sigel took a leading role in the crucial effort of the city's German population to preserve Missouri for the Union.[67] Yet support beyond Missouri was essential to Sigel's meteoric rise to high military command and transfer to Virginia. House Representative John Carlisle of loyal western Virginia pressed Treasury Secretary Salmon Chase to bring Sigel east: "Siegel is the man we want. I would not give him for 50 Rosenkranz's [General William S. Rosecrans] or 100 Fremonts'."[68] Radical Republican senator Charles Sumner likewise petitioned Lincoln to appoint Sigel as Frémont's replacement in Missouri, especially in light of the need to placate ethnic loyalties. "As a German he would be most acceptable in St. Louis," Sumner wrote, "where there are so many of that nation."[69]

Passed over for high command in Missouri, Sigel was free to take a command in Virginia. Distinguishing himself in the West—like Pope—"in a series of engagements," Sigel was "a diminutive person, but well-knit, emaciated by his active career. As a general he was prompt to decide and do, and his manner of dealing with Confederate property was severer than that of any [native-born] American." In Virginia, Sigel "battered the splendid mansion hotel of Sulphur Springs to the ground, [after] somebody discharged a rifle from its window."[70]

Sigel's counterpart at the head of II Corps was Nathaniel Prentiss Banks of Massachusetts, a man who worked from early youth in a factory as a "bobbin boy" before entering the world of politics and rising to governor of Massachusetts.[71] Banks thus related to his soldiers convincingly as a common man. During a visit to the 3rd Wisconsin's camp, he was, as one observer said, "one of the pleasantest generals we have here. He has less pride in him that some of his subordinates in rank, always shakes [hands] with the officers and asks the boys how they are etc."[72]

One reporter found Banks "a fine representative of the higher order of Yankee."[73]

Banks's appointment among the first major generals of volunteers satisfied New Englanders' expectations of influence in the Union's high command. Banks nevertheless would join McDowell in gracefully and patriotically accepting the promotion of Pope over his head. "General Pope of the west has been placed in command of all our forces," Banks wrote his wife. "He is junior officer to all of us. This is the first time it has been done in that way. It does not trouble me much. If it is possible to help on the war—by this means I shall be glad."[74] Unique among the corps commanders of Pope's army, Banks's diary for 1862 is available to historians. Among memoranda about military matters and other minutiae, Banks sprinkled personal and political comments. In early July, he scribbled a note about the reconstruction of southern states: "How to re-construct the Gov't. *Show your power.*"[75] After sending messages to Quartermaster General Montgomery Meigs regarding shelter tents and to Pope about outposts to guard against cavalry raids and guerrilla attacks, Banks noted, "our men have not seen enough of the sun and the rain to be good soldiers. They think too much. The less thought the better—not to make them machines but to give them endurance—Dr. Antiself, Med. Doctor."[76] A West Point martinet could not have better registered his opinion of the proper role of enlisted men to march and fight and not think.

At the helm of the army's largest component—III Corps—was its most senior West Point graduate, McDowell, whose commission as a major general predated Pope's. A member of General Winfield Scott's staff, he was a logical choice to command the Union Army gathering at Washington. An 1838 West Point graduate, McDowell had the dubious distinction of watching defeat snatched from the jaws of victory by his classmate Pierre Beauregard at Manassas in July 1861.[77] During that engagement, McDowell gave his army excellent Napoleonic tactical orders for an offensive consisting of a feint with the army's left wing followed by a devastating blow from the right wing as it executed a flank march. The fatal flaw of the otherwise brilliant battle plan was that it lacked trained and experienced soldiers and competent generals to carry it out, a problem McDowell pointed out to Lincoln to no avail in 1861.

Political realities and public pressure for the northern army to march "on to Richmond" impelled Lincoln to push McDowell's army into action well before the general believed it was ready in the summer of

1861.[78] In the weeks before First Bull Run, McDowell was seen doing staff officer work (searching for mislaid cannon at the railroad depot, for instance), which did not prevent him from formulating a good battle plan despite an inadequate staff complement.[79] McDowell's successor, George McClellan, was granted far more time to train his army.[80]

Following the defeat at Manassas, McDowell demonstrated great restraint when dealing with southern civilians, restraint any War Democrat could appreciate. Take, for instance, his response to the looting of Mary Custis Lee's property at Arlington House. The mansion of Mary Custis and Robert E. Lee across the Potomac from Washington, D.C., once the home of George Washington's stepson, was occupied by Union troops. Mary Lee entrusted care of the mansion to the slave Selina Norris Gray and her husband when she fled south. They protested to McDowell "when officers began to abscond with the mansion's treasures, whereupon McDowell ordered everything removed to Washington and placed in safekeeping at the patent office."[81]

By 1862 McDowell was persona non grata with General McClellan and his inner circle, seen as too close to the president and too far from his fellow West Point alumni. On January 10, with the president, the cabinet, Congress, and the northern people increasingly impatient with the lack of action by the Army of the Potomac, and McClellan ailing from typhoid fever, McDowell was called to a special council of war to discuss plans for a new campaign against Richmond.[82] When the general arrived at the White House, he found the president, the secretaries of state and the treasury, the assistant secretary of war, and Brigadier General William B. Franklin (one of McClellan's closest subordinates).[83]

After detailing the depressing present "State of affairs," Lincoln admitted that he visited "McClellan's House and the General did not ask to see him," but he must talk to "somebody." Lincoln then asked the generals what they would do with the large force gathered outside Washington, with emphasis on speedy action. McDowell responded "that the question as to the *when*" of army movement "must be preceded by the one as to the *how* and the *where*." He proposed to "organize the army into four army Corps" and move on Richmond in an overland campaign. Franklin hemmed and hawed. He confessed "he was in ignorance of many things necessary to an opinion on the subject," but "on being asked by the Presdt. if he had ever thought what he would do with the army" if he led it, the general admitted he had. He would leave a force to protect the capital and take the bulk of the army to the "York river to operate on Richmond," a loyal defense of his friend's pet project.[84] Franklin undoubtedly reported to McClellan all that transpired, including McDowell's dismissal of McClellan's campaign.

Lincoln remembered McDowell's proposal to take McClellan's division-based army structure and add a new bureaucratic and command level by forming four corps. When McClellan implemented his final plans preparatory to the move to the Virginia peninsula, the president forced the corps system on him. McClellan wanted to wait until after the first battles of the campaign, when the signal contributors to the anticipated victories would have demonstrated their worthiness for corps command, but he was overridden. McClellan almost certainly would not have selected any of the Army of the Potomac's five initial corps commanders: McDowell, Samuel Heintzelman, Erasmus Keyes, Banks, and Edwin Sumner.[85] Banks's V Corps was left behind when the army boarded ship for Richmond, and McDowell's I Corps—later the III Corps of the Army of Virginia—was left at Fredericksburg by presidential command. Fighting losses and reinforcements enabled McClellan to form two new corps (V and VI) and place two of his most loyal generals, Fitz John Porter and William Franklin, at their head. John Pope would encounter many difficulties with Porter and Franklin in August.

Politics internal and external plagued McDowell by the start of McClellan's campaign, adding to his "unpleasant notoriety." His selection of junior officers for his staff won him no favors among McClellan's West Point clique. One was the son of the anti-slavery Republican and military governor of Washington, James Wadsworth. The choice of Craig Wadsworth was simple, as his father had served with McDowell as a volunteer aide at First Bull Run; still, as a partisan Republican and military amateur he annoyed McClellan.[86]

McClellan's hostility pushed McDowell into the Republican camp. Fellow Ohioan Salmon Chase was a constant friend, and a staff officer noted that Rhode Island's Republican Governor William Sprague—who later married Chase's daughter—visited the general.[87] "None bore ingratitude so stolidly," a journalist noted of McDowell. "He may have flinched, but he never replied; and though ambitious, he contented himself with subordinate commands. Some called him a traitor, others incompetent, others a plotter. . . . Implacable, dutiful, soldierly, rigorous in discipline, sententious, brave—the most unpopular man in America went on his way." If a Republican general "has a thorny path to tread," McDowell "has been treated worse than any other."[88]

Hearing that McDowell had been thrown from his horse and was “hurt some,” a caustic western soldier commented, “I think some times it is a pitty he did not breake his neck or something worse.”[89] McDowell did not strike back at his legion of tormentors until long after the summer campaign. He did continue his detail-chasing habits from the previous summer; McDowell’s staff would credit him with saving valuable supplies on the retreats from the Rapidan and Rappahannock lines.[90]

The generals (and colonels) who commanded the divisions and brigades in the corps of Sigel, Banks, and McDowell reinforced the army’s Republican character. Of the thirty-six commanders down to brigade in the three corps involved in the Second Manassas Campaign, six were present at First Bull Run as generals, regimental, or battery commanders. They ran the gamut from army commander McDowell to brigade commander Robert Schenck; from colonels Leopold von Gilsa, Julius Stahel, and Adolph von Steinwehr (commanding the 8th, 41st, and 29th New York Infantry Regiments, respectively), to battery commander James Ricketts. Another three—Abner Doubleday, Samuel Crawford, and Truman Seymour—awaited exchange after the surrender of Fort Sumter and so missed the war’s first major battle. At the head of all, striding into the martial and political chaos of the disparate Union forces in the Shenandoah Valley and northern Virginia, was Major General John Pope.

# 2 John Pope Takes Command

John Pope was—like Abraham Lincoln and Jefferson Davis—born in Kentucky.[1] He was connected to the first Republican president by his father, a judge who presided over a number of young lawyer Lincoln's cases in Illinois, and was related to Mary Todd Lincoln by marriage. Crucially, Pope was also linked to Republican Salmon Chase via his father-in-law, who shared a hometown with the treasury secretary.[2] He was also an ardent Republican himself. Captain John Pope spent the weeks before Lincoln's inauguration awaiting a court-martial. He stood accused of violating the Fifth Article of War for calumniating President James Buchanan, a Democrat, in a speech given in Cincinnati. Pope attacked Buchanan for failing to respond decisively to the secession of the Deep South. Fortunately for Pope, the lame duck president dismissed the charges, although if he had not, congressional Republicans might have made Pope into a political martyr and then propelled him to high command in 1861.[3] Pope was released in time to escort the president-elect on the train ride east from Illinois to Lincoln's inauguration in Washington, a journey fraught with rumors of an assassination attempt. Following the successful if tense inauguration, Illinois governor Richard Yates pressed the new president for high military rank for his constituent. Yates sought a brigadier's star for Pope in June 1861 and two-star (major) general rank after the fall of Island Number Ten.[4]

Brigadier General Pope faced his first major challenge in northern Missouri in July 1861, his first assignment as a general. As he assumed command of a military department, Pope was immediately plagued by guerrilla or partisan bands who were sabotaging and hampering the movement of supplies and troops.[5] Probably the most crucial impact of this activity was the drying up of supplies to Radical Republican General Nathanael Lyon's aggressive campaign in southern Missouri.

Pope required lessons in the intransigence of southern civilians, as well as on the need of his soldiers to forage. One colonel landed in hot water for allowing his famished soldiers to requisition food from local farms. "How dare you take private property for the use of your regiment?" Pope stormed. "How dare you go through the country pilfering, arresting men, taking possession of horses?" When the colonel pleaded military necessity due to spoiled government rations, Pope replied, "You should starve in your tracks before you touch private property." Facing court-martial, the colonel found in Pope a "narrow martinetism with a decided proclivity to slaveocracy. In condemning me for feeding my men, from necessity, upon rebel flour and beef, and for using a few horses against the traitors of the country, Gen. Pope disregarded the self-evident truth that 'war must feed war.'"[6] A few months of ambushed patrols and burned railroad bridges convinced Pope to change his tune. On July 21, 1861, Pope issued his first major public decree, targeted at the civilians in the Department of Northern Missouri.

"It is very certain that the people living along the line of the North Missouri Railroad can very easily protect it from destruction, and it is my purpose to give them strong inducements to do so," Pope declared. "I therefore notify the inhabitants of towns, villages, and stations along the line of this road that they will be held accountable for the destruction of any bridges, culverts, or portions of the railroad track within 5 miles on each side of them. The settlement will be held responsible [for any damages], and a levy of money or property sufficient to cover the whole damage done will be at once made and collected." Pope also acknowledged the asymmetry of knowledge between Union soldiers and local residents. It was impossible for troops "even to ascertain the names of the criminals engaged in this kind of work, although they were well known to everybody in the neighborhood. If people who claim to be good citizens choose to indulge their neighbor and acquaintances in committing these wanton acts," they must be held accountable in their place by occupying forces.[7]

Clay Mountcastle has deemed Pope's decree "legally perilous," one for which he could have been "prosecuted for criminal conduct" in a Missouri civil court. Pope, however, was merely repeating counter-guerrilla army policy during the Second Seminole and Mexican Wars, although this time applying them to (erstwhile) citizens of the United States.[8] Pope's military superiors were unlikely to nullify his policy nor were his subordinates, and no court was likely to challenge it. Michael Fellman has argued that Union soldiers in Missouri "believed the enemy was everywhere and everyone" and that most of the civilian population "secretly supported the guerrillas."[9] They probably also appreciated that Pope did not intend to send them on wild goose chases after elusive guerrillas who melted back into the civilian populace. "The system of pursuing the perpetrators of these outrages can lead to no good results while so large a body of people sympathize with them," Pope informed his superior, John Frémont. "It is a war which can only be ended by making all engaged suffer for every act of hostility committed."[10]

Pope attempted to implement this policy through a creation of the French Revolution: the formation of Committees of Public Safety in the department's towns. The "respectable citizens" were held liable for the maintenance of the peace, with taxation and property loss in case of failure. The general reasoned that "once the secessionists understand that upon peace in their midst depends the safety of their families and property, we shall soon have quiet again in North Missouri."[11] Mountcastle contends that Pope did not realize Missouri's citizens were more focused on self-preservation than the preservation of property and, at any rate, guerrilla reprisals were more threatening than those proffered by Federals.[12]

Although he was initially leery of endorsing Pope's harsh decrees, continued guerrilla activity pushed Frémont to act, and by August 30 he had declared martial law throughout the state, most controversially ordering the emancipation of the slaves of disloyal masters. This was too much for the president, who sent a military commission to investigate and, upon its findings, removed Frémont. Pope remained in Missouri but was sent to the southeastern corner of the state for the winter. His force was renamed the Army of the Mississippi and by April of the new year, it had captured an important Confederate garrison on the Mississippi River.[13]

The commanding general of the Army of the Mississippi was "pugnacious and confident and conceited," wrote one historian. This view was shared by at least one of the general's overburdened administrative officers.[14] "I do not think much of Gen. Pope as a man yet I consider him a good General," his chief commissary officer in the Mississippi army wrote. He considered Pope a "wicked profane and overbearing old scallawag," and his transfer to Virginia was a relief.[15]

After Pope's Army of the Mississippi captured Island Number Ten, Radical Republicans pounced on the opportunity to replace the disappointing George McClellan with a professional officer with bona fide anti-slavery views loyal to the Republican Party. They exhorted the president to bring Pope east to invigorate the Union Army with his aggressive leadership style and accomplish what McClellan proved incapable of doing: capture Richmond. New York merchant Alexander T. Stewart—one of the nation's wealthiest men—joined Illinois senator Orville H. Browning to press Pope's case. Soon after their interview with Lincoln, Clara Pope informed her husband that he was a shoo-in for the command of the forces under Frémont, Nathaniel Prentiss Banks, and Irvin McDowell, and might replace McClellan himself. Word of the appointment quickly followed.[16] Pope was an instrument in congressional radicals' hands to destroy slavery and punish Democratic Confederates, while the general sought military glory and to supplant Democratic generals like McClellan.

GENERAL POPE. "Well, Sir; who are you, and what do you want?"
STRANGER. "I am—aw—Aid-de-Camp to GENERAL STONEWALL JACKSON. The GENERAL sends his—aw—Compliments, and wishes to know if you can let him have a few Bottles of *Rose-Water?*"
GENERAL POPE. "Tell the GENERAL that this Concern has changed hands; and the present Head of the Firm has *given up the Rose-Water Branch of Business,* as he finds it *don't pay!*"

Cartoon from *Harper's Weekly,* August 9, 1862

General Pope. "Well, Sir; who are you, and what do you want?"

Stranger. "I am—aw—Aid-de-Camp to General Stonewall Jackson. The General sends his—aw—Compliments, and wishes to know if you can let him have a few Bottles of *Rose-Water?*"

General Pope. "Tell the General that this concern has changed hands; and the present Head of the Firm has *given up the Rose-Water Branch of Business,* as he finds it doesn't pay!" (Courtesy of Washington and Lee University Library Special Collections)

John Pope officially assumed command of the newly designated Army of Virginia's three corps on June 26, 1862. In mid-July, he decided to make his intentions plain to the men and officers of the new army, which he did by a proclamation written in his own hand. He informed his new command of his research as to "your whereabouts, your condition, and your wants," which explained his continued absence. "Let us understand each other," Pope proclaimed. "I come to you from the west, where we have always seen the backs of our enemies; [where the] policy has been attack and not defense. I presume that I have been called here to pursue the same system, and to lead you against the enemy. It is my purpose to do so," Pope assured his men, "and that speedily. I am sure you long for an opportunity to win the distinction you are capable of achieving. That opportunity I shall endeavor to give you."[17]

The general then announced his expectations for his new command. "Meantime I desire you to dismiss from your minds certain phrases which I am sorry to find much in vogue amongst you. I hear constantly of taking 'strong positions and holding them,' of 'lines of retreat,' and of 'bases of supplies.' Let us discard such ideas. The strongest position a soldier should occupy is one from which he can most easily advance against the enemy. Let us study" the lines of retreat the Army of Virginia can force the foe to travel, "and leave our own to take care of themselves. Let us look before us, and not behind. Success and glory are in the advance; disaster and shame lurk in the rear. Let us act on this understanding, and it is safe to predict that your banners shall be inscribed with many a glorious deed." If general and soldiers understood one another properly and acted accordingly, he trusted, in Napoleonic fashion, that "your names will be dear to your countrymen forever."[18]

Historians have noted the critical response of soldiers and officers to Pope's supposedly fatuous and self-serving rhetoric.[19] Many of the sources cited, however, were written months, years, or even decades after the fact. The contemporary letters and diary entries of most of the officers and men on this subject were complimentary, or at least hopeful that Pope's words were a portent of aggressive and victorious campaigning.

"We hail the coming of General Pope with much satisfaction," a Wisconsin major wrote shortly after the announcement of the formation of the Army of Virginia.[20] "Thank Heavens we have at last got but one commander in this valley," a captain from Massachusetts wrote. "I don't know much about Genl Pope but any one man can conduct affairs here better than they have been conducting by the dozen—more or less—who have been pulling and hauling against one another here." The captain was confident that Pope and Franz Sigel were fully the "equal" of Stonewall Jackson.[21] Enlisted men applauded the prospect of "war in earnest," as promised by Pope and supported "by the Government and no false notions of mercy to save the scoundrels that have caused this war."[22] An Indiana cavalry corporal interrupted a day of reading Tennyson to express "pleasure with Genl. Pope's Address" in his diary on July 16. The noncommissioned officer (NCO) thought the new general "seems an energetic—'go ahead' man—such an one, as this department needs, and has ever needed, and has never had!" McClellan's generals, he thought, "have paid too much attention to reviews and inspections and parades—to strong positions—and defensive works, lines of retreat, and bases of supplies. And not enough to the weaknesses of the Enemy." If McClellan and his ilk were "beautiful theorists," they lacked anything "of the practical warrior about them. We have been outgeneraled here—for the simple reason that we have had energetic men to contend with" and no "go ahead" men to oppose Jackson.[23]

Pope's July 14 proclamation was by no means his first. Less than a week after taking command—but a full month before meeting his soldiers in person—Pope issued the first of a stream of orders demonstrating that his advent in the eastern theater meant the commencement of war in earnest. This order was to the army's commissary officers, restricting rations to "only bacon, salt, coffee, sugar."[24] Its meaning was quickly apparent to those affected. "Some important movement is contemplated probaly and it is to save transportation" that the rations have been so curtailed, wrote an officer in the 3rd Wisconsin.[25] This initial order lasted mere weeks, falling afoul of the basics of supply and demand. The commissary officers "tried it [for] a few issues and then came back to the regular rations again." The failure of this initiative hardly prevented the general from "carrying on a terrible paper warfare which is making him famous."[26]

At least one of Pope's directives might have given the Army of Virginia's medical director conniptions. "Gen'l Pope insists upon having all the sick carried along on the march in ambulances, teams or afoot," a Maine officer in II Corps noted on July 25. "This although very bad for the [truly] sick is an excellent measure for keeping those only a little indisposed on duty."[27] Those soldiers who possessed high morale and a keenness to see battle received a fillip from this message from army headquarters, namely that all soldiers must do their duty. They would not have to shoulder the burden dropped by malingerers and shirkers shamed into marching in the ranks by the threat of a bumpy ride in ambulances.

Although much of Pope's rhetoric was just that, a significant material contribution of the general's came with his decree changing soldiers' tents. Many of the army's regiments were accustomed to using large Sibley tents, which accommodated sixteen men each.[28] These tents were comfortable but cumbersome to transport, and were not conducive to rapid movement. They had their uses but far from the battlefield. A Hoosier sergeant sitting in a hospital was pleased with his surroundings though anxious to return to the field. "We are in large nice tents, with nice beds to lie on, and everything was very comfortable. There are sixteen in the tent with me."[29]

Pope desired for his army to shelter more in line with what western soldiers used on campaign.[30] Enlisted men were accordingly provided with half of a shelter or "dog" tent; two soldiers would pair up to button together and fashion a single tent just large enough for two. McDowell first pushed this initiative with his own corps in mid-May, and Pope then applied it to Sigel's and Banks's corps. A few regiments were already equipped with shelter tents—thanks to farsighted governors or generous colonels—when Pope took command. A soldier in the 7th Wisconsin noted that they could now "carry our tents on our backs. They button together. They are very nice, a new invention."[31] But this order entailed a change for most of Pope's regiments. "We are now in McDowell's Corps," a member of the 13th Massachusetts wrote, "and I learn there is to be a new order of things; he intends taking away our [Sibley] tents and substituting the smaller ones, such as the men carry on their backs."[32] The so-called shelter tent halves weighed five pounds, "and each man will be required to carry one on his back; so that the labor heretofore performed by horses will now be transferred to the men." He was sure that "the new tents are but a very poor protection against the weather."[33] A corporal in Banks' corps noted in July that his regiment was ordered to turn in their tents. Eleven days later they received new tents. "They are a fine thing[,] being but a fly."[34] Soldiers throughout the army noted the change and its import: hard marching and active campaigning were coming.[35]

Whatever the intentions of Pope's reform, weather still impacted army morale beyond the control of any general, and heavy rainfall dampened soldiers' spirits in their smaller shelters. "We are experiencing a long, severe rain storm," a Harvard-educated lieutenant of the 2nd Massachusetts wrote. "With the men, it is particularly hard, as they have now lost their comfortable Sibley tents and have only small shelter tents in their places, which afford them very little protection" from the elements.[36] A captain concurred, declaring the "nasty little shelter tents almost worse than nothing at all and I am afraid will cause much sickness among the men" during prolonged damp or cold weather.[37]

Officers maintained a modicum of private luxury in their canvas housing even as the army sought to cut down on impedimenta and the length of its wagon trains. Two days after Pope's ascendancy, the company commanders of at least one of McDowell's brigades were issued wall tents, which were more spacious than shelter tents if smaller than a Sibley, and provided privacy denied to enlisted men. This new comfort indicated to one Wisconsin captain that no forward movement was envisaged in the near future.[38] Yet the same order that all other tents must be turned in hit officers' basic camp comforts hard. "Officers trunks are not allowed to be carried and there" was "a general shipping off of trunks," even if they were allowed to retain "one of their old tents to each company," which would likely be appropriated by the captain.[39] "Our tents are partly taken away; the officers crowd into a diminished number, and the private have, or are to have, 'shelter tents,'" a chaplain recorded.[40] The lieutenants of each company had to rely on the generosity of their captain for shared use of the single permitted wall tent.

Officers of the 2nd Massachusetts did not allow the loss of their camp luxuries to dissuade them from enjoying life. The day before their men turned in their Sibley tents and they themselves sent away their trunks, the surgeon and two lieutenants rode into Warrenton. Lieutenants Charles Morse and Robert Gould Shaw "took tea at the 'Warren Green Hotel,' regaling ourselves on iced milk and corn-bread, finishing the evening by smoking our cigars on the piazza." Although "each officer [was permitted] to keep only a small valise and roll of blankets," they took the inconvenience in stride.[41]

Inconveniences to volunteer officers and enlisted men in the form of tenting and baggage restrictions certainly reduced the size of army trains. "Few are probably aware how very cumbersome these trains are," noted one officer. "Even when the transportation is reduced to its minimum standard, a division of ten thousand men will require something like forty ammunition and fifty forage and subsistence wagons, twenty or thirty ambulances, and about sixty regimental and head-quarter wagons." On top of that the horses drawing each wagon needed forage, requiring additional transport. "Thus I have seen it stated that the wagon-train of the army of the Potomac would extend at least fifty miles," noted a Maine soldier.[42]

An allied reform was the conscious effort to cut down the size of the army's baggage, supply, ammunition, and ambulance wagon trains. A

Massachusetts soldier credited McDowell with chivvying his division commanders in early June—before the arrival of Pope—to pare back their wagon trains. Nothing should be taken "but ammunition, subsistence, forage and cooking utensils." McDowell unfavorably compared the mobility of his units with those of Stonewall Jackson, who "marches thirty miles a day, and that we can never catch an enemy with a train filled with trumpery," as a member of one of his New England regiments noted.[43] Thirty years after the campaign, the historian of the 13th Massachusetts noted that "our service under [McDowell] began at a time when [we] still retain[ed equipment] what in the years 1863–4 would have been considered luxuries."[44]

A 13th Massachusetts soldier noted that once McDowell's reforms were fully implemented there would be "but five wagons to a regiment; the officers to give up their trunks, and we [soldiers] are to be cut down in every way—brought to a level with the regular army."[45] "I have been overhauling my knapsack and throwing out everything I do not absolutely need," Warren Freeman wrote. "It now weighs eighteen pounds, and to this will be added an extra pair of shoes, and a shelter tent weighing five pounds. McDowell is much opposed to a baggage train."[46] The positive aspects of McDowell's reforms were credited to Pope; the negative ones were put on the luckless McDowell, which failed to dispel volunteer soldiers' distrust of McDowell, who was still saddled with the blame for the defeat at Manassas the previous July. Some of McDowell's men felt they already carried enough in their knapsacks though. "They are puting on to[o] much style in this Brigade to suit my mind," a soldier from Indiana wrote. "They want every man to carry an extra pair of pants and shoe and coat." His regiment was not issued the new clothes, and "if they had it would have been thrown away."[47]

Not all regiments in Banks's corps could be immediately equipped with shelter tents just because Pope signed an order to that effect. This necessitated the temporary retention of Sibley tents, although the permitted regimental allowance was slashed. In early July, Banks added up the transportation allotments for his units. Brigade trains contained thirty-five to forty wagons, while regimental trains now consisted of fewer than thirteen wagons. "McClellan corps carries 5 days rations with 5 wagon to each Regt. One ration weighs 2 lbs."[48] Pope's decrees that the army should be constantly ready to march with several days' rations on hand meant that the number of commissary wagons could not be reduced, so brigade and regimental trains had to be cut back somehow. "Two [Sibley tents] taken away from every Company, so as to lighten all of the baggage wagons," a musician of the 5th Connecticut noted on July 15.[49]

As it turned out, Pope and his staff did not practice what they preached regarding personal baggage. A headquarters staffer claimed that the army headquarters constituted "a full brigade" in size, or one to two thousand men.[50] In August, a staff officer visiting army headquarters observed "almost a regiment of orderlies holding the staff horses" for the dozen general officers meeting with Pope.[51] When Pope visited the army for the first time, a New Englander noted that he "travels in great state, he and his staff having a camp of *75 large tents* and over 100 wagons. He goes through the country like a little king."[52] This may have been a scaled-back version of the baggage train accompanying McClellan's headquarters, but not by much. Fortunately, when Confederate cavalry commander J. E. B. Stuart's troopers raided Pope's headquarters wagon train in August, they lightened the load for Pope's headquarters' beasts of burden, relieving the army commander of his dress uniform.

While implementing his "western" strategy in Virginia, Pope searched for promising western officers to assign to his new army. Hobnobbing with radical politicians in Washington in June, Pope encountered fellow Kentucky native John Buford. Pope was surprised that Buford was still a major and found an opportunity to promote him to brigadier general and commander of one of Pope's three new cavalry brigades.[53] The fact that Buford's brother Napoleon had served well under Pope during the recent Mississippi campaign enhanced Buford's worthiness.[54] Buford, who possessed "a voice and tone" of command "that was not to be disobeyed," proved a credit to the new army's mounted arm in scouting and rear-guard actions throughout the summer.[55]

Pope reorganized the Army of Virginia's cavalry units, forming them into brigades attached to the three infantry corps and so rendering them more effective as scouting units in the army's effort to bring the enemy to battle on favorable terms.[56] He assigned as chief of cavalry for the army Vermont-born, decorated Mexican War veteran Brigadier General Benjamin Stone Roberts.[57] Roberts's first responsibility was to rid northern Virginia of Confederate guerrillas and spies. Pope's experience with the depredations of western guerillas left him with little patience for eastern partisan rangers and their civilian supporters.[58] While serving in Missouri, Pope witnessed the sanguine nature of guerrilla warfare and experienced the problems of dealing with an intransigent civilian population. The draconian measures laid on Missouri civilians—loyalty oaths followed by eviction upon refusal, reprisals for guerrilla raids, and the summary execution of civilians caught using arms against Union troops—were soon implemented in Virginia, with cavalry at the tip of Pope's spear.[59]

Pope took great care in the selection of his staff, considering political sensibilities and rewarding personal friends and allies from the antebellum army. If Pope could not handpick his three corps commanders—or was indisposed to make any changes at the highest echelon of his new command—he did decide who administered the army and delivered his orders to its constituent parts.[60] Key to tackling the new army's administrative challenges were the members of his headquarters staff.

Pope selected a regionally representative set of staff officers hailing from western Virginia, loyal border states, New England, the mid-Atlantic, and western states. While McClellan selected his aides-de-camp from loyal West Point alumni, his father-in-law, and even exotic French aristocratic exiles, Pope favored West Point graduates and volunteers whose competence had impressed him during his western campaigns in Missouri and on the Mississippi.[61] Frémont's headquarters staff was, like McClellan's, filled with flamboyant aides—many of them nattily dressed Europeans—but this changed after Frémont's huffy resignation at the prospect of subordination to Pope and his replacement by Franz Sigel. Frémont's staff officers were swiftly dismissed from service following his resignation.[62] George David Ruggles, an 1855 West Point graduate from New York, was at the core of the Army of Virginia's headquarters as Pope's chief of staff and adjutant general, a hefty responsibility for an officer not yet thirty in 1862. Pope brought Maryland native Thomas Andrew McParlin east from Chicago to serve as his medical director.[63]

During the month before he left Washington to take command of the new army in the field, Pope made use of Buford as an inspector general and summoned Banks's Virginian aide, David Strother, to familiarize him with the territory.[64] The selection of another loyal Virginian as a member of Pope's military family could be seen as a personal insult to the general's opponent, Robert E. Lee. Colonel Louis Henry Marshall, an 1849 West Point graduate, was a nephew of Lee's, the son of the rebel general's older sister, Anne, but had befriended Pope during a prewar surveying mission. "I could forgive [Marshall] fighting against us, if he had not joined such a miscreant as Pope," Lee wrote to his daughter.[65]

Ohioan Thomas C. H. Smith, another of Pope's choices to staff his headquarters, spent the first months of the war as a lieutenant colonel commanding the 1st Ohio Cavalry at Louisville and Lebanon, Kentucky.

Not a West Pointer, Smith graduated from Harvard College in 1841. He participated in the siege of Corinth, Mississippi, with Pope following the Battle of Shiloh and then followed the general east to the Army of Virginia.[66] Pope inherited an inspired chief of military railroads and construction, previously recruited by Irvin McDowell, a general whose contributions to the Union war effort remain overlooked. West Point graduate Herman Haupt convinced McDowell and Secretary of War Edwin Stanton that—like the armies in northern Virginia—the duties of supplying and transporting Union forces needed to be consolidated. Problematic railroad stock and tracks in Virginia and acts of sabotage perpetrated by rebel guerrillas complicated the task of supplying mobile Union forces. McDowell and Stanton concluded that Haupt was just the man for the job.[67] Pope, however, did not see the need for Haupt's services at the head of "a separate and independent department," leading to Haupt's resignation. Only after the repulse at Cedar Mountain in early August did Pope apologetically reinstate Haupt.[68]

Another German American, this one from the Grand Duchy of Baden, was belatedly appointed Pope's chief of artillery. Hubert Anton Casimir Dilger was too young to participate in the 1848 revolutions but graduated from Baden's military academy at Karlsruhe and made a name in Baden's artillery corps before migrating to Cincinnati. By 1862 he was the commander of a battery of Ohio artillery serving in western Virginia; on July 22, Dilger was assigned to Pope's headquarters as artillery chief.[69] In establishing an army-wide artillery chief, Pope was following McClellan's prescient appointment of Henry J. Hunt as the Potomac army's artillery reserve commander, which bore fruit in the last of the Seven Days Battles.[70] Dilger lacked Hunt's experience and seniority—batteries were commanded by captains, making them Dilger's peers rather than subordinates—but his appointment was a reflection of his promise.

The artillery of the Union Army of Virginia needed a physical overhaul and better ammunition, as well as centralized leadership. A captain on Franz Sigel's staff was "very busy with the Artillery" on June 29, "trying all the Artillery of this Division and reporting their condition, efficiency etc." as his general assumed command of what was previously John Frémont's corps. "The Amm[unitio]n is all so poor that nothing can be done with it," he reported.[71] By late August, though, this staff officer was performing battlefield miracles—if he can be trusted in singing his own praises—with Sigel's artillery. Confederates "think I am a regular born Artillerist here and I can just control the whole Artillery of the fight as I have done on several occasions," he wrote. "In the heavy fight [on the banks of the Rappahannock] I cut a road through the woods and brought two pieces on their flank which they did not expect and drove them from their position." Sigel "is the man. [He] always sends for me when anything is to be done. *He gave me Two Regiments and Two* [artillery] *Pieces and told me to outflank them and worry them* as much as possible."[72]

Although Pope wasted no time organizing his headquarters staff, he did not join his new army until a full month after arriving in the East. He spent that month profitably, at least from a political standpoint, quartered in Washington and building a rapport with Secretary of Treasury Salmon Chase and congressional Republicans. Pope's "vanity was apparent to the most shallow observer, and although he was brave, clever, and educated, he inspired distrust by his much promising and general love of gossip and story-telling." A reporter compared Pope and Lincoln: "He had all of Mr. Lincoln's garrulity (which I suspect to be the cause of their affinity), and none of that good old man's unassuming common sense."[73] Pope's rhetorical bombast and political machinations aside, his Washington headquarters appeared utilitarian and modest enough to a Pennsylvanian reporter who visited on July 12. The general was ensconced in "a quiet brick house, convenient to the War Office, and the only tokens of its importance were some guards at the threshold, and a number of officers' horses, saddled in the shade of some trees at the curb." Pope's headquarters, even as he campaigned for greater military responsibility and political visibility, was more in line with Ulysses S. Grant's headquarters two years later than that of Pope's showy contemporary George McClellan. "The lower floor of the dwelling was appropriated to quartermasters' and inspectors' clerks, before whom a number of people were constantly presenting themselves, with applications for passes—sutlers [merchants allowed to accompany the army to sell goods to soldiers], in great quantities, idlers, relic-hunters, and adventurers, and, citizens of Virginia, solicitous to return to their farms and families." Most belonging to the last category were "rebuffed, as Pope had inaugurated his campaign with a show of severity, even threatening to drive all the non-combatants out of his lines, unless they took the Federal oath of allegiance."[74]

Pope's sojourn in Washington put him in the right place at a melancholy time: the death and funeral of Secretary of War Edwin Stanton's infant son. One of General Pope's staff officers, recently transferred from McDowell's headquarters to serve as Pope's chief topographical engineer, noted that his brother-in-law, Quartermaster General Montgomery Meigs, and he "expect[ed] to go to the funeral at an early hour to-morrow morning. Genl. Pope said he would go with us—out near Tenallytown, some 5 or 6 miles from here." Three days later, the officer confirmed to his wife that Pope was present at the funeral.[75] Also present were President Lincoln and several other members of his cabinet. In fact, on the coach ride to the funeral, Lincoln first revealed to several cabinet members his intention to emancipate at least the slaves of disloyal masters.[76]

In Washington Pope drafted his initial proclamation and the various general orders that soon followed it. Both the authoritative historian of the Second Bull Run campaign and Pope's biographer note that the general's rhetoric-turned-policy was "a calculated outgrowth of the Federal government's changing approach to the war," and Pope "a political weapon wielded by the administration."[77] Pope showed his intended public announcements to Lincoln, who tacitly agreed with them—or at least chose not to oppose them.[78]

"Have you considered the order I proposed to issue yesterday which directs all male citizens living within the lines of the army under my command," Pope wrote to Lincoln on July 23, 1862. "Such as take the oath of allegiance and give sufficient security for its observance to be allowed to remain at home." Conversely, all men who refused the oath were "to be conducted South, with a notification that if hereafter found within the lines or in the rear of U.S. forces they will considered and treated as spies?"[79] The president raised no major objections, and Pope's proposal was transformed into policy within forty-eight hours.

The day before his new command was announced, the general gave a speech attacking slavery and McClellan's generalship to the House of Representatives. Two weeks later, Pope testified before the Joint Committee on the Conduct of the War. Asked whether he anticipated his upcoming campaign would be purely defensive, Pope's reply delighted the committee's radicals. "I mean to attack them at all times that I can get the opportunity," he promised.[80] Unlike McClellan, Pope did not have his sights set on the White House, but he intended to drum up support for a Republican war policy in Virginia. His first recruits in this campaign were abolitionist politicians seeking to transform civil war into revolution.

Although a tiny minority of northerners were abolitionists in 1860, the secession of southern states and the year of costly civil war rendered them prophets worthy of honor in northern public opinion in the summer of 1862.[81] Their humanitarian influence was reflected in the efforts of antislavery politicians—elected officials professing varying degrees of racial egalitarianism—whose congressional ranks grew in the 1850s. Once the Civil War began, the most radical discussed the possibilities of persuading the president to move more stridently against slavery, and if the president could not be moved, to supplant him with a more suitable candidate in 1864.[82] Among their most influential leaders were Treasury Secretary Salmon Chase of Ohio, Senator Charles Sumner of Massachusetts, and Representative Thaddeus Stevens of Pennsylvania.

Chase, deeply disappointed that Lincoln was the Republican Party's nominee for the presidency in 1860 instead of him, early on cultivated West Point alumni who might win the war and enhance his chances for the White House in 1864.[83] It was largely at Chase's recommendation that the president selected the West Point Ohioan McDowell to head the first federal army in its ill-fated drive on Richmond in July 1861. McDowell remained an active commander in the Union war effort in 1862, and was the senior (and only West Point–educated) corps commander in the Army of Virginia. The McDowell and Chase families were close from the 1850s, and the widowed Chase often sent his teenage daughters to visit the McDowells.[84]

Historians have identified McDowell as a Democrat in his political leanings, though such a claim is difficult to confirm, and the West Pointer's political views hardly kept Chase from befriending the officer.[85] If not an anti-slavery Republican, McDowell was still unwelcome in McClellan's West Point clique, and he remained in the good graces of the ascendant Radical Republicans. Chase quickly warmed to Pope upon his arrival in Washington in June. In conversation with Chase, the general argued that slavery must be destroyed, and "it was only a question of prudence as to the means to be employed to weaken it." The "means" included shifting the costs of war fully upon southern civilians, to make them feel the hard hand of war.[86]

Chase acted as a power broker, a key link between military and political radicals, perhaps a necessary byproduct of his presidential ambitions. He endeavored to ingratiate himself with important representatives from the regional and ethnic constituencies of northern radicals. As an Ohioan, Chase cultivated West Point graduates from his home state for high command in the first year of the war, including McDowell and McClellan (a transplant) in the eastern theater. Out west, where the bulk of Ohio soldiers served, Chase corresponded with the Buckeye Republican general James Garfield and other promising, politically connected Ohio generals.[87] On June 3, 1862, for instance, Chase wrote to assure McDowell that the "confidence of both the President and Stanton in you is unshaken," but he also encouraged McDowell to increase their confidence "by future activity and energy. Never say 'die'! Speak of difficulties only to express resolve to overcome them. [A] little hearty boasting sometimes is very well."[88] Chase was well aware of McDowell's weaknesses and tailored his advice to aid the general in overcoming them. "He is too indifferent in manner, and his officers are sometimes alienated by it. He is too purely military in his intercourse with soldiers," Chase noted after Second Bull Run. "There is apparent hauteur: no, that is not the word—rough indifference expresses better the idea—in his way towards them, that makes it hard for them to feel any warm personal sentiments toward him."[89]

Battlefield victories gained by Union generals from Ohio trumpeted the prestige and presidential aspirations of the treasury secretary. Ohio bordered on the mountains that separated eastern from western states, and on a major river that divided North from South, and Chase promoted the careers of Ohioans serving in both theaters of war. William Tecumseh Sherman—foster son of a powerful Ohio political family—wrote Chase of the implacable nature of the war at hand: "When one nation is at war with another, all the people of one are enemies of the other." No abolitionist, Sherman nonetheless advocated taking the kid-gloves off when dealing with a recalcitrant civilian population that supported Confederate regular troops and guerilla insurgents.[90] For decades a resident of Cincinnati—with its large German American population—Chase was keen to gain the support of German Republicans, foremost among them Carl Schurz.[91]

During the maneuvering prior to the Republican Party convention of 1860, Chase tried assiduously—but without success—to gain Carl Schurz's support for the Republican presidential nomination. Although he ended up supporting William Seward, Schurz represented the interests of Radical Republicans by visiting Lincoln in the White House to support Chase for a cabinet post. Schurz may have reminded the new president that he himself would also make an excellent cabinet member. Unhappy with his initial posting as U.S. minister to Spain, Schurz enlisted the help of the treasury secretary to garner a commission as a brigadier general in command of a brigade of mostly German American troops in the spring of 1862.[92] Interestingly, Lincoln took Schurz aside before he assumed his command to request that Schurz keep Lincoln apprised of important developments in the army occupying northern Virginia. After all, Schurz was assigned to serve under the first Republican presidential candidate, John Frémont, and the president—keeping most of his Republican presidential rivals close by in his cabinet—liked to keep an eye on a rival in the field, namely Frémont.[93]

If a few generals like Benjamin Butler, David Hunter, and Frémont promoted blatantly anti-slavery policies in occupied slave territory—Frémont and Hunter attempted to unilaterally free the slaves in their military districts despite Lincoln's opposition to such action—they were the junior partners in a martial-political alliance of Radical Republicans. From the first months of the war, Radical Republican politicians expressed displeasure with the Democratic proclivities of West Point–trained generals.[94] Republican senator Henry Wilson claimed that no fewer than 80 of 110 brigadier generals serving in the Union armies were Democrats, and that all but one of the armies "is under the control of a general opposed to the present Administration."[95]

While Pope and his new Republican army confronted the Army of Northern Virginia near Fredericksburg, congressional radicals demanded "generals with ideas," commanders who on the battlefield were "almost irresistible because swayed by the great invisible forces" of Republican ideology.[96] The strong minority of anti-slavery generals in Pope's command presented a test case for an army commanded by men of anti-slavery "ideas" and the conviction that punitive measures must be taken against traitors. Banks's and McDowell's acceptance of Pope's command was evidence of ideology trumping traditional military protocol, since both were senior to him by date of commission. The obeisance of two of the army's three senior generals in favor of (civilian) executive prerogative over decades' old military precedent was not countenanced in the Army of the Potomac. If these political generals prevailed in combat, they would provide proof that McClellan and other Democratic generals should be sacked in favor of nonprofessional Republicans. Chase's faith in Republican generals like Pope, Banks, and Sigel was vocalized in the halls of Congress by Charles Sumner and Thaddeus Stevens.

Five years before civil war began on a national scale, blood was spilling in a civil war between pro- and anti-slavery settlers on the western frontier and in the Senate chamber of the Capitol. Attacked by South Carolina representative Preston Brooks, Sumner was beaten within an inch of his life. The public caning of Sumner led to the Republican broadside "bleeding Sumner and bleeding Kansas," waking northerners up to the brutality of violence-prone southerners.[97] By 1862, Sumner was lamenting the string of victories in the western theater. "We are too victorious; I fear more from our victories than our defeats," he confessed in his diary. "There must be more delay and more suffering . . . before all will agree to 'let my people go': and the war cannot, must not, end till then."[98]

Fortunately, the war in Virginia was stalemated, due to the milquetoast efforts of Democratic West Point graduates.

Stevens, chairman of the influential Committee on Ways and Means, was firmly established as "a symbol of change for his countrymen" by the time Congress adjourned for the summer of 1862. Stevens constantly agitated "for an end to slavery, the enrollment of black troops, a vigorous prosecution of the war, and its financing through legal tender notes."[99] He expended a great deal of time and energy to improve the future prospects of African Americans, concerning himself with both free and enslaved. While Pope faced Lee's army near Fredericksburg—and with the preliminary emancipation proclamation in his pocket—Abraham Lincoln met with a group of black ministers and urged them to consider emigration to Panama. Stevens was aware of the proposal for free blacks to settle in the Chiriqui region. Hearing that the president had granted it credence, Stevens warned Lincoln (through Chase) of the many flaws of the scheme, and Lincoln sent a senator to assess the feasibility of the enterprise.[100]

Boston abolitionist Wendell Phillips vocalized the wishes of abolitionists for a political-military alliance of radicals. Phillips demanded "a proclamation of freedom, war on war principles to be conducted by such men as Sumner, Stevens," and Chase. These anti-slavery politicians would be aided "by Hunter, Sigel, and Fremont in the field," for "no emancipation policy is of any value unless its earnest and downright friends are put at the head of affairs."[101] "Earnest" friends of emancipation occupied key military roles by summer. The commandant of the forces in Washington, James Wadsworth, of the abolitionist stronghold of upstate New York, was an anti-slavery general and Republican appointee.[102] And by July radical favorite John Pope commanded the second largest Union army in Virginia.

Radical Republicans in Congress worked overtime to provide Republican generals like Pope with more ammunition to attack the root causes of secession and undermine the foundations of Confederate strength. The disappearance of the southern states' Democratic congressmen during the secession winter of 1860–61—rendering both houses Republican strongholds—simplified their task.[103] The longer the war lasted the more traction party radicals gained in their efforts to transform the war into a revolution, even if conservative and moderate Republicans remained a force to be reckoned with in Congress. The legislative body handed Pope two major legislative gifts in mid-July 1862, a clear sign that Radical Republicans were in the ascendant. Two weeks after the formation of the Army of Virginia—and following months of fiercely partisan and ideological debate—Congress passed and Lincoln signed the Second Confiscation Act. This law authorized the confiscation of the property of supporters of the southern rebellion, including their slaves. The human property of Confederates was declared "forever free of their servitude" when they escaped to Union lines or if they resided in Confederate territory occupied by Union forces.[104] The "most striking feature of the . . . Act was its sharp distinction between the confiscation of other property and the emancipation of slaves," writes historian Eric Foner.[105]

On July 17, the president signed Congress's amendment to the Militia Act of 1795, authorizing Lincoln to employ African Americans in "constructing intrenchments, or performing camp service or any other labor, or any military or naval service for which they may be found competent."[106] While many Republicans, including the president, were skeptical that slaves possessed the courage to face their masters in combat, moderate Republicans "lined up behind the proposal." Maine senator William Fessenden, a moderate Republican, stunned radical colleagues when he spoke in favor of the new act; his support "marked a crucial turning point."[107] "When *he* moves, it signifies that the whole glacier has started," a journalist wrote of Fessenden.[108] The question remained whether Lincoln would evolve fast enough in his stance on emancipation and punitive measures against rebels to satisfy Radical Republicans.

In early July, a third party joined the conflict between senior Union generals. Lincoln announced his choice of a new general in chief as soon as he returned to Washington from a trip to the Virginia peninsula to inspect the Army of the Potomac. The president saw a force severely reduced and thrown back from Richmond during the costly Seven Days Battles, convincing him that George McClellan had forfeited the strategic and tactical initiative. Lincoln appointed West Point alumnus Henry Wager Halleck to coordinate the disparate Union armies, particularly the armies of Virginia and the Potomac, which were separated by Virginia's rivers and the Confederate Army of Northern Virginia. An expert on military policy, Halleck (nicknamed "Old Brains") had previously served in the western theater as John Pope's superior and as McClellan's subordinate.[109]

McClellan unambiguously opposed Halleck's appointment, considering Halleck's promotion "a slap in the face. It *is* grating to have to serve under the orders of a man whom I know by experience to be my inferior."[110] Halleck arrived in Washington on July 23, about a week before Pope left the capital to join his anxious army, and held meetings with the president, Secretary Stanton, and generals Pope and Ambrose E. Burnside.[111] Pope held Halleck in low esteem for his failure to attack the Confederate Army in Corinth with more alacrity in the weeks after the Battle of Shiloh, but was pleased to have a superior officer standing between himself and McClellan. After all, the Army of Virginia simply did not have the numerical strength to take on the Army of Northern Virginia on its own; a junction with all or a significant part of McClellan's army was necessary before any offensive action could be taken.

Aside from establishing good relations with the president, general-in-chief, and prominent Radical Republicans while in Washington, Pope also needed to create a rapport with two members of the War Department: Edwin Stanton and Montgomery Meigs. Secretary Stanton was a prewar Democrat. Brought into Lincoln's cabinet to replace the corrupt Simon Cameron, Stanton served briefly in James Buchanan's lame-duck cabinet during the secession winter and was initially friendly to McClellan.[112] Yet Stanton resolved to run a War Department focused on winning the war by supporting vigorous offensives. "As soon as I can get the machinery of the office working, the rats cleaned out, & the rathole stopped, we shall *move,*" Stanton wrote to journalist Charles A. Dana. "The army has got to fight or melt away; and while men are striking nobly in the west, the champagne & oysters on the Potomac must be stopped."[113]

By June 1862, Stanton was fed up with McClellan's excuses as to why he could not take Richmond by the time Pope arrived in Washington, which Pope duly noted. Stanton was characterized by his "fierce determination, instantaneous decision and execution, remorseless concentration, and a savage capacity for labor that despite perpetual ill-health made him, in the opinion [of one Democratic opponent] the greatest lawyer of his time." He was also "the most dynamic, if not the most admirable, member of Lincoln's cabinet."[114]

Pope may not have anticipated great reliance on the services of Quartermaster General Montgomery Meigs in the upcoming campaign, committed as he was to having his army subsist on supplies confiscated from rebel civilians, but the capable Meigs did his duty. However, perils beyond the purview of quartermasters loomed: guerrilla activity, rebel cavalry raids, and the audacious attacks of Stonewall Jackson on Pope's supply depots threatened the army's lifeline at a crucial moment. Pope's failure to protect his line of communications left tens of thousands of Union soldiers hungry and critically low on supplies fifty miles from the overflowing supply depots at Washington, a unique situation in the Civil War's eastern theater.[115]

If he did not see his troops until early August, Pope did make efforts to gain a better understanding of the geography of the anticipated campaign. Less than a week after his arrival in Washington, the general recalled Banks's staff officer David Strother—a loyal Virginian—to the capital. Pope questioned Strother closely regarding "the county of Culpeper and the adjoining counties," with the aim of concentrating the Army of Virginia—anticipated to comprise eighty thousand men—at Charlottesville. Once gathered together in full force, the army would move forward to "menace Richmond and Lynchburg and the canal and railroad lines along the James, at the same time protect the Valley and Western Virginia."[116] Strother found the new commanding general an improvement over Banks. He also noted that Pope was chummy with the radical abolitionist and western general Ormsby Mitchel, "a very small man with a boyish face and manner" yet wearing "a major general's shoulder straps."[117]

The soldiers in John Pope's new command awaited his advent in the field with great interest. The experience of a year of army life, the intransigence of the civilian population of northern Virginia, and firsthand exposure to slavery had radicalized the common soldier. Increasingly willing to see "the hard hand of war" applied to Confederate civilians, they accepted their roles as face and fist of a changing war policy toward the rebellious populace.[118] They were dismayed by the Union failures on the peninsula and in the Shenandoah Valley but confident that "blame for the prolongation of this strife" does not rest "with the rank and file of the army." This left open the possibility that "McClelland" was not "the great chief that we had hoped for." A trooper in the 1st (West) Virginia Cavalry believed "there is something rotten in Denmark."[119]

Unlike the men serving with the Army of the Potomac, the men in Pope's army—particularly those of I and II Corps—were used to campaigning under the double disadvantages of a violently hostile civilian population and an aggressive military opponent.[120] The men in the newly organized army had spent the previous months marching up and down the Shenandoah Valley, chasing or being chased by Stonewall Jackson's rebel forces, and almost always meeting defeat when battle was joined. It was obvious that their generals could not match Confederate leaders like Jackson. "We have too many Major Generals in this valley and too few men," a Marylander wrote home in mid-June.[121] "Thank Heavens we have at last got but one commander in this valley," a company commander from Massachusetts wrote his wife. "I don't know much about

Genl Pope but any one man can conduct affairs here better than they have been conducting by the dozen—more or less—who have been pulling and hauling against one another here."[122] They were tired of rough handling by the rebels and hoped that a new and vigorous commander—perhaps a West Pointer *and* a Republican—could bring victory.

Many of the soldiers in the three corps were encouraged when their new commander issued proclamations and general orders to exhort—or shame—his new command to perceive their duties and their enemy differently. "He is a man of action," a III Corps soldier commented of Pope in July, "and will take advantage of any circumstance to strike a blow."[123] "Gen'l Pope is just the kind of man we want," another soldier enthused.[124] "I think placing Pope in his present position was the very best thing that could be done," a soldier in the 94th New York wrote his father. He was weary of McDowell's "imbecility."[125] Plenty of the soldiers in the army expressed a lack of confidence in their generals—particularly III Corps Commander Irvin McDowell—rendering Pope's aggressive bluster a breath of fresh air and a cause for renewed hope for the frustrated volunteers. Some of the enlisted men claimed that McDowell must be a "traitor."[126]

Pope's final proclamation, General Order No. 13, stipulated that soldiers found their proper duty on the battlefield, and no more of their "force and energy should be wasted in protecting private property of those most hostile to the Government."[127] Pope's "last order, relating to guarding the private property of rebels, and the abolishment of it," wrote an Ohioan, "is the best thing that has been done yet, I think." He was tired of enduring "all kinds of weather protecting [Virginians'] property while they have their sons in the rebel service fighting against us."[128] A sergeant from Indiana felt that the general was saying that "the army was enlisted to put down the Rebellion and Not to guard Rebles and their property," and this policy change "Should have been Done long ago." Pope's order was in line with Indiana political general Lew Wallace's recent speech that West Point graduates were wanting in the "backbone and Nerve" demonstrated by "the private Soldier"; Pope had the courage to fight treason with harsh justice.[129] "Gen. Pope is very popular and everybody approves his course," claimed a man in McDowell's corps. "Every one says the orders he has published are just the thing."[130]

The historian of the 10th Maine noted that General Order No. 11—requiring southern civilians to swear an oath of loyalty to the U.S. government—"gratified us exceedingly for a while," and General Order No. 13 "called out a hearty amen in all our corps."[131] "I hope the order" requiring "every citizen to take the oath of allegiance, or leave the state," will be "carried out to its *fullest* extent," wrote a Hoosier to his parents. He wished the oaths applied to the women of Warrenton, Virginia, who "fairly turned up their *noses* at *us* as we passed through" in late July. He similarly praised Pope's order to "live on the resources of the country," which he believed "will cut short the *provisions* of the rebels" and bring Virginia's civilians to their senses as the "Government which has protected them so long" withdrew its benevolence.[132]

Of course, not all members of the new army, particularly many of the more conservative (and most especially the West Point clique) officers, approved of General Pope's policy changes. Brigadier General Marsena Patrick, a brigade commander in McDowell's III Corps and future provost marshal of the Army of the Potomac, complained that Pope's addresses were "very windy and somewhat insolent."[133] "General Pope's bombastic proclamation has not tended to increase confidence," wrote a major in the 6th Wisconsin; "indeed the effect is exactly contrary," at least among officers who shared his Democratic proclivities.[134]

The response to Pope's heated rhetoric and ironfisted policies toward disloyal civilians was almost equally negative in the Confederate Army of Northern Virginia and the Union Army of the Potomac. Robert E. Lee, commanding the main Confederate Army in Virginia, labeled Pope "a miscreant" and vowed to "suppress" Pope, his army, and his draconian measures, which struck Lee as Republican policies achieved by military means.[135] Stonewall Jackson saw Pope's "cruel and utterly barbarous orders" as heralding a "new phase of the struggle" and left "Lee in great perplexity how to meet it." Jackson told Lee that despite being "nominally" under McClellan's command, Pope was "right under the eyes of Mr. Lincoln, violating all the so-called principles of modern warfare." Pope's policy, so different from McClellan's "mode of warfare . . . in strict conformity to the usages of civilized nations," demonstrated that Pope was "manifestly expecting to supersede McClellan and desolate the South." Jackson proposed a new method of campaigning to deal with the Republican general, turning away from McClellan's forces to concentrate on and destroy Pope's force.[136]

Pope's Potomac rivals also planned his demise. "I regret to see that general Pope has not improved since [West Point days]," wrote McClellan's close friend Fitz John Porter. Pope "has now written himself down as what the military world has now known, an ass."[137]

# 3 An Army of Brigades

John Pope's new command existed largely on paper. He faced an unenviable task: too few men to defend too much territory, including the Shenandoah Valley and forward defenses of the capital along the Rappahannock River. Worse, George McClellan expected to commandeer the army's largest corps as the key reinforcement in the capture of Richmond. This corps held the Rappahannock line. The uncertainty over whether and when Pope would lose his force's strongest corps plagued him, and the situation was complicated because the birth of the Army of Virginia coincided with the second of the Seven Days Battles, when Lee "captured the initiative" from McClellan.[1] As McClellan's army weathered fierce offensives, he clamored for reinforcements from Pope to save his army. Two of Pope's corps had previously formed part of the Army of the Potomac, molded since August 1861 by McClellan, the "Young Napoleon" to whom their officers and men retained a lingering loyalty.[2] Pope's task was to unite his corps while defending Washington and the Shenandoah, reinforcing McClellan, and threatening Richmond. Multiple factors worked against cohesion, including the speed at which the Army of Virginia was formed, restructuring in response to the fortune of battle, regional loyalties, and continual jockeying for position.

Armies of 25,000 men (or more) fought the early skirmishes and battles of the American Civil War, but these combats usually degenerated into duels between opposing regiments. An army comprised several corps, which each consisted of two or three divisions; each division contained two to four brigades; each brigade consisted of two to five regiments; each regiment had ten companies; and each company upon recruitment contained eighty to one hundred officers and men. While the company was the basic recruiting unit, the regiment was the essential fighting unit. The outcome of battles often rested on the individual training and willpower of regiments and their colonels. Some armies—most notably the Army of the Ohio, in the analysis of historian Gerald J. Prokopowicz—

never outgrew the provincialism of state-organized volunteer regiments to operate effectively as a larger force.[3] Later renamed the Army of the Cumberland for service under William Rosecrans, the Army of the Ohio was, like the Army of Virginia, formed to liberate a state (Kentucky) from Confederate occupation, and retained the stamp of its state of origin.[4] Organized from three corps-sized "armies" that never coordinated effectively in the Shenandoah Valley, Pope's army lacked the time to learn to operate as an army.

At the brigade-level—in no small part due to the attention of dedicated West Point–educated brigadiers—the Army of Virginia was able to go toe to toe with the best Robert E. Lee's army could throw against it. In this developmental level of the hierarchy of operational effectiveness, Pope's army was little behind McClellan's vaunted Army of the Potomac and its Napoleonic use of divisions. From August 1861 to February 1862, the brigades and divisions of the Army of the Potomac had a full six months to train its regiments in combined maneuvers and for the congruent parts to familiarize themselves with one another. McClellan had learned at West Point the importance of trained infantry divisions.[5] Those divisions—based on the French Napoleonic organization—could be combined with cavalry brigades and artillery battalions to form self-sufficient, combined-arms corps.[6] McClellan was reluctant to form army corps, however, until his divisions had seen active campaigning.[7]

The tiny size of the antebellum army, moreover, and its primary use against small forces of indigenous foes on the western frontier did not allow for the training and combat testing of divisions that would combine into *corps d'armée*. Rarely was a unit larger than a regiment assembled in one place prior to the Civil War. Four months of active campaigning, on the other hand, enabled McClellan's units to put their training into practice.

As one historian has noted, after the Peninsula Campaign, "both Union and Confederate forces had achieved a reasonable level of tactical competence at the brigade and regimental levels, adequate march discipline, and reasonably good unit cohesion. The coherent coordination of different units at the division and corps levels," however, "tended to tax the leadership ranks of Civil War armies so severely that even victorious armies usually could not obliterate their opponents in an open-field battle."[8] None of Pope's three corps commanders, for instance, demonstrated much tactical ability. At least three of the eight infantry divisions of the army, however, were led by competent generals. John Reynolds of the Pennsylvania Reserves, as well as George Greene and Alpheus Williams of Nathaniel Prentiss Banks's corps, demonstrated inspired leadership of divisions. But, as a colonel of the Pennsylvania Reserves noted, "the principal business of a division commander in [Pope's] campaign" appeared to be "looking for some one to give [him] orders!"[9] Additionally, Union armies in Virginia underwent major changes in the weeks leading up to the formation of Pope's army: new corps were formed, and divisions were cannibalized to fill the new formations. Upon congressional rejection of his promotion to major general of volunteers, for instance, James Shields's division broke up as it marched to Alexandria. Some of his brigades went to reinforce McClellan on the peninsula, while others were reassigned to divisions in Banks's and Irvin McDowell's commands.[10] Louis Blenker's division of German American regiments was also cannibalized when he fell under a cloud of scandal, although its brigades all remained under John Frémont's (and then Franz Sigel's) overall command.[11]

Republicans led no fewer than six of Pope's infantry brigades, most flamboyantly the amateurs Robert Milroy and Abram S. Piatt and West Point graduate Abner Doubleday. If not the most militarily effective generals at the start, they learned on the job. Their battlefield liabilities were more than balanced by the solid-to-brilliant performance of nonpartisan West Point brigadiers Samuel Crawford, George Gordon, John Gibbon, George Meade, Zealous Tower, and cavalry brigadiers John Buford and George Bayard.

The experience of the Army of Virginia's cavalry brigades epitomizes the brigade-level cohesion of the army. Pope reorganized the cavalry in his army into three brigades, one attached to each army corps.[12] Pope appointed Benjamin Stone Roberts, who had only been a general for ten days, as the army's chief of cavalry, but Roberts effected little in the coordination or direction of operations in his brigades. His recent promotion, moreover, meant he was junior in rank to two of his three brigade commanders, Bayard and John P. Hatch. Among veterans of the prewar regular army, Roberts had a reputation for accomplishing the minimum required to keep his commission. One of Pope's engineers used to joke "about some of his ways of *shunning* military duty etc.," but now, in wartime, the engineer saw Roberts in a new light, as "a very good officer and a man of many excellent qualities."[13] Roberts proved more effective as a sort of inspector general for the army's cavalry, however, than as the commander of Pope's overworked mounted arm.

After Banks's II Corps was mauled at Cedar Mountain in early August, its cavalry brigade was reassigned to provide scouts for the two divisions of Ambrose E. Burnside's IX Corps, which joined Pope's army, and to add muscle to the two mounted brigades used to screen enemy cavalry.[14] As the army's eyes and ears, the three cavalry brigades could expect to encounter rebel guerrillas as well as regular Confederate cavalry. Although Pope concentrated his cavalry to a greater degree than McClellan ever did, he is still faulted for not going far enough.[15] That assessment is rather unfair to Pope and the Army of Virginia, which had the old forces' dual defensive responsibilities for the distinct regions of the Shenandoah Valley and Fredericksburg. Pope could only unite his corps under threat of a major Confederate offensive. So long as his three corps were dispersed, each needed a dedicated cavalry force for reconnaissance purposes.

The two generals at the helm of Banks's and McDowell's mounted brigades brought to the important tasks of scouting and counterinsurgency years of experience gained while fighting Native Americans with the regular cavalry. "Gen. Bayard has had a great deal of experience in fighting Indian Guerrillas and probably he understands how to fight Virginia Guerillas also," a Pennsylvania cavalryman noted. "He has in his brigade two regiments of cavalry a Battalion or four companies of the Bucktails and a battery of flying artillery or Mountain Howitzers. It is called the flying brigade because the Bucktails can travel nearly as fast as our cavalry," as their knapsacks were hauled by wagon.[16]

The men and officers of the cavalry brigades were the first to experience the sort of active campaigning Pope's decrees envisaged. In late July, a squadron of the 1st New Jersey Cavalry crossed the Rappahannock River at Raccoon Ford on the initiative of a mere lieutenant. Soon after, his patrol "struck the enemy, who rushed down upon us and pushed us into the river. A big burly chap made me his special object of attack. In the melee he lost his saber, yanked his scabbard off and hit me on the head, which quite stunned me. I was well defended by my men." The patrol returned to the other side of the river with three wounded. The lieutenant was concerned that he faced a reprimand for scouting without orders, but General Bayard only remarked, "You were quite inquisitive. Inquisitiveness brings experience."[17]

Pope's contribution to the mounted arm of the Union's eastern armies was understated compared to that of McClellan, but more useful in both strategic and tactical senses. Pope envisioned each brigade as the eyes and ears of the corps to which it was attached, able to screen an advance or delay pursuit. McClellan's antebellum analysis of the use of cavalry on the battlefield was certainly impressive enough. When the Crimean

War broke out in Europe in 1853, Secretary of War Jefferson Davis sent a delegation of army officers to study the conflict. Captain McClellan of the 1st Cavalry was a part of the mission, focusing his study on the Russian and Austrian cavalry. The most lasting impact of his mission was the McClellan saddle, "modeled upon the Austrian pattern, which remained the official saddle of the United States mounted troops until the end of its horse-cavalry days."[18] He also wrote a study of European cavalry as well as a field manual for cavalry.[19]

A major problem with McClellan's manual was his insistence that "the strength of cavalry is in the spurs and sabre," the mounted charge; on the densely wooded terrain of northern Virginia, this simply was not true.[20] However aged and infirm he may have been, even General Winfield Scott knew that Virginia's terrain required a major departure from European cavalry practice.[21] Despite the months McClellan spent (or wasted) planning his Peninsula Campaign, and for all his antebellum study of European cavalry, he planned little and inadequately for the use of his cavalry. McClellan took a mere dozen regiments of cavalry to scout for 210 infantry regiments and some 60 artillery batteries, and then poorly used them.[22] McClellan failed to learn the lessons of the Peninsula Campaign, moreover, and did not use his cavalry well during the Antietam Campaign either. Not cavalry scouts but footsore infantrymen from one of Pope's old Indiana regiments stumbled on Lee's secret orders and gave McClellan an opportunity to catch Lee's divided army at Sharpsburg.

Pope's more sizeable mounted units with the three disparate commands in northern Virginia nonetheless also were outmatched by their rebel counterparts in the Shenandoah Valley. Much of this was due to the poor initial choice of cavalry commanders. Other reasons included the inexperience of the volunteer Union cavalrymen, the skill of Confederate cavalry commanders and rebel horsemen, and the daunting topography and size of the campaign territory. The small army under Banks, the main victim of Stonewall Jackson's campaigns during the spring of 1862, contained the equivalent of three cavalry regiments under the command of Brigadier General John Porter Hatch. A West Point graduate and artillerist in the prewar army, Hatch reported to McDowell from a posting in Annapolis as "Chief of Cavalry" of his corps on March 18, and took his whole staff with him. Hatch was happy with his sedentary post in Maryland, "but my place is in the field and unless I get a chance to do something the war will close and I find myself a Captain" again in the tiny regular army.[23]

A week later Hatch was in Washington but unsure of his next command; "I may be put in command of a Brigade of Infantry or I may be kept as Chief of Cavalry," he noted. Hatch claimed he would be "satisfied with any position they may determine to give me," though, and seemed more concerned about his former regular army battery stationed in New Mexico, which had lost heavily in a recent skirmish. While he applied for the command of the small relief force to be sent to New Mexico, he was convinced "it will probably be given to some politician who will manage to make some reputation out of it."[24]

By April Fool's Day, Hatch knew he was being transferred to Banks's command; however, he was under the impression he would have "a very fine" command, "consisting of seven mounted Regiments," rather than the three he actually led.[25] Banks heaped praise on his chief of cavalry "for the spirit infused into his troops during the brief period of his command, which, by concession of friend and foe, had been made equal, if not superior, to the best of the enemy's long-trained mounted troops."[26] Banks's assessment is questionable, however, as it was written after his force was chased into Maryland and barely escaped annihilation at Winchester.[27] In truth, as Banks had admitted earlier, his mounted arm was "mostly inexperienced men and untrained horses weak in numbers and spirit—much exhausted with night and day work."[28]

While recuperating and re-equipping his brigade, Hatch noted that the civilians of western Maryland treated Union soldiers "with the greatest kindness," and he was convinced that "there is no secession feeling in this portion of Maryland."[29] General Lee would have been well advised to obtain this intelligence before invading Maryland in September. Unlike white Virginians, western Maryland "farmers staid at home and attended to their farms and the consequence is instead of weeds as high as a mans head we find corn, potatoes fruit of all kinds and many grain and haystacks," a soldier from Wisconsin observed.[30] A week before the birth of the Army of Virginia and the start of the Seven Days Battles, Hatch confidently informed his sister that "if Fremont makes a junction with us we will be strong enough to meet any force that can be spared [by Jackson] to meet us." He was realistic enough to recognize, however, that if McClellan "is defeated we will be compelled to evacuate once more."[31]

Ten days later Hatch noted major shifts in the Army of Virginia. "The recent change in the organization of the Army gives great satisfaction to all but the [corps] leaders. Genl. Fremont has done what the President undoubtedly desired he would do, that is 'asked to be relieved from duty.' I think he will resign." Sigel was likely to follow Frémont, which Hatch hoped would happen. "We can get along without Dutch generals or Dutch soldiers, and it is a great pity that any were ever taken into service." As for the new commander, "I know Pope well, believe him to be a man of talent, and I hope he will prove capable. One commander were it an inferior one is better than three." Hatch had a West Pointer's contempt for his corps commander though. Banks "is a good man for a politician, but is no general, having no confidence in himself and little military talent." While Banks was "mortified at having a junior put over his head," Hatch was confident that he "will not make a difficulty about it."[32]

Pope, on the other hand, discovered with his army's first cavalry raid that Hatch was not suited to the command of an intrepid raiding and scouting force. Lincoln had promised Hatch a major general's commission if he succeeded, sufficient motivation to execute a daring raid when he set off with five cavalry and two infantry regiments on July 17. Intelligence showed that Hatch would not face any significant enemy forces, but he failed to use his mostly mounted units to gain further intelligence, was surprised by an enemy force, and returned to camp.[33] A key sign that Hatch was not fit to command a lightning cavalry raid was the inclusion of infantry, artillery, and even a wagon train in his striking force.[34] Pope was oddly restrained in his criticism about the raid, however; he provided detailed instructions as to how cavalry raids should be conducted and gave Hatch a second chance. Hatch botched that one as well.[35]

By July 29 Hatch had been relieved and sent to Wisconsin Republican Rufus King's infantry division, a lateral transfer rather than a demotion. The general was fortunate not to be transferred away from combat commands entirely and relegated to commandant of a garrison. Admitting that his brief career as commander of the advance guard of Pope's army "did not give satisfaction," Hatch blamed his lack of success on his troops. "They are not reliable. I shall be better pleased with my new command." Hatch also now had "no confidence in Pope, and shall be astonished if with all his bluster anything is done."[36]

Hatch's replacement was General Buford, rescued by Pope from a desk job and put in more fitting roles as an inspector general and then at the head of an active cavalry force. Buford, like McDowell's cavalry chief George Bayard, had served in the old army and spent the immediate prewar years fighting Native Americans on the Great Plains with a regiment of dragoons (mounted infantry).[37] Although promoted three ranks at one jump, Buford did not make any major sartorial changes, unlike most of his old army peers. He continued to wear a Kentucky hunting shirt and a similarly well-worn dark blue blouse with his large tobacco pipe sticking out from a pocket, complementing his tanned complexion and unoiled moustache, although at some point he acquired a coat with the appropriate general's stars and buttons.[38] Infantrymen in Banks's force noticed the marked change in the corps cavalry that Buford represented. The new general dressed and rode differently from the other dandies on horseback, as if he understood that war was a serious business and not a parade ground affair.[39]

Buford and his two colleagues still had their work cut out for them, as the majority of their troopers lacked carbines to engage enemy cavalry and infantry at long range. Pistols and sabers were fine for cavalry charges, but carbines were needed for scouting duty and dismounted action against enemy infantry. The few carbines available to cavalry regiments were usually inferior models that often malfunctioned in the field. Frémont's entire cavalry brigade was equipped with only sabers and pistols. A major of the 1st Maine Cavalry in Bayard's brigade noted that in the heavily forested "topography of the country, it is next to impossible to encounter our foes successfully, as he is never in a position where saber and pistol can be used," and his unit had only seventy-two carbines.[40] A squadron of the 2nd New York received twenty-two Sharps carbines on June 22, but fewer than half of the troopers in the unit were issued first-rate carbines. Most made do with Colt or Beales revolvers.[41] The squadron of Indiana cavalry attached to McDowell's corps exchanged second-rate revolvers for top-of-the-line Colt army revolvers on August 10, and eleven days later was issued new carbines—though no record exists as to what model these were.[42]

Just how undermanned and outmatched Pope's cavalry were was evident in early August, when the three brigades had to picket and patrol the banks of the Rapidan and Rappahannock Rivers on both flanks of the infantry corps. The four thousand men of Bayard's and Buford's brigades—minus the hundreds of men on detached duty as generals' escorts, orderlies, and couriers—had to patrol a line of more than forty miles along the Rapidan alone. Their task was to prevent J. E. B. Stuart's cavalry from launching one of his famous raids around the army—and wreaking havoc in the army's supply trains—as well as to delay and report any flanking movement by masses of fast-marching rebel infantry, Stonewall Jackson's vaunted "foot cavalry." Frequent skirmishing with rebel cavalry and constant riding wore out both horses and men.[43] Sigel's cavalry chief reported that his men and horses were in no better shape than those of Bayard and Buford, weakened by hard riding and poor feed for the horses. By August 29, most of the surviving horses could not be ridden.[44]

Intra-army misunderstandings also undermined the morale of the average trooper. A sharpshooter in the garrison of Fredericksburg noted in mid-July the lack of appreciation infantry division and corps commanders had for cavalry. "Everything here is quiet the Cavalry Scouts occasionally bring in a prisoner or two to be let go again by the Officers in command if it goes on in that way much longer there wont be many Prisoners brought in the Cavalry Boys say and I don't blame them."[45] By the time battle was joined at Manassas, Buford and Bayard had informed Pope that in their commands "there was not 5 horses to the company that could be forced into a trot." The day after Second Bull Run, Pope sent a desperate telegraph to Henry Halleck: "I need cavalry horses terribly. Send me 2,000 I need them badly—worse than I can tell you."[46]

Buford's cavalry brigade did provide the Army of Virginia's commander with one major intelligence coup, along with a fine feather for the cap of General Buford, by literally capturing Stuart's feathered hat. On August 16, Buford's brigade crossed the Rapidan, rode around Jackson's right flank, and occupied Orange Court House. Two of Buford's regiments rode on in a southeasterly direction along the railroad route to Richmond. At Verdiersville on the evening of August 17, they overran Stuart's headquarters, almost capturing the general and taking his fancy cloak, ostrich-plumed hat, and adjutant (Major Norman Fitzhugh). On Fitzhugh were documents revealing that the main body of Robert E. Lee's army had joined Jackson's force and was now planning to encircle and destroy Pope's army. This intelligence, sent posthaste to Pope's headquarters, precipitated a rapid withdrawal from the Rapidan to the Rappahannock. This coup almost certainly saved the Army of Virginia.[47]

Although the cavalry reforms initiated by Pope, Bayard, and Buford were altering the way that Union troopers campaigned and viewed their role in the war effort, infantrymen were slower to believe any real changes were occurring. The old notion that the infantry did the hard marching, bleeding and dying while cavalrymen rode away from hard combat as fast as their horses could carry them, died hard.[48] "The [1st] Michigan cavalry have a woman whom they carry around horseback and with their band and this woman, reduces war down to a farce," a lieutenant of infantry wrote. "I saw once the band and this woman, a half dozen officers with the remains of a terribly decimated Company [following] in the rear. Said someone '*That's rather a large head for so small a body.*' Very pert I thought."[49] Men in the infantry brigades led a less romantic life on campaign.

"My brigade is as good a one as in service," a reinvigorated John Hatch wrote on August 9. Hatch was "gratified by the kind feelings expressed by my old cavalry command, when I parted with them. One Regt. escorted me out of town and I was cheered as I left camp." But he was happier as an infantry brigadier. Hatch was now a devoted McClellanite. Although McClellan's failure to take Richmond was "a mystery," Hatch noted that Burnside's corps had arrived, and thought Burnside—a friend of McClellan's—would "superceed Pope if he is unsuccessful. Pope has not the confidence of us old soldiers."[50]

The shift proved most profitable for Hatch's career. His popular division commander, Rufus King, was subject to epileptic seizures, and one struck as two of his brigades were engaged by Stonewall Jackson's divisions at Groveton on August 27. As the senior brigadier, Hatch took command of the division the next day and led it through the Second Bull Run and Antietam campaigns.[51] Hatch would have his revenge, and indeed uttered the brief elegy on Pope's army command; on the afternoon of September 2, as Pope and McClellan met at the outer fortifications defending Washington to pass authority over the retreating army, Hatch rode up to his division. Within Pope's hearing, Hatch shouted, "Boys, McClellan is in command of the army again! Three cheers!"[52] The weary men responded with loud enthusiasm.

Some West Point brigadiers were strict but earned their men's respect by their attention to detail. While still a colonel, Fort Sumter veteran Abner Doubleday inspected his regiments in the early spring. "Inspection of arms by Col. Doubleday who condemnd our guns," a soldier in the 88th Pennsylvania noted. He "broke some of our bayonets and rammers in trying them."[53] As a West Point graduate, Doubleday was trained to pay attention to basic equipment and its upkeep, a detail that politically appointed generals with no military experience were likely to overlook.

Unlike Hatch, Doubleday owed his promotion to his Republican political connections. Even before battle was joined at Manassas in July 1861, Doubleday's relatives appealed to Radical Republicans in Congress to support his promotion to brigadier general on the grounds of his political loyalties. "When you reflect that there are not more than twenty such Republican officers in the U.S. Army, it is time that those who have been true to their principles under the opposing circumstances surrounding them should be remembered," a relation wrote to Michigan Republican Zachariah Chandler. "We ought to have officers to command our army whose heart is in the work like Captain [Nathanael] Lyons of St. Louis and Captain Doubleday of Fort Sumter."[54]

Brigadier General Abner Doubleday. (Library of Congress)

The soldiers serving under brigadiers like Doubleday and Hatch took great interest in their commanders. The men of Hatch's infantry brigade may have liked their new brigadier but such was not always the case. "Nothing is so pleasant as to have a popular General," a member of the 10th Maine in Banks's corps wrote of John Pope. "A change in our Brigade commander would have hurt no ones feelings. It is a pity that in the multitude of Brigadiers, that those of merit should not receive good positions, and meritorious troops be well Brigadiered."[55] The denigrated officer was surgeon-turned-general Samuel Crawford. "I saw Crawford for the first time yesterday," a Massachusetts captain wrote in July; "he is a very fancy looking individual indeed he was assistant surgeon at Fort Sumter and got his Brigadiership for that but I do not imagine he knows much about military matters."[56] A musician in the 5th Connecticut recorded an unpopular order by General Crawford in July: "Regt. were all searched for Pistols and all that were found were confiscated by Order of Corporal Crawford, as all the boys called the General. He isn't thought much of in the Brigade."[57] A Maine lieutenant was still running down Crawford in early September. He compared Crawford with McDowell, who was universally unpopular after Second Bull Run: "The Government must put McDowells and Crawfords and all politicians in the back ground and promote men who show ability."[58]

State rivalries could and did play a role in the preference or dislike that common soldiers and volunteer officers held for their brigade, division, and corps commanders. As the Union armies did not follow the Confederate example of forming brigades composed of regiments from the same state, such invidious comparisons were almost inevitable.[59] The three brigades of the Pennsylvania Reserve Division faced initially the least problematic relationship with their brigade and division commanders, as all were organized in the Keystone Commonwealth.[60]

Brigades in which all the regiments hailed from disparate states were fodder for discord when a new brigadier was appointed from among the regimental commanders, as the soldiers often believed there was favoritism toward a particular state. One solution was to appoint a West Point–educated brigadier general promoted from the regular army, as in the case of North Carolina native John Gibbon's assignment to command a brigade in McDowell's III Corps composed of one Indiana and three Wisconsin regiments. In Gibbon's case, however, the western volunteers initially united in their dislike for a regular officer's draconian rules and exacting standards.[61] Geographical divisions beyond the state level could also come into play; western soldiers sometimes resented eastern commanders, and vice versa.

Such rivalries were presumably not eased by biases at the highest level. In implementing his western, hard-war policies in Virginia, Pope betrayed a tendency to play favorites when comparing western and eastern soldiers. Since in his rhetoric he proclaimed the superiority of western to eastern soldiers, so Pope expected to find the western troops in his new army to be made of sterner stuff than the easterners. "The Genl is not very pleased with his present command," an Illinois officer on Pope's staff informed his father on the day the general began reviewing his new army, "and I can not find fault with him for not liking it." If the Army of Virginia comprised a "sufficiently large [force] to make a good fight, they are a different material from our western men: seeming more willing to retreat, than advance."[62] Fortunately, the western regiments appeared solid enough. A private in the 3rd Wisconsin noted that upon passing his regiment in a division review in early August, Pope remarked that this was "a fine regiment." When Banks informed him that this was a Wisconsin unit, Pope commented that "all the Wisconsin Regiments that he seen was very fine regiments."[63] Pope was predisposed to look to the few western regiments in his army to provide a fighting elite.

In mid-August, rumors circulated among the soldiers of John Gibbon's brigade of Indiana and Wisconsin regiments. "Gen Pope wants to see the western troops so it is said," commented a private in the 7th Wisconsin.[64] "Gen. Pope assured Gen. Gibbon that his (Gibbons) Brigade was the *best* he ever saw," a Wisconsin officer noted after a morning review of his unit by Pope and McDowell.[65] The westerners' brigade commander proudly transmitted Pope's opinion to the men: "Pope said that Our Brigade was the best in the service, the largest & best looking men."[66] Pope's comments, uttered barely a week after he joined the army, made an important early impression.[67] Events on the battlefield at Groveton on August 28 proved Gibbon's all-western brigade was indeed combat effective; they inflicted heavy casualties on a foe that outnumbered them two to one.[68] At no other engagement in the campaign of the Army of Virginia did units of Pope's army inflict heavier casualties on the foe.

Pope was not alone in praising western units as superior to their eastern counterparts. Maryland native and West Point graduate Colonel Samuel Carroll favored the 7th Indiana above the eastern regiments in his brigade. "He takes a great interest in our Regt.," a sergeant informed his parents, even to the extent of holding a special drill in the evening just for the 7th, "and says it is the 'Star of the Brigade.'"[69] "Again we are brought under the command of an Eastern man, who has no sympathy whatever with Western troops," an enlisted man in the 66th Ohio wrote of the promotion of Pennsylvanian John W. Geary to command his brigade. "The Western men will fight bravely under an officer whom they like, and in whom they have confidence," the Ohioan wrote his local newspaper, "but to seek a General in Pennsylvania, of all the States, does not accord with their ideas at all. We have seen too many Pennsylvania troops already," to possess any "confidence in their fighting abilities."[70] The common soldiers were usually more concerned with the travails of daily life than the politics of high command, but the origins and ideas of their commanders clearly mattered to some.

Ethnicity was a source of conflict in the organization and operation of higher-level units in the Army of Virginia as well. "I want time to apply myself to getting my Division in good condition," Robert Schenck wrote after losing command of I Corps. "My German Brigade requires attention."[71] Two days later he announced a plan "to try a little disapline by closer and more immediate command, on the Dutch part of my Division.

Oh! if I had nice independent command of my own, with good troops, of good American material altogether, how much more easily and satisfactorily I could get along!"[72]

The men of Pope's army viewed their brigades as the fundamental political unit of their martial society, where men from different states debated politics, marched, drilled, and fought together as members of a volunteer army dedicated to the preservation of republican government. This did not negate the importance of small-unit cohesion, particularly when volunteer regiments consisted of companies raised in one county or even a single town. Yet soldiers found it hard to pay attention to the status of men outside their own regiment. "I presume you see . . . frequent mention made of the [1st] Maine Cavalry," a Massachusetts infantryman wrote home. "They are said to be composed of superior men, to be ambitious of excelling in the art of arms, etc. Well, I confess to feeling more interest in troops that come from near my own home, than from a section of country where I am an entire stranger."[73]

Men with friends or relatives in other regiments from the same state expressed concern about their movements and made efforts to visit them. The unit most frequently referred to in letters home was the all-western brigade commanded by North Carolina Unionist John Gibbon, consisting of one Indiana and three Wisconsin regiments. This is not surprising as the largest contingent (49) in this study's 250-man source base were the Indiana and Wisconsin members of what was later known as the Iron Brigade. The runner-up, with 35 officers and men, was the unit of Pennsylvania Reserves, a division of three brigades that served in both McClellan's Peninsula and Pope's Second Bull Run campaigns.[74]

Coincident with the ascendancy of Pope was the institution of regular brigade drills, held on a weekly basis. "Things keep about the same except we have a brigade drill two hours in the forenoon and the regiment is formed in light marching order at sunrise every morning," a Wisconsin corporal wrote.[75] For a month, General Marsena Patrick's brigade camped near Falmouth on the Rappahannock. He "established his headquarters near the front of [a fine natural drill ground], where the various regiments of his brigade, [were] constantly under his eye." Brigade drill was held every morning immediately after reveille, "from five to seven," and—tryingly for bleary-eyed and empty-stomached soldiers—before breakfast.[76]

Another brigade in Patrick's division suffered regular drills under the exacting eyes of a different West Point graduate. "We are 'up in the early morning' and [assembled by] 7 o'clock in fighting order, paraded for brigade drill by Gen. Gibbons," one captain noted on July 16. "This is the first attempt the 'Brigadier' has made at drilling his 'Western Brigade.'"[77] "It appeared that Gibbon [was] determined to prepare us for some sanguinary conflict," a Wisconsin sergeant complained. "This morning he drilled us over two hours and a half." It was the second straight day Gibbon had held a long brigade drill and the fourth brigade exercise in six days.[78] "We are having brigade drills every morning at 7 a.m.[,] splendid drills," another soldier wrote. "I do not think there is a brigade in the army that can beat us in it."[79]

Despite "extremely hot" weather, a sergeant in the 75th Ohio noted the continuance of drills at all echelons of Franz Sigel's corps on August 8. "While on drill, we have Battalion drill every day, Sunday excepted, and company drill in the afternoon, Brigade drill once or twice a week and Division drill once a week, and review, or rather maneuvering as if we were engaged in a grand battle by Sigels whole command."[80] An Indiana officer in Banks's corps noted drills at all levels in early August, from a single regiment to the entire corps: "We are drilling constantly going through all the maneouvers of Batalion Brigade and Army corps drill, had two army corps drills last week commanded in person by Gen Banks." A "general Review of the whole corps" was held in which Banks's men were "Inspected by Gen Pope who appeared among our lines for the first time he looks like he had the right grit about him," wrote the officer.[81]

One of McDowell's aides, Joseph Willard, formerly a prominent Washington hotelier, joined Pope's chief of cavalry in an August 16 inspection of III Corps' cavalry brigade, commanded by George Bayard.[82] Probably the most exciting part of cavalry brigade drills, for observers and participants, was "a charge on an imaginary foe, with sabers drawn and glistening in the sun." At least one infantryman thought "they looked as [though] they could sweep every thing before them."[83] The effect of such a charge on an organized infantry foe was rather different from parade ground appearances though. The 1st Pennsylvania Cavalry discovered the futility of this sort of mounted charge at Cedar Mountain on August 9 when they charged a Confederate infantry line to cover the retreat of Banks's infantry and took a hundred casualties from a single volley.[84]

Radical Republicans Salmon Chase of Ohio, Thaddeus Stevens of Pennsylvania, and Charles Sumner of Massachusetts represented the geographical alliance of westerners, denizens of the mid-Atlantic, and New Englanders that coalesced to elect the first Republican president. The

Army of Virginia, led by a Kentucky-born West Point graduate, consisted of the three northern constituencies combined with loyal border staters from Maryland and western Virginia who may not have voted for Lincoln but were determined to preserve the Union. They were joined by allies from south of the Mason-Dixon Line: thousands of African American contrabands who formed an unarmed auxiliary branch of the army, providing vital labor and military intelligence for an occupation force surrounded by a hostile civilian population. At a critical moment, Pope's army represented the realization of the dream of abolitionists like Wendell Phillips and a nightmare brought to life for Democrats like McClellan and Confederates alike. A single grand victory near Manassas would not only wipe out the stain of First Bull Run but enable Pope to supersede McClellan as commander of the Union armies in Virginia and usher in a presidential policy of emancipation.

John Pope lived up to some of his rhetoric, ordering his corps commanders to pitch into the enemy heedless of their position or strength at Cedar Mountain and Second Bull Run, without regard to lines of retreat or defense. At Second Bull Run, General Robert E. Lee's "desire ha[d] been to avoid a general engagement," but Pope's aggressive focus on the rebel army rather than a McClellan-like obsession with the rebel capital forced Lee to accept a full-scale battle.[85] As a western cavalry trooper in Pope's army put it in 1862, "our Potomac Generals have paid too much attention to . . . strong positions—and defensive works, lines of retreat, and bases of supplies" but "not enough to the weaknesses of the Enemy."[86]

The second battle at Manassas was a repeat of the first, however, and a tragedy for the Union war effort, which had been poised to become a war of emancipation rather than preservation of antebellum sectional compromise. Running from June 26 to September 1, the campaign coincided with the birth and death of Pope's army. After a few weeks of planning and reorganization, Lincoln decided that McClellan must retreat from Richmond to reinforce Pope. In mid-July the Army of Virginia therefore advanced from the Rappahannock to the Rapidan River to hold a defensive line and await McClellan's army. An August 6 advance on the railroad junction at Gordonsville spurred Stonewall Jackson to counterattack. He faced Nathaniel Prentiss Banks's II Corps at Cedar (or Slaughter) Mountain on August 9. Following Pope's aggressive rhetoric, Banks's men attacked Jackson, but superior numbers told, and Banks was driven back on the rest of Pope's force with a loss of 2,300 against Jackson's 1,300 casualties.[87]

Two weeks of skirmishing followed along the Rapidan and then Rappahannock defensive lines. To break the stalemate before McClellan's legions could reinforce Pope, on August 26 Lee sent Jackson's wing of the rebel army around Pope's right flank to destroy the Union supply depot at Manassas Junction. Pope sent his entire army haring after Jackson on August 27, ignoring the other wing of Lee's army for the next three days.[88] Two corps from McClellan's army (III and V) joined Pope's columns as they converged on Manassas. Having feasted on Pope's supplies, Jackson's corps took up defensive positions along an unfinished railroad cut north of the First Manassas battlefield. After ambushing one III Corps division on August 28, Jackson's force weathered disjointed offensives by Pope's army on August 29.[89] The rest of Lee's army joined Jackson by that evening, and following more abortive Union advances, counterattacked on the next afternoon and drove the Union army (which suffered over ten thousand casualties to Lee's eight thousand) from the battlefield. After a brief skirmish at Chantilly on September 1, the armies of Virginia and the Potomac retreated to the defenses of Washington, where McClellan assumed overall command.[90]

# 4 Generals, Officers, and Citizen-Soldiers

BRIEF AND MILITARILY unsuccessful as was the lifespan of the Army of Virginia, its story illuminates the significance of politics in the Union Army's ranks, motivating its leaders, determining relationships and rivalries, and demonstrating the forces that affected not only the conduct of war but government policies as well. Politics permeated the views and actions of generals, officers, and citizen-soldiers alike.

The forms in which politics were expressed for generals and officers derived in part from their different statuses. An officer gained promotion to general via nomination by the president, an appointment subject to the "advice and consent of the Senate."[1] John Pope's promotion and his command, as well as his policies, were beholden to the support of Republican politicians. Officers—ranking from second lieutenant to colonel—were subdivided into field and company grades. Field officers—colonels, lieutenant colonels, and majors—were chosen by their governor or fellow officers; company officers were elected by their men. These distinctions indicate to whom these officers owed their status.[2]

The political stance of generals influenced their military decisions, their possibility of advancement, and their relationship to their troops. Generals' political views were visible to southern civilians and northern soldiers alike as they performed occupation duty. This was particularly clear in Fredericksburg, a strategic town occupied by Union forces. In a single week in May, three different generals—all from Irvin McDowell's corps—held the military governorship of the town. Discipline-obsessed and Democratic West Point graduate Marsena Patrick left town on May 23. The post was taken over by the Republican Abner Doubleday, the only one of nine commissioned officers stationed at Fort Sumter in 1861 to have voted for Abraham Lincoln the previous fall.[3] "I feel sad," Patrick wrote, "at the thought that these helpless families are to be left to

Brigadier General Marsena Patrick (*center*) and staff. (Library of Congress)

the tender mercies of an Abolitionist." Doubleday was disgusted with Patrick's kid-glove policies in a nest of rebel sympathizers. "I found it quite impossible to carry out a policy, the effect of which was simply to discourage the Union men and favor the rebels." Doubleday protected Unionists and facilitated the flow of contrabands across the Rappahannock to freedom behind Union lines. Two days later Doubleday's superior replaced him with John Reynolds, an apolitical yet anti-abolitionist West Point graduate who resumed Patrick's practices.[4]

The majority of the generals of the Army of Virginia were West Point graduates, professional rather than political generals. Twenty of the thirty-four generals in the army graduated from the military academy. They were, by seniority of rank and then alphabetically: McDowell, Pope, Christopher Augur, George Bayard, John Buford, Doubleday, John Gibbon, George Gordon, George Greene, George Hartsuff, John Hatch, Rufus King, George Meade, Patrick, Henry Prince, John Reynolds, James Ricketts, Truman Seymour, Samuel Sturgis, and Zealous Tower. West Point alumni were heavily concentrated in McDowell's III Corps, in which thirteen of fifteen generals were graduates. In Nathaniel Prentiss Banks's corps, five of eight generals attended West Point, while Franz

Sigel's corps trailed with none of its seven generals boasting a West Point education. All but seven of George McClellan's generals were West Pointers by August 1862. Professional officers of the antebellum army, inured to glacial promotion rates, were sensitive to issues of seniority, an obsession that began at the moment of graduation from West Point, when final class standing determined a cadet's regular army branch. Top graduates joined the highly prestigious engineer or artillery arms, branches carrying prestige but slow promotion rates; the rest joined the infantry or cavalry.[5] As historian William B. Skelton notes, the Corps of Engineers—the army's most select group of top-ranked West Point graduates—was the most politically active branch of the antebellum army. This trend was certainly borne out in the highest echelons of the Virginia army. Both John Frémont and John Pope—prewar topographical engineers—campaigned for power within the regular army while cultivating ties to the Republican Party.[6]

Meteoric promotion could occur in time of war, but politics was a surer route to promotion than combat. Officers who advanced further and faster than their classmates due to political connections rather than bravery excited jealousy. Volunteer officers saw how jealousies over rank from the antebellum army bled over into the Union Army's command structure, with potentially deadly results for soldiers. "Politics rules everything and the number of political appointments to the army which passed the senate the last two days of the session was sufficient to disgust an honest man," wrote one officer.[7] Many officers and enlisted men deplored West Point graduates' handling of the war. "If it were not for the *Regular Army,* the war would be over in 60 days," an Ohio officer groused.[8] Political generals shared their subordinates' disgust with professionals. "If the Devil had swallowed [West Point] 40 years ago, this rebellion would have been crushed Months ago," wrote one. "Our Genls. would now have been governed by common sense instead of West Point Slavery."[9]

The father of a Wisconsin officer supervising engineering work ordered by McDowell was asked why the general did not march from Fredericksburg to help McClellan capture Richmond. "McClellan jumped McDowell in the way of promotion," the officer replied; "a regular never forgives another man for jumping him in the way of promotion." He claimed that when McClellan left for the peninsula with orders for McDowell to follow, "McDowell and his friends cheated little Mc out of fifty thousand of his best troops."[10] In truth, Lincoln held McDowell's corps back when he found that the force McClellan had left in place to protect Washington, D.C., was smaller than promised.[11]

Five of the sixteen political generals—half Republicans, half Democrats—in David Work's recent study of these men served with Pope. All were Republicans: Banks, Frémont, Sigel, Robert Schenck, and Carl Schurz. Six of the generals were in the western theater that summer and ten in Virginia.[12] Of the eight Democratic generals Work analyzed, three were with or near McClellan on the peninsula, none with Pope. Political officers in the Potomac army learned to accept that promotion to general within the army was largely on the basis of McClellan's criteria: battlefield bravery, West Point pedigree, and personal loyalty. Generals of suspect loyalty like Banks and McDowell were shunted to backwater commands. Whenever possible, McClellan imposed the antebellum army's promotion criteria on his West Point–dominated force, a clear departure from the partisan promotions endemic in the Army of Virginia prior to Pope's arrival, which Pope had little choice but to accept. Pope lacked the ten months McClellan enjoyed to shape the army to his will. If he could not prevent volunteer regiments from democratically electing their officers, McClellan imposed competency exams and demanded West Point's emphases on discipline and drill from those seeking promotion to general.[13] Only two of his infantry brigades included regular regiments (a single regular infantry battalion served with Pope), but the other thirty brigades and their volunteer officers accepted the regular rules for advancement.

If most political generals in Pope's army identified as Republicans, brigade commander John W. Geary was an example of the "War Democrat" general in Banks's II Corps. Geary "occupied a leading place in the Mexican War, and was afterward Mayor of San Francisco." He worked "with the Southern wing of the Democratic Party," an alliance he rethought in 1861, "and was quietly ambitious, promoting the agricultural interests of his commonwealth."[14] As territorial governor of Kansas in 1857, he informed a Democratic newspaper that the hard working "white man, with his intellectual energy, far reaching science and indomitable perseverance," was the "peculiar object of my sympathy."[15] One Pennsylvania journalist found Geary "a fine exemplar of the American gentleman, preserving the better individualities of his countrymen, but discarding those grosser traits which have given us an unenviable name abroad." Nevertheless, he was subject to the demands of partisan politics. "The bias of party, which in America diseases the best natures," affected Geary. "He was prone to go with his party in any event, when his fine intelligence would have prompted him to an independent course."[16] Still, Geary possessed the "utmost confidence and respect" of a lieutenant in the 3rd Maryland: "He is not aristocratic enough to suit some tastes and is rather petulant, but the latter results from his disgust at every thing that evinces anything other than *pure* patriotism."[17]

By the summer of 1862 northern journalists were engaged in a war of words over the proper strategy and tactics for the Union war effort, exchanges that gained heat because many, if not most, newspapers were organs of political parties. As historian Bernard Weisburger notes, "according to journalistic accounts Civil War fighting men had the temperamental instability of operatic leads. They burst into either tears or 'oaths' at any unusual development in the news, [and] one could find an army to suit one's taste merely by selecting the right journal of fearless and impartial opinion."[18]

Debates in the press over military leadership centered not on quality but "amounted to a struggle between those who anticipated emancipation as the ultimate goal of the war and those who would refrain from meddling in any manner with the institution of slavery."[19] "The politicization of military questions introduced potentially catastrophic conflicts in the upper reaches of the Union's military and political leadership," notes historian Wayne Wei-Siang Hsieh. "Frustrated by McClellan's mixture of conservative politics and military lethargy, the most ardently anti-slavery segments of the ruling northern political party" joined with Republican generals, newspapers, and citizen-soldiers to reconstruct the traitorous South. After all, "McClellan's old army allies hardly helped matters by using 'military science' as a partisan club to pound Radical Republicans in open political combat," particularly when "military science" entailed kid-glove treatment of southern whites, their old political allies.[20]

Full-time journalists employed by the *New York Herald* or *Tribune* reported on army-level events from the perspective of generals, which businessmen and politicians in the major cities found relevant. These prominent newspapermen were welcomed for the benefit their positive (or inflated) reports of battlefield sagacity and valor could have on the career of an officer by publicizing heroism to influential political "friends." "We have with us a newspaper correspondent and on him our [prominent] friends at a distance must depend for military news," a staff colonel at army headquarters noted in early August.[21]

Political generals were particularly dependent on the good graces of their home-state constituents and worried incessantly as to how their battlefield valor (or lack thereof), as reported in newspapers, affected their reputations. Journalists from prominent newspapers thus had politically minded generals at their mercy. Division commander Rufus King, a Republican from Wisconsin, was sensitive to the coverage of his military career by newspapers in New York, Washington, and Wisconsin. "The feeling is very strong against McClellan in very many places," a West Point graduate from New York noted in July. "Even King gets a slap" from the Republican-run *New York Tribune,* one of King's brigadiers penciled.[22] King's subordinate was "disgusted" at the ways newspapers held his commander's will hostage to the agendas of Radical Republicans. Appalled by his soldiers' looting, a brigade commander wanted to send out guards to arrest thieves, but "Gen. King has sent me an Order to withdraw my guards from all Rebel property and houses. He is frightened at the attacks of Newspaper writers and the *Tribune* and Pope's Order for political purposes."[23]

The most important newspaper, in Pope's mind, was Horace Greeley's *New York Tribune,* and at least two *Tribune* men rode with Pope. Greeley's weekly paper was read by Republicans across the northern states. Historian James Ford Rhodes claims that to read the *Tribune* was to understand the 2 million men who voted for Lincoln in 1860.[24] Pope had good reason to support Greeley's reporters; they paraded his aggressive strategy and rhetoric before the eyes of Republicans far from the battlefields. Unlike McClellan, "Pope is one of the stirring sort of men," the *Tribune* boasted the day after he received his new army, "and will not be likely to stand on the bank of the Potomac until all the water has run down before crossing."[25]

As early as December 1861, during an address at the Smithsonian Institute, Greeley looked directly at the president and declared that the primary objective of the war must be the destruction of slavery. Lincoln appeared unmoved. The president felt compelled to respond, however, when Greeley issued an open letter to the president while Pope's army faced off with Lee's across the Rappahannock River. The "Prayer of Twenty Millions," published on August 20, claimed, "What an immense majority of the loyal of your countrymen require of you is a frank execution of the law of the land, more especially the Confiscation Act. That act gives freedom to the slaves of rebels we ask you to render it due obedience by publicly requiring all your subordinates to recognize and obey it."[26]

Pope hardly ignored powerful Democratic newspapers in his quest for favorable press, though. The influential Democratic *New York Herald,* edited by James Gordon Bennett, overtly puffed McClellan in hopes of seeing him as Lincoln's Democratic opponent for the 1864 presidential election. It supported Lincoln during the summer but vigorously attacked Secretary of War Edwin Stanton, prompting at least one epistolary defense of the secretary from Lincoln.[27] The *Herald* blamed McClellan's defeat on the peninsula on Radical Republicans, demanding—in the name of a "furious" and "indignant" public—the immediate purge of all "radicals" from Lincoln's cabinet.[28] The *Herald*'s chief correspondent with the Army of Virginia was Frank Chapman, from whom Pope and his "radical" subordinates could hardly look for fair coverage.[29] Chapman was known for false reportage, to "appear to be in at the big events, whether there or not. I do not think he was anywhere near the battle of Cedar mountain," a colleague noted.[30] Pope also permitted George Townsend—a writer for Democratic newspapers in Philadelphia and New York known for fair journalism—to join his forces in the field.[31] Reports from a fair-minded Democratic journalist could balance those of a charlatan, in Pope's eyes.

Although leaks from newspapers, regardless of their political leanings, could pose a major threat to vital military operations, Pope sought to remain in the good graces of friendly reporters and newspapers. This remained true despite telling George W. Smalley of the Republican *New York Tribune* that Henry Halleck had sent him a "peremptory order to remove all reporters from his army, stop all telegrams" and all nonofficial mail.[32] On August 14, three northern newspapers based in urban centers printed compromising information that gave the rebel army an opportunity to crush the Army of Virginia well before any elements of McClellan's army were available to reinforce it. "Before a tent had been struck, or a division put in column for march," the *New York Tribune* and *Philadelphia Evening Bulletin* published stories declaring that the Army of the Potomac had left Harrison's Landing and the peninsula. The *New York Times* printed a similar story the next day.[33] Learning the lesson of August 14, General-in-Chief Halleck issued an order to expel all reporters from the Army of Virginia, hoping to prevent another leak. Pope carried this order out on August 22. Smalley said he would leave camp at once, but the general assured him it was not necessary, as "this is not an official interview" and that he had yet to make his mind up about enforcing the order.[34] Smalley took the hint and left army headquarters, laying low for several days, continuing to report, and tenting with a friendly officer before gaining an appointment as a volunteer aide to a division commander. Not all reporters fared so well; one was arrested nine times before getting beyond the lines of the Army of Virginia.[35] According to a *Chicago Times* reporter, two reporters for the Democratic *New York Herald* left the capital for Warrenton, Virginia, the day after a mass of reporters arrived following expulsion by Pope, yet these newcomers traveled with passes issued personally by the general.[36]

The respect of the soldiers under their command was of concern to both generals and officers, if more significant for the latter. No general in the army enjoyed a better reputation among the citizen-soldiers under his command than the Republican political general from Wisconsin, Rufus King. A dozen of King's fellow Badgers (of the fifty Wisconsinites' papers reviewed for this study) noted his popularity, which was visible when he took over Frémont's corps. The officers of a mostly Wisconsin brigade assembled at King's division headquarters to bid him farewell. A private in the 7th Wisconsin noted this gathering and imagined they "felt pretty bad about his going away."[37] "I do not think the change" to a general from Banks's corps "is a fortunate one for the Division," wrote a Wisconsin officer.[38] King traveled to Washington, where he convinced Lincoln of his desire "to remain with his old division of which he had the full confidence both of officers and men."[39] "Gen. King is a man that was beloved by all belonging to his command," a private summed up.[40]

Another Republican general, Robert Schenck, was keen to remain popular with the men under his command. Despite deploring the indiscipline of his German units, he found himself "universally popular with the 'Dutch'" and his Yankee units. "If Washington City and West Point shared in this regard, I should get forward" in rank. "It is a consolation though to have the confidence and admiration of the officers and men with whom I march and labor and fight, and quite a compensation for slights or want of appreciation elsewhere."[41] A regimental commander from Schenck's home state appealed to this sensitivity in imploring the general to transfer his regiment to Pope's army. The colonel hinted that he and his men had "lost confidence in both" their Ohioan brigade and division commanders. "It is in your power, to make Eight hundred and fifty Ohio men happy by" transfer to his command, he told the political general.[42]

Field and line (or company) officers shared the ideologies and interests of their soldiers who held some influence over their careers. By the summer of 1862, field and—to a greater extent—company officers largely were frustrated by the obligation imposed by their generals to protect Virginian civilians' property when those civilians taunted them and aided both regular and irregular Confederate forces. The major division between field and line officers was the electoral basis of their office. Colonels were initially appointed by the governor of the regiment's home state, while the other field officers, the lieutenant colonels and majors, were elected by the officers of the regiment but required the approval of their state governors. Line officers—captains, first, and second lieutenants—were directly elected by the enlisted men of their regiment, though again subject to gubernatorial approval. The constituencies for the various officer ranks played important roles; the officers looked to their men for support and sought to keep them satisfied.

As each state's governor determined who assumed the mantle of field officer, an individual regiment's officers and men might well object to that choice, sometimes vehemently. On July 6, 1862, the 1st Rhode Island Cavalry was informed that Governor William Sprague—sixteen months from becoming Treasury Secretary Salmon Chase's son-in-law—had appointed a major from a New York cavalry regiment as their new commanding officer. "Never was a camp thrown into greater commotion and indignation," noted the regiment's chaplain. "This sensation had its spring in our appreciation of Lieutenant-Colonel [Willard] Sayles, and the Governor's pledges to us. When the report was substantiated by official documents, nearly all the officers handed in their resignations, and well-nigh mutinous purposes broke out in the ranks."[43]

Most of the resignations were refused; however, the two field officers (a lieutenant colonel and a major), who were most directly disappointed by the governor's failure to promote a Rhode Islander, were allowed to resign. Less than a week previously the governor had visited the regiment and "promised us recruits and repeated, what had been before pledged to us, that all promotions in the regiment should be members of the command."[44] The new colonel was not only not a Rhode Islander but a foreign military officer. Within two weeks of his arrival, though, "the ill-feeling towards" Colonel Alfred Duffie "had given way to admiration."[45] A commissary sergeant in the regiment was terse but positive in his initial assessment on July 9: "Col. A. N. Duffie took command today. He is a Frenchman. Smart."[46] In frequent Napoleonic decrees to his regiment—not unlike those of Pope—Duffie praised his men and claimed, "the proudest satisfaction a commander can feel is mine," namely "seeing the proficiency of his command in discipline, in drill, and in soldierly exercises."[47]

Colonel Alfred Duffie. (Library of Congress)

The relationships between the field officers of a regiment could be fraught due to the differing political backgrounds of their appointments and promotions. While the field officers were initially appointed by the governor of the unit's home state, replacement colonels, lieutenant colonels, and majors were selected by the popular vote of the regiment's officers, though still subject to gubernatorial approval. While the field officers of the 1st Rhode Island Cavalry resigned over their governor's decision to appoint a colonel from outside the regiment and the state, not all field officers gave up their commissions so easily.

James B. Post, the lieutenant colonel of the 95th New York, a regiment whose "morale and discipline is being greatly impaired by" sentry and railroad guard duty, engaged in a protracted dispute with his colonel, who in turn feuded with the brigade commander. Colonel George H. Biddle "don't want to leave [Brooks Station, Virginia] and quietly uses his influence to remain. You see he is in command of the station and has not been with the regiment an hour. He is very jealous and tenacious of his authority, and frequently makes himself very ridiculous. Many of the officers are disgusted." It was "a very peculiar position for me, being next in authority" yet powerless to act. While doing his duty, Post observed "that the q[uarte]r master has an undue and pernicious influence with the Colonel, and the qr master is anything but a favorite as he is a politician at home and cant seem to be happy without having somebody by the ears."[48] The quartermaster remained a thorn in the side of the regiment's second-in-command for the next month.[49]

"You cannot wonder that at times I feel rather inclined to try and get a different regiment but I am trying to stick by as long as I can," the regiment's lieutenant colonel confessed to his sympathetic spouse. "The Colonels conduct is known at Washington and I very much fear if he gets into a tantrum sometime he may get into trouble, particularly as" the West Point brigade commander, "Genl. Doubleday is a regular army officer and won't stand any nonsense."[50] If disgusted with his colonel, Post was pleased with his brigade commander. "The General thinks us the best regiment in his brigade and we all like him very much except Col. Biddle whose behavior is absurd and rediculous in the extreme," he noted. Biddle's long term as an independent commander of a detached force "has made him very impervious and he swears at his men and officers horribly. He don't like the General because he got us into his brigade and it breaks up his comfortable and independent position. His conduct for the past two days [was] so unbearable" that Post and Major Edward Pye would have resigned their offices, along with "the best of the officers and we will [not] just on the eve of a march to make any imputation against the credit of the regiment." Despite the conduct of his officers, Biddle "allows a lurking suspicion to linger that there is a conspiracy against him." Finally his subordinate decided to reply. Post and the major "decided to show we don't want his place, nor [to] be under him unless he will behave himself," and went to Doubleday to ask him to intervene. If this informal method failed, formal complaints would follow, forcing the colonel's arrest and Post's promotion, leading Biddle's toadies to "say I had attained my object. No!"[51]

Within two weeks of penning the above letter, Post was in de facto command of the regiment, "the Col being disabled and gone to Bekans Station in care of the sick and baggage. And I think it gives quite as much satisfaction to the Genl as to the officers and men of the regt to have it so as the old col is in his dotage and has greatly disappointed all of us." Biddle's closest ally, the regimental quartermaster, was also mysteriously "lying sick in Washington," but this was of limited relief as Post now had to command the regiment and mind its supplies.[52] Doubleday accepted the testimony of the lieutenant colonel and major against their colonel, making it convenient for Biddle and his crony to beg a leave of absence on the basis of ill health.

Generals, particularly those who started their Union military careers as colonels of volunteer regiments, obviously were not above interfering in regimental affairs. The lieutenant colonel of a Pennsylvania regiment forced his men to endure a grueling march on July 6, such that "if a man left the ranks for a drink of water when a halt was not ordered this wretch would make them *pour it out,*" a soldier in the unit wrote. Only one in three of those who started out on the march arrived at its destination with the unit's colors. When the brigade commander, formerly the regiment's commander, found out, he was livid. "I am happy to say that Genl. Geary told Lt. Col. [Hector] T[yndale] that if he ever dared to march his men in that inhuman manner again, he would have him *cashiered,*" a witness penned. "Bully for Geary!"[53]

Some of the acrimony between John Geary and Tyndale stemmed from the stark difference in their political views. Tyndale was an early member of the anti-slavery Free Soil Party; he escorted John Brown's wife to see her husband as he awaited trial in Virginia and again when she brought the revolutionary's body home to upstate New York.[54] Geary was a partisan Democrat and relied on politicians from Pennsylvania to attain military rank in the Mexican and American Civil Wars.[55]

Field and line officers engaged in a great variety of political squabbles, whether over election campaigns for promotion or presidential politics. The colonel of a volunteer regiment was often the lightning rod for discontent and division among his regiment's officers. Many of the officers and men of an Indiana regiment in Banks's corps were deeply disturbed by the special relationship between their colonel and the regiment's civilian sutler, a close relative of his.[56] Indeed, the colonel of another regiment in the same brigade put the Indiana colonel to shame by "cleaning house" for the Hoosiers, so to speak. In the spring of 1862, enlisted men of the 3rd Wisconsin "smelled some whiskey in the sutlers tent belonging to" their Hoosier neighbors and proceeded to get drunk. The 3rd's colonel heard the noise, arrested the sutler, "and immediately confiscated his whole property, 4 fine horses, and 4 mules and 2 wagons and all his stock of goods" as the sutler had violated army regulations for the sale of liquor to soldiers.[57]

Many of the Hoosier regiment's officers resigned their commissions in the summer of 1862 as a result of conflict with their commander. "We have been here 16 days and during that time six Officers have resigned to return to Hoosierdom," one of the regiment's lieutenants wrote his father from Front Royal, and "at that rate there will be some chance for promoting soon."[58] By July 10, the lieutenant colonel and major of the regiment "both proffered their resignations and the Colonel has been compelled by his officers to promise to resign and there isn't a man in the regiment probably of any education," a lieutenant wrote. "I can find 20 sergeants in our regiment better qualified than the present Colonel," the Harvard alumnus sniffed.[59]

The colonel of the Hoosier regiment was not only unpopular but evidently incompetent from a military standpoint. The "unfortunate 27th Indiana regiment which is always doing something wrong, insisted upon keeping up its reputation" during Pope's first review of Banks's corps. "We were to salute by Brigades when the Pope rode down the lines; 1st the second Brigade and then our own. But when Geary gave the command to present arms, old [Silas] Colgrove repeated it," although his unit was not in Geary's brigade, "and the instructions I had carefully given him about the three ruffles and a march and the colors drooping, he put in faithfully but in the wrong place," an exasperated staff officer wrote. "Fortunately the General [brigade commander George Gordon] didn't see it until it was too late to remedy it, but then he sent down a savage order to old Colgrove which I by good luck didn't have to carry."[60]

Many colonels looked with eager anticipation for the opportunity to trade their eagle-motif shoulder straps for the stars of a general, but making that leap often required a shift in patronage. Regimental commanders required the approval of their state governor, but hopeful generals required support at the national level, in the form of congressional and presidential approval. In the early months of the war Lincoln was careful—as in the selection of his cabinet—to nominate generals broadly representative of the various regions and states, not forgetting loyal southerners. The officers and men of a regiment could support the promotion of their colonels as adding to the luster of their home state's contribution to the national war effort, or despise a colonel who seemed more interested in seeking higher command than in their wellbeing.

Soldiers could and did expect their officers—particularly their colonels—to inspire them with stump speeches. Speeches presented the major experiential and entertainment opportunities that antebellum Americans had for engaging in politics at the local and national levels, with plenty of opportunities to question, heckle, or otherwise express their opinions.

Audiences regularly attended speeches and debates involving a single speaker lecturing for an hour or more.[61] Any literate person could read a newspaper's coverage of candidates' speeches, but to attend a speech or debate was to engage in politics as part of a wider community and to interact with the candidates.

The men of the 6th Wisconsin accosted their colonel—already in bed—to deliver a speech on July 4. "Who is there?" the colonel gruffly replied to the crowd of boys gathered around his tent. "The sixth regiment" was the response; "we want a speech." The colonel consented but asked them to "wait til I get my britches on. He came out buttoning his britches and made the boys a short but funny speech," an orderly sergeant recorded, "told them what good soldiers they were and what great servise they had done their country did you not lay at Arlington all winter in mud up to your knees." Had the regiment "not marched and countermarched the country all spring and summer and [was it] not now guarding the gray widows of Fredericksburg and so and so forth."[62] Despite grogginess and possibly fighting a hangover, the colonel fulfilled his duty with a series of rhetorical questions reinforcing his audience's self-identity as loyal citizens and good soldiers.

On a swelteringly hot day in early August, another Wisconsin colonel addressed his tired and sweaty regiment. After a march of seventeen miles and a halt for lunch, the colonel ordered the men to gather around him: "Men: again you are called on for work. Genl Pope does not order you forward but he solicits you to do so. Since Saturday noon his force has been standing under arms and for nearly 48 hours without rations." He appealed to those willing to soldier on to remember that their pain was for the gain of their fellows. "If on the march tonight your backs ache, your feet blister, if you become weak and faint from fatigue, just remember almost 40,000 of your friends [and] comrades are looking with anxious eyes for the cloud of dust that shall mark the course of your approaching column, and keep pegging right on."[63]

The officers at generals' headquarters—aide-de-camps, adjutants, and chiefs of staff—served as their generals' eyes, ears, and mouthpieces in the field.[64] Staff officers were a special breed of officer, occupying a liminal world as the go-betweens from headquarters to unit commanders. They earned the jealousy of combat officers in the infantry regiments for the luxuries they shared with generals, living as they did at brigade, division, corps, or army headquarters. One of the siblings who owned Willard's Hotel in the federal capital, for instance, was sent by McDowell on several occasions to nearby "plantations" to confiscate ice for headquarters' use, a luxury that an infantryman could only dream of on sultry July and August days.[65]

Nepotism in the selection or promotion of staff officers never failed to offend other hopefuls for the post. A cousin of the newly promoted General George Gordon was offered promotion to captain on Gordon's staff. This relative was already a lieutenant and one of his aides, and aware of the enemies he would make should he accept. "I told him I wasn't fit for it and hoped that would end it. But [Gordon] recurred to it again and seems very desirous I should have it." Yet the general's selection "is giving the office to a young and inexperienced man, when there are several officers who have seen much more service and deserved it more. If I take it, it will provoke complaints of partiality to his family, and as it seems to me, is unjust toward [the] regimental Adjutant."[66]

No small amount of political wrangling went on between staff officers and their generals, as well as between line officers and politicians at state and national capitals. A considerable number of staff officers were appointed by generals as favors to the governors and congressmen who aided the generals in their campaigns to attain their stars; as such, the staff member could also be the eyes and ears of the political patron at headquarters. So long as relations between general and politicians remained amicable, disgruntled staff officers could do little harm in that area, though they could still leak damaging information to the press.

Massachusetts governor John Andrew warned former governor—now General—Nathaniel Prentiss Banks that a "young officer" who was too "free" in his "conversation" with a reporter contributed to a damaging article on Banks's performance in the Shenandoah Valley. Particularly troubling was the fact that the "young officer" was a major on Banks's staff.[67] Banks put up with this albatross on his staff until mid-July: "I want very much some good [staff] officers with me, but I cannot get them. [Major R. Morris] Copeland has gone. He is a species of demon, more resembling in appearance and mind the Infernal spirit than any man I have seen."[68] Major Copeland proclaimed his innocence to the end, at least in official correspondence directed at his general. "A thunderbolt has fallen on me from the clear sky and without any intimation that there was any charge against me I am dismissed [from] the service," Copeland complained to Banks in mid-August.[69] Banks's corps had been decimated at Cedar Mountain five days before, so Banks had more important matters on his mind than a loudmouthed former staff officer. Copeland may not have made a good—or discreet—staff officer, but he

Lieutenant Robert Gould Shaw of the 2nd Massachusetts, friend of Major R. Morris Copeland. (Library of Congress)

already had a reputation as a landscape architect and was a friend of the Shaws, a prominent Boston abolitionist family whose eldest son, Robert, served in Banks's corps.[70]

Banks searched far and wide for new staff officers, with little success. "Are you still at Liberty to join [my] Staff," Banks telegraphed a captain in the 71st Pennsylvania in Sumner's II Corps on the peninsula.[71] Catholic abolitionist Orestes Brownson contacted Banks in late July on behalf of his son, a captain on John Frémont's staff now in limbo while the general waited for a new assignment, as the captain "wishes to be on active duty, and would prefer active service on your staff to remaining idle at New York."[72] A fortnight later Captain Edward Brownson wrote Banks to inform him that the secretary of war supported his return to active duty: "Mr. Stanton will immediately add me to your staff if you consent. My father wrote to you desiring it. I respectfully solicit it."[73] Banks did not accept Captain Brownson's offer with alacrity, possibly from a concern about allowing the son of a prominent abolitionist on his personal staff. He later changed his mind to take Brownson, but the captain had given up "all hope of being so fortunate as to be your Aide," and accepted an appointment in the Washington garrison instead.[74]

If some staff officers proved a constant trial to their general, others were well and truly integrated in the general's "military family," and to lose a staff aide to wounds or capture struck home. "Poor [William] Wilkins was missing," a II Corps division commander wrote of one of his staff captains in the wake of the fight at Cedar Mountain, so devastating to Banks's troops. "He was seen safe after the fight coming from the right where I sent him. He probably was run upon by the Rebel pickets when alone and captured. We heard the next day he was a prisoner. He is not wounded. I miss him greatly now," the commander added, since Banks was injured in an equestrian accident "and on the following day turned over the command to me," leaving the general with endless paperwork and duties and a diminished staff to perform them with. The corps adjutant general was wounded, and the adjutant generals of both II Corps divisions were out of action from wounds or capture at Cedar Mountain, leaving the corps severely short-staffed.[75]

A Civil War regiment's complement of officers may be compared to the U.S. Congress.[76] The three field officers formed the Senate, while the thirty line or company-grade officers comprised the House of Representatives. If one extended the analogy, the 640 to 800-plus soldiers and NCOs constituted the (male) voters of the regiment's home state. Like the army, Congress was an all-male organization: "Most congressmen came to the capital alone, leaving their wives and families back home; they were not paid enough to do otherwise."[77] A few officers could afford to bring wives with them on campaign, but soldiers' families were not allowed with the army.

The turnover of senators and representatives was high, just like that of the officers in volunteer regiments. Not a few officers hoped that a stint in the Union Army in defense of the nation would lead to eventual election to Congress. The extent of their representation and the constituency that elected them distinguished representatives from senators, and company from field officers. In the nineteenth century, members of the House of Representatives sometimes referred to themselves as the "immediate representatives" of the people in their home districts, as opposed to members of the Senate, who represented the state as a whole and were usually elected by the state legislature, not by the voters of a single district.[78] Representatives—and line or company-grade officers—could be expected to be more interested in the immediate concerns of their larger constituency of voting but unelected folk (privates and NCOs in the case of company officers) than senators (or field officers). Field officers concerned themselves with the opinions—and votes—of the line officers and state governors far more than with the gripes or suggestions of enlisted men. Even as the Capitol's dome was under construction during the war years, so the volunteer officer corps, and especially its relations with enlisted men accustomed to democratic debate and votes, was a work in progress.

Company-grade officers—captains, first, and second lieutenants—were the most democratically selected of all Union officers. Although state governors still approved their commissions, this usually was a rubber stamp as the popular vote of the enlisted men and NCOs of their companies was the real arbiter of their selection. As the "lower house" of the regimental "Congress," the company officers were much more likely than field officers to emerge from the noncommissioned ranks as the war wore on. Captains and lieutenants were the key to leading and inspiring the small-unit cohesion of locally raised companies to enable regiments to function and fight as a single unit.

If elevated by their men, company officers were nevertheless, like field officers, paid significantly more than their men. Out of their substantial pay, however, they had to provide their own food and the salary of a servant. Nevertheless, the large pay increase was a major motivation of enlisted men seeking an officer's commission. An Ohio corporal encouraged his father to seek a commission to make a quick buck. "The money is just what you want to pay your debts with and it can be as easily obtained from the government as any business you can do. If you inlist you get good wages and," the NCO wrote, "when you see you can stand it no longer you can Resign it is perfectly honorable and your privlidge. Mother can spair you for a year or two for the sake of having money enough to make her comfortable for years after you return."[79]

Officers and enlisted men shared a common view of the core qualities a good officer should possess. He should be both "courteous and gentlemanly" in his conduct. European military officers were expected to be born to their rank, as many western European armies relied heavily on their aristocracy to form their officer corps. The military academy at West Point annually graduated a few dozen men to be officers and gentlemen, insufficient to lead even the small prewar army. Expanded into a volunteer force numbering in the hundreds of thousands, the Union Army required that craftsmen and clerks learn to lead men, and quickly. If the United States did not breed gentlemen, the trusted men of its town and country yeomen could learn to become officers, with "courteous and gentlemanly conduct" in the treatment of both inferiors and superiors the key to leading men who bestowed rank via the ballot box. Effective leaders "commanded the respect of both Officers and Men," and the loss of these men was widely felt because of the difficulty of finding suitable replacements.[80] An English observer noted in early 1862 that "there is no physical degeneracy about a race which could produce such as those which formed the army of the Potomac" in its camps outside of Washington. "I have seen the armies of most European countries; and I have no hesitation in saying that, as far as the average raw material of the rank and file is concerned, the American army is the finest." However, the officers "are, undoubtedly, the weak point of the system. They have not the military air, the self-possession which long habit of command alone can give; while the footing of equality on which they inevitably stand with the volunteer privates, deprives them of the esprit de corps belonging to a ruling class."[81]

Officers below the rank of general suffered a general lack of information from on high, and thus indulged in a great deal of gossip. They desired ardently any tidbit of news, including newspaper articles. "We are expecting *to advance* now," a Maryland officer wrote home on July 6. "Orders and hints indicate that we may look for more decisive measures. It is a remarkable fact that we learn more of ourselves from the papers than we ourselves can know unaided by other than orders."[82]

The surgeon of a Pennsylvania Reserve regiment admitted to his wife in mid-August that he was in the dark as to his unit's next destination: "We are in great suspense as to where we are going, one supposition is that we are to ship for Charleston another to North Carolina and the third and most plausible back to the defense of Washington." The physician hoped Washington was their destination, as South Carolina was not a desirable post during the present "sickly season."[83] Members of the Pennsylvania Reserves, the peripatetic reinforcements for George McClellan's and then John Pope's armies in June and August, respectively, could be excused any confusion as to their next assignment. "We are now in Gen. [Ambrose] Burnside's Corps and I am glad of it I do not like [Fitz John] Porter and still less McDowell," a soldier in the 9th Reserves wrote from Fredericksburg on August 20. "We have changed considerably first under . . . McDowell then Porter and now Burnsides. I hope we will stay in Burnsides Corps."[84] The soldier was mistaken, as his division was only making a stopover at Fredericksburg en route to rejoin Irvin McDowell's III Corps.

Political conflict was hardly limited to officers. Plenty of politicking occurred in the enlisted ranks. Common soldiers sought promotion as noncommissioned officers, and NCOs sought commissioned rank and the higher pay that accompanied shoulder boards. To gain advancement though, privates, corporals, and sergeants needed to cultivate the support of other soldiers, as well as the officers. Enlisted men who lost out in elections found that new officers and NCOs were far more solicitous of the desires of soldiers who had voted for them than erstwhile opponents. "I made an effort to better my position as you probably know but failed as I generally do," a Wisconsin soldier wrote his mother from a hospital. "The soft-headed, bass-wood men, the pets and dogrobbers of the commissioned officers"—the ones who supported the newly elected officers—"are the lucky ones" who could ask for and receive a discharge or furlough.[85]

Ambition festered into a disease for men desiring to "better themselves," their rank, and their pay. "If there is any possible way to better my circumstances I wish to do so," a Wisconsin corporal keen to become an officer wrote home. "Promotion is slow now, not near so fast as formerly here." His attempt to win a regular army commission "seems to have 'played out,'" but he hoped for a commission with a new regiment on the basis of a recommendation letter signed by all three of his regiment's field officers. He lamented that he was "only 3d Corporal and there are five Sergeants and two Corporals between myself and the Shoulder Straps."[86]

When his father suggested seeking the aid of an influential Madison, Wisconsin, politician who did not know the corporal personally, the soldier noted that he was "a total stranger to him, and I cannot ask any favors from" a stranger "in so direct a manner." After all, "Mr. [Samuel D.] Hastings not knowing anything of myself will not feel very interested in my case. Although he will probably hand the [recommendation] to Governor [Edward] Salomon, that I presume will be the last of them."[87] If in late June the corporal temporarily swore off "working for any position," less than a month later he was back to his plotting. Now he identified "the opponents I have in this company." Unfortunately his Company was "principally composed" of "cursed thickheads and of which the 1st and 2nd Lieutenants lead the van in lack of intelligence, education, or even common sense."[88] Hope sprang anew in mid-August, though, when the major of his regiment transferred to a new Wisconsin unit.[89] Active campaigning culminating in the Battles of Second Bull Run and Antietam kept the office-seeker from further politicking until mid-September.[90]

The two Badgers' rank-related funks were hardly unique. Another Wisconsin soldier believed his company commander was actively scheming to keep him in his lowly rank. "The captain looked at me with a look of malignant triumph" when the promotion of two corporals was announced, the soldier wrote. His name was not read out, and the captain "evidently thinks the whole aim of my life is office holding." After gaining his own election to company command, the captain seemed determined to keep others from enjoying the privileges of officer rank: "He probably will keep me in the ranks for some time in order to show me 'that he has the discretion to detect an office seeker and knows how to punish one.'"If the soldier failed to gain promotion in the army, he hoped "one day to be [the captain's] peer—aye more than his peer—in civil life."[91] By the time Pope took command, this soldier was a corporal but found plenty in his new rank to deplore, as he was now company cook, a thankless job in his mind.[92]

Women also campaigned with Pope's army, adding to the political, racial, medical, and intelligence activities of the Republican force. While this study centers on the male musket- or sword-carrying members of the army, women of all social classes, black and white, played a significant role in the life of this army, sometimes in overtly political ways. Jessie Benton Frémont, wife of John Frémont, was the most prominent woman attached to the army—however briefly—to attempt to radicalize the war effort.[93]

In 1861, Frémont had asked his wife to read his declaration of martial law and the emancipation of slaves owned by rebellious Missourians. She warned him that Lincoln would react negatively.[94] When John Frémont's unilateral decision to emancipate slaves in his military district was countermanded in Washington, Jessie Frémont decided to defend the proclamation. She approached Lincoln in person to defend the general's act and convince Lincoln of the military necessity of freeing the slaves of traitorous masters. The president claimed that Frémont "should never have dragged the Negro into the war. It is a war for a great national object, and the Negro has nothing to do with it."[95] Afterward, Frémont told a confidante she lacked "Mr. Frémont's patience and I get ill and heart sore. I can but think that if the President had had one interview with Mr. Frémont there never would have grown up this state of injury to the public service." She continued, "two honest men can quickly understand each other." However, Lincoln's "good brain and bad heart" could not transcend racial conventions, although she blamed "the evil minded of the Cabinet" more than the president.[96]

Other wives played key roles in helping their husbands gain their stars. The wife of German revolutionary Carl Schurz, though opposed to her husband's involvement in another military conflict, took advantage of a chance meeting with Secretary of the Treasury Salmon Chase to gain his support for Schurz's quest for a command. "This state of uncertainty is most painful to both of us, especially as the recent victories of our army make it probable that the war will soon be ended. My own private wish is to go back to Europe," Mrs. Schurz wrote to the treasury secretary, but she accepted that "Mr. Schurz desired very strongly to enter the army and to remain here."[97]

At least one western officer lacked John Frémont's "patience" and bluntly told his wife to leave politics to men, where politics "belonged." "You write me so much politics, that my brain keeps *muddled* and I fear that you are dealing with matters, that you will find rather disagreeable and perplexing," a major with Democratic leanings wrote his wife. "My advice to you is, that you were not designed for a politician, and had better steer clear of the troubles incident to political maneuvering. There are but few females who have an especial political influence who preserved a very enviable reputation."[98] He represented the common middle-class view that women and men occupied different spheres, and that politics belonged to the dirty and dangerous public world of men.[99]

An Ohio colonel held a more enlightened view of the partnership between husband and wife and women's political views. If he confessed his indifference to the "opinions of persons for whom I do not care," he was "sensative" to the opinions of loved ones. "I know that in Society husbands and wives differ on religion and often vital questions and 'get on' after a manner. I believe there is no true marriage without a union of the mind and soul—and this belief was all that kept me from marrying a protestant." While fighting to preserve the national Union, "I felt that no true *union* could exist between two who differed so essentially in thought and principle. Was I right?"[100] On his wife's answer seemed to hinge the future health of their nation as well as their marriage. He was disturbed to find that his wife disagreed with him on the propriety of the abolition of slavery. "We ought to communicate our thoughts and feelings," the colonel argued, wishing "our whole hearts were united in this hour of gloom—it would help us to carry our burdens. But if not, we must get on with our troubles as best we can without that consolation." He did not insist—as did the Wisconsin major above—that she surrender to his will: "You may think and write as you please; I am done with reproof—but I hope never to become indifferent to your thoughts and opinions. That would be a sad day."[101]

Dozens of army wives accompanied the troops, particularly officer's wives, who, it was felt, brought a higher moral tone to the camps than the spouses of common soldiers. Fanny Ricketts even wrote General James Ricketts's official reports for him. She shared some of the dangers of accompanying the army onto the battlefield, joining in her husband's imprisonment in Richmond after his battery was overrun at First Bull Run, and was once again on the plains of Manassas with a Union Army thirteen months later.[102] "Genl. Ricketts wife was on the field," noted a Pennsylvania soldier on August 30, and the "heroic [wife] went to Richmond Prison with her husband."[103] Others played more traditional roles, far from the battlefield. The wife of Ricketts's corps commander comforted Irvin McDowell after he faced defeat for a second time at Manassas. The wife of an engineer on Pope's staff and Helen McDowell conferred at West Point shortly after receiving news of Second Bull Run, and both wrote their husbands consoling letters: "He seemed very much pleased when he spoke of [the letter]—poor fellow. I am glad that he should have so good a source of comfort now that the world seems turning against him," noted Colonel John N. Macomb, Jr., the engineer on Pope's staff.[104]

One woman sought to accompany the officers and men of the Army of Virginia each time it faced battle, though she counted no husband, father, son, or brother in its ranks. She desired from an early age to follow her militia captain father's footsteps as a soldier, and cited patriotism as the reason for her medical relief efforts when her sex prevented her from joining the army. Clara Barton aided more fighting men of Pope's army than any other woman—and arguably more than many male physicians—as they lay wounded on Virginia battlefields.[105] Barton was politically aligned with moderate Republicans desiring "the restoration of the Union *as it was.*" She trusted Lincoln would accomplish this, "unless the resistance of the South prove so obstinate, and prolonged, that the abolition or overthrow of slavery follow as a consequence."[106]

One of the few female government employees in 1862, Barton clerked in the Patent Office. She observed firsthand the woeful state of insufficiently provisioned and incompetently staffed army hospitals in Washington and resolved to do something.[107] General George McClellan's decision to attempt an amphibious end-run leading to a war-ending attack on Richmond stymied Barton's hopes of accompanying the Army of the Potomac on an overland campaign from Washington. But the formation of the Army of Virginia offered her renewed hope.

After securing a pass to aid "the sick and wounded" of the Army of Virginia, on July 18 Barton embarked on an eleven-day tour of New Jersey and Massachusetts to raise funds and acquire supplies. By early August, Barton was ready to set off from Washington with two hired assistants.[108] For the next month, Barton proved time and again more determined and efficient in her contributions to the war effort than many officers. Resolved to bring her supplies to the battlefield of Cedar Mountain, Barton shrugged off officers' warnings that she faced capture. "I fail to see any more danger to me than for our disabled men," Barton replied.[109]

A surgeon from a Pennsylvania regiment assigned to Franz Sigel's I Corps welcomed the arrival of Barton and her supply wagons to the Cedar Mountain battlefield. James L. Dunn was "covered with blood from head to foot" after performing endless amputations and informed Barton that his field hospital had run out of every sort of dressing and bandage. These supplies Barton replenished. "I thought that night," Dunn wrote, "if heaven ever sent out a homely angel, she must be one, her assistance was so timely."[110] Two weeks later, the army was again battling the Confederate Army, this time near Manassas Junction. As the lion's share of available ambulances was with McClellan on the peninsula, Pope's army was lacking in this department when it marched into battle. The War Department pressed into service hacks, omnibuses, hay wagons, and private carriages. Medical staff trained to deal with the ten thousand casualties incurred in fruitless frontal assaults on Stonewall Jackson's position were also in short supply.

Medical director Andrew McParlin had an appeal printed in newspapers and nailed to hotel bulletin boards of the "pressing need for the services of surgeons and nurses (male) to attend the wounded of the great battles" at Manassas. Hundreds of volunteers reported to Alexandria for rail transport to the battlefield, but many were too intoxicated to aid the suffering and dying soldiers.[111] Barton found her way to the frontline hospitals, sober and pressing through the detritus of the army's retreat. Barely evading capture in moving his patients from the battlefield and setting up a field hospital at Fairfax Station, Dunn again encountered Barton, who once more arrived as if a heavenly apparition with desperately needed medical supplies. She alighted from a train to "supply us with bandages, brandy, wine, prepared soup, jellies, meals, and every article that could be thought of" to relievc the suffering of the wounded.[112]

Many more women—black and white—followed Pope's army or interacted with its units in Virginia but remain nameless to historians. Hundreds of self-emancipated slave women cooked for and washed the clothing of Union soldiers.[113] Thousands of white southern women confronted the men of the army, contesting Unionist ideology and Pope's increasingly harsh policies. Blatantly pro-secession statements and politicized actions brought them perilously close to crossing the line of gender conventions, when they would forfeit the protection that "civilized" men granted to dependents.[114] "We don't blame any Woman here for being Secess[ionist] as they all have Husbands Fathers and Brothers in the Suthern Army and it is but Natural for them to Simpathise with them," a captain wrote his wife. "But they must learn not to insult and misuse the vary men that they are Protected by [for] they are in our Power."[115]

Generals, officers, and soldiers shared a good deal of sentimentality, particularly when writing home to their wives and children. As dire as the war effort seemed, soldiers and officers exhorted their children to obey their mothers and excel in school.[116] "In your last letter home you asked me to send you home some of my hair," a Pennsylvania sergeant wrote, acknowledging his wife's request, "but I have it so close to my head now that I wood have to have it shaved off." After all, "a man out hear has to take care of him Self or the lice wood carry him of[f]."[117] Sentimentality had its limits.

# 5 Constituents in a Republican Army

THE FIERCE PARTISANSHIP of the citizen-soldiers with the Army of Virginia can be traced to their demographic origin. The bulk of the army organized by John Pope—its rank and file—was the best martial representative of the white men who voted for the Republican Party in 1860. The army was also more demographically representative of the armed Union war effort in the summer of 1862 than the Army of the Potomac. George McClellan's army was an overwhelmingly northeastern force of Yankees and New Yorkers; only 11 of 138 volunteer infantry regiments originated outside the northeastern region. This preponderance may be seen in the six infantry brigades composed entirely of regiments from the Democratic Party–dominated constituencies of Irish immigrants, and residents of New Jersey, Philadelphia, and New York City serving in McClellan's army. These units formed almost a fifth of McClellan's infantry force of thirty-two brigades. None of Pope's twenty-three brigades fit this Democratic mold.[1] Even so, Pope's army was on balance eastern, and fully two-thirds of its infantry regiments originated in New England, New Jersey, New York, or Pennsylvania.[2] The other third hailed from border (Delaware, Maryland, and Virginia) or western states (Indiana, Ohio, Michigan, and Wisconsin). Until the return of the all-Pennsylvania division from service with V Corps on the peninsula on August 22, the army was 36.4 percent non-northeastern. The major constituencies rendering the Army of Virginia unique among northern armies were border state Unionists, Unionist Virginians, German Americans, and westerners. The soldiers were aided by thousands of self-emancipated slaves, who constituted an unarmed but politicized auxiliary to the army, and a welcome labor force.

The seventeen states contributing infantry regiments to the Armies of Virginia and the Potomac contained a free population of 18,017,773, according to the 1860 census.[3] The nine states of the northeastern region (Connecticut, Maine, Massachusetts, New Hampshire, New Jersey,

New York, Pennsylvania, Rhode Island, and Vermont) contained about three-fifths of the base at 10,704,668. The border and western states (Delaware, Indiana, Maryland, Michigan, Minnesota, Ohio, Virginia, and Wisconsin) comprised the other two-fifths. As such, the twenty-eight non-northeastern regiments—31 percent of the Army of Virginia's infantry force—corresponds much more closely to the 40 percent of the free population residing in non-northeastern states in the sample than the 8–12 percent in the Army of the Potomac. This balance was more extraordinary still because more than two-thirds of the free population of Virginia resided in the portion that seceded in 1861.[4]

The Army of Virginia's ninety infantry regiments were unevenly distributed between three army corps. Irvin McDowell's III Corps contained the bulk of the army's regiments and had been the largest of McClellan's corps when organized as I Corps of the Army of the Potomac. The II Corps was the lightweight among the three, a major liability when it faced Stonewall Jackson's wing of Robert E. Lee's army alone at Cedar Mountain.

Franz Sigel's I Corps comprised twenty-one infantry regiments, four regiments and two battalions of cavalry, and nine artillery batteries. It was the most western of the corps, with nearly half (ten) of its infantry regiments hailing from outside the mid-Atlantic and New England regions. Nathaniel Prentiss Banks's II Corps held twenty-two infantry regiments, four cavalry regiments, and six artillery batteries. His corps was nearly as non-eastern as Sigel's, with ten foot regiments originating in the western or border states. If on paper it was larger than Sigel's corps, however, Banks's force suffered severely in the Shenandoah Valley during the spring and was seriously under strength; fewer than eight thousand men took the field at Cedar Mountain in August.

Even before the Pennsylvania Reserve Division returned from the peninsula, McDowell's III Corps contained thirty-two infantry regiments, five cavalry regiments, and ten artillery batteries. It was the most lopsidedly northeastern of the three corps, with twenty-six foot regiments (81.25%) recruited from the mid-Atlantic or New England regions. As of August 22, when the Pennsylvania Reserve Division returned, the corps claimed forty-six infantry regiments and fourteen batteries, and its eastern dominance grew to 84.8 percent among the infantry.[5]

Yet regiments marching on paper did not mean full, battle-ready regiments in the flesh. The Pennsylvania division, 9.1 percent of the infantry strength of the Army of the Potomac during the Seven Days Battles, suffered 20 percent of the entire army's casualties, twice its "fair share."[6]

The division also was badly reduced in numbers by disease while on the peninsula.

The three corps of the Army of Virginia contained thirteen cavalry regiments as well as one cavalry battalion from Connecticut, a squadron from the 3rd Indiana, one company of the 3rd West Virginia, and thirty-two artillery batteries. The sixteen cavalry formations were proportionately even more western and southern than the ninety foot regiments. Six of these mounted units were recruited outside of New England and the mid-Atlantic states.

The army's three corps possessed an estimated maximum strength of 45,000 at the beginning of July, but it could never hope to muster this total, with thousands of men in the hospital or on guard duty on any given day. If properly coordinated, Pope's army could expect to overwhelm just about any corps-sized force Stonewall Jackson might bring into the Shenandoah Valley, but not stand up to the entire Army of Northern Virginia. Pope's officers were aware of the challenge of engaging Lee's full army. "No one here seems to know what Pope's plans are but my idea is that we shall not do much of anything until a large force is concentrated here—we have now about 25,000—and then we shall move towards Gordonsville and threaten Richmond," a Massachusetts officer wrote.[7]

"If our Regiments were full we would have a splendid Army under Popes command," a Midwestern officer in Banks's corps noted on August 4. "In Banks Division we have six Brigades. Now you would think that was quite [a] formidable force, but in those six Brigades there is not more than ten thousand men whereas there ought to be twenty thousand."[8] One of Pope's staff officers estimated in early August that the army numbered "thirty six thousand effective men." He reached this estimate by "counting *dutch, negro's* and the *Staff;* the last making a full brigade," a tongue-in-cheek comment. "We have men enough to accomplish our object and present a bold front before Richmond" but not to attack Lee directly, the officer concluded.[9] Enlisted men shared his concerns. "The men are afraid that a largely superior force will be brought to bear upon us from Richmond," a corporal noted. "These apprehensions would not be indulged in had we confidence in those at the helm" in Washington. "We do not fear an equal force but we do fear superior Generals."[10]

"We are slowly but surely moving towards Richmond feeling our way as we go along," a captain of the 88th Pennsylvania noted on August 7. "Our army though in considerable force is not sufficiently strong for any emergency which I think is one reason for moving cautiously."[11] Two days after the Battle of Cedar Mountain, where Pope's army took two thousand casualties, the same captain took a cautionary tone in analyzing the strength of the army: "Pope has not over Fifty Thousand men not over Twenty five Thousand here, or near him. Hereafter he will have to watch the enemy better if he wants to beat him."[12] Not until the last week of August did sufficient Union reinforcements—in the form of McClellan's III and V corps and the Pennsylvania Reserve Division—arrive for Pope to assume the offensive against the combined wings of Lee's army.[13]

This study uses the personal accounts of 250 soldiers and officers as a source base for information on the army. These members of the Army of Virginia represented less than 1 percent of its strength, but their stories provide some insight into an otherwise unwieldy human machine. Of course, the 250 men selected—largely on the basis of the accessibility of their diaries and letters—are by no means completely congruent with the geographical representativeness of the army as a whole, let alone the officer-to-enlisted ratio. Organizationally, fully 60 percent (151) were in III Corps, 26 percent (65) with Banks, 11 percent (27) in I Corps, and 3 percent (7) at army headquarters. Almost 46 percent of the officers and men in the sample hailed from outside the mid-Atlantic and New England regions, as opposed to just under a third of the entire army. Only 61 percent of the men (152 of 250) were enlisted—private through sergeant major—as opposed to at least 90 percent in a "normal" Civil War army. Because officers and noncommissioned officers were required to be at least functionally literate, they are likely to be over-represented in any archive of Civil War veterans' personal papers. Staff officers and regimental commanders are particularly overrepresented.

The four categories of non-northeastern contingents that rendered the Army of Virginia so different from McClellan's army require further study to flesh out the Republican character of Pope's army. They are listed in the order in which they are discussed: men from Border South states, Unionist Virginians, German Americans, and westerners. Be aware, however, that individual soldiers and officers can and do overlap categories.

The Border South states comprised Delaware, Kentucky, Maryland, Missouri, Tennessee, and Virginia, along with the District of Columbia. Tennessee and Virginia seceded, however, and only western Virginians (dealt with later) contributed to the Army of Virginia. Federal armies in the eastern theater, moreover, never contained units from Kentucky or Missouri.

The Border South thus contributed only three infantry regiments, the Purnell Legion of nine Maryland companies, and a Maryland cavalry regiment to the Army of Virginia. Men from Delaware, the District of Columbia, and Maryland also marched in other units of the army, with Marylanders predominating. The most underrepresented geographical segment in this project, therefore, is the soldiers of the border states. Men of the Delaware and District of Columbia regiments left no records in the archives consulted.

When politicians in Richmond voted to secede in May 1861, western Virginian "Unionists were ready to secede from secession and create a loyal government either for Virginia or for a new and separate state." In June, delegates set up a "restored" government at a Wheeling convention. The Wheeling governor, Francis H. Peirpoint (later Pierpont), took office on June 20, 1861. Peirpoint's "Northern-born wife was something of an abolitionist, and he himself, unlike most Virginia Unionists, had anti-slavery leanings."[14]

By April 1862, Peirpoint reported "eleven regiments of infantry, two regiments and one battalion cavalry, [and] three batteries artillery" furnished by western Virginia for the Union war effort. Some eleven thousand Virginia volunteers thus served in Union armies in June 1862.[15] No fewer than five infantry regiments, a cavalry regiment and two squadrons from another mounted regiment, and an artillery battery composed of western Virginians—half of all Virginia Unionists in arms—marched with the Army of Virginia. Many recruits from Ohio and Pennsylvania also served in those units.

A disproportionate number of German Americans appointed generals in the Union armies were "Forty-Eighters," veterans of the liberal European revolutions of 1848 who emigrated following their defeat. Yet the vast majority of German-speaking immigrants who volunteered to save the Union were not Forty-Eighters. Indeed, prior to the Irish potato famine and subsequent accelerated immigration from Ireland in the 1840s, the various German-speaking states that comprise modern Germany provided the second-largest source of immigrants to the United States (after Great Britain). Through the spring of 1862, the single largest concentration of German American soldiers was in Louis Blenker's division, which consisted of seven New York and four Pennsylvania infantry regiments, a New York cavalry regiment, and four batteries in three brigades.[16] These eleven regiments, which served in John Frémont's Mountain Department, were predominantly but not purely German American in composition.

"Blenker's division were the *enfans perdus* of the Federal army. Their commander even then enjoyed a most doubtful reputation, and the men justly or unjustly shared in the repute of the General. They had been moved as far away from Washington as possible, and not without cause," an English observer noted in early 1862. "In the Potomac army commanded by McClellan" prior to its embarkation ships bound for Richmond, "the number of foreign regiments was at that period extremely small, and almost all of them were attached to Blenker's division."[17]

The Englishman found the camps of Blenker's division to be "filled with the black sheep of every nation under the sun. The word of command had to be given in four languages," and the regimental officers were foreigners "almost without exception. Both men and officers were a fine daredevil looking set of fellows, and might doubtless have been made excellent soldiers with strict training. The difficulty was that with a volunteer organization," the "stern discipline necessary to break the troops" of their democratic predilections was wholly lacking.[18] In July, Blenker's division was broken up, and its brigades formed the core—eleven of twenty-one regiments—of Sigel's I Corps.[19]

The most (in)famous Union regiment recruited from numerous communities of patriotic immigrants was initially a part of Pope's army. The 39th New York, or Garibaldi Guards, was probably the most diverse "foreign" regiment in Union service, with three companies of Germans, three of Hungarians, and one each of Swiss, Italians, French, and Iberians (Spanish and Portuguese), all formed in New York City.[20] Originally led by a Hungarian colonel, it was part of Blenker's division before being transferred to Banks's corps. The Garibaldi Guards were sent to garrison Harpers Ferry in early July, missing Cedar Mountain and Second Bull Run.[21]

Blenker's division labored under two black marks. Its men were known as indiscriminate looters of civilian property and as European mercenaries whose service demonstrated the moral bankruptcy of the Union's cause to pro-Confederate Virginians. The majority of the enlisted men volunteered to fight for their adopted country from the same sense of patriotism that motivated their Anglo-American comrades; however, a number of officers did fit the bill of swords-for-hire. An English tourist met officers in Blenker's division "who had served in the Papal brigade, the army of Francis II, the Garibaldian expedition, the British and Spanish legions, the wars of Baden, [and] the Morocco campaign."[22] At Frémont's headquarters, *Daily Telegraph* reporter Edward Dicey met an old acquaintance from Europe, "Major, Colonel, General, or whatever his rank now may be, Von Traubenfass," a model European mercenary.[23]

"Where and in what strange medley has Traubenfass not been involved?" the journalist from England asked. "He has served, of course, in the Spanish legion—in the wars of the Rio Grande—in the Schleswig-Holstein campaign. He has been in the service of a half dozen Indian princes," with "a perfect galaxy of orders from deposed potentates. When I met him last, twelve months before, he was a general in the Garibaldian army, and received a very handsome salary for his unknown services." Von Traubenfass was subsequently "projector, manager and secretary of an Italian railroad, which was to connect Sicily with the mainland." Seemingly within an hour of arriving in Wheeling, he persuaded General Frémont of his military bona fides and "was instructor of cavalry, or inspector of horses, or military commissioner in the army of the United States," and assumed that this civil war "would not last much longer." Once the Union won, he would move on to the next country in need of his services. "What nation he belongs to, who he has been, where he comes from, or what his age is, are all questions I have often asked in vain, and doubt if he knows himself."[24]

Historian Jon Gjerde has noted the explosive growth of the northwestern United States in the half-century before Abraham Lincoln's election. Barely a quarter of a million in 1810, the white population of the Old Northwest reached 1.5 million by 1830. "In the three decades prior to the Civil War the five states in the Old Northwest expanded to nearly 7 million inhabitants, an increase that exceeded the white population growth in the two centuries between the foundation of Jamestown and the Louisiana Purchase," according to Gjerde. "The states in the region thus contained over one-quarter of the American population on the eve of the Civil War."[25] For this study, Illinois, Indiana, Iowa, Kansas, Michigan, Minnesota, Ohio, and Wisconsin are designated as "western" states; soldiers from these areas are overrepresented in the sample of 250 officers and men.

A total of eight infantry regiments and portions of two cavalry regiments hailed from west of Ohio, with another twelve infantry and two cavalry regiments from the Buckeye State. Indiana and Wisconsin contributed equally, with four infantry regiments each, along with a regiment of cavalry from Michigan and a troop (two squadrons) of Indiana cavalry. Among eastern armies, the Army of the Potomac alone boasted a regiment from Minnesota.[26]

The Army of Virginia contained the only brigade of all-western soldiers serving east of the Appalachians. Not yet known as the Iron Brigade, John Gibbon's Indianans and Wisconsinites of McDowell's III Corps was the tallest brigade in the eastern theater as measured by the average height of the men. Only the 27th Indiana in Banks's II Corps could measure up to them, and their brigade's average height—aided by the 3rd Wisconsin—was spoiled by the bantam men in the 2nd Massachusetts.

From a territorial population of about 42,000 in 1800, Ohio grew explosively to 230,760 a decade later, and by 1825 its residents numbered 800,000. By then, Ohio stood as the fourth most populous state in the United States. Although Ohio remained a predominantly rural and agricultural state, by the antebellum decades it could no longer be designated part of the frontier.[27] The state can be divided into at least two obvious north-south regions. The anti-slavery stronghold of the old Connecticut Western Reserve on the state's northern tier along Lake Erie included Cleveland and Oberlin, while the southern region bordering the Ohio River contained a blend of pro-slavery southern-born settlers and German Americans in and around Cincinnati. Ohio contributed a hefty number of regiments to the war effort, behind only New York and Pennsylvania, and most Ohioans served in western armies. No fewer than ten Ohio regiments served with Pope in June, but none were with the Army of the Potomac.

Abolitionist, disappointed Republican presidential candidate, secretary of the treasury, and 1864 presidential hopeful Salmon Chase hailed from Ohio. From the outbreak of hostilities in April 1861, Chase vied to place Ohio men in places of influence in the war effort. He was particularly successful in promoting Ohioans to the command of the eastern army in the first year of the war. McDowell and McClellan owed much to Chase's patronage. He undoubtedly hoped that if one of "his men" won the war and saved the Union, he would be the logical choice for the White House in 1864, though the victorious general would pose a challenge. By July 1862, however, Chase and fellow anti-slavery Republicans were fed up with McClellan's lackadaisical efforts to take Richmond and his conservative opposition to emancipation, and Chase found Pope a welcome replacement, even if he was not from Ohio.

Had Jackson and Lee not attacked Pope so rapidly in the wake of the evacuation of McClellan's army from the peninsula, reinforcements marching to the Army of Virginia would have rendered it even more heavily Ohioan. General Jacob Dolson Cox, a graduate of the abolitionist-founded and interracial Oberlin College in Ohio, commanded the "Kanawha Division" composed of seven infantry regiments, all from Ohio, sent to reinforce the army from western Virginia. Hearing of indiscipline and a lack of initiative in the Army of Virginia, Cox eagerly offered his services: "In view of the report that disciplined troops are wanted at the East, I call your attention to the fact that my division is among the best-seasoned and oldest troops in the field, and are desirous of joining the principal column."[28]

Cox's offer was not altruistic; the general sought the glory that could accompany proximity to Washington, reporters, and politicians. "The boys are all well and in fine spirits and anxious to join Pope, hoping to have a hand when Richmond falls," and undaunted by the prospect of the two-hundred-plus-mile march from western Virginia to the vicinity of Fredericksburg, wrote one of the division's cavalry escorts.[29] One of Cox's colonels aided the general's quest for a transfer to Virginia, writing division commander Robert Schenck in I Corps and promising the Ohio political general his fellow Buckeyes "would pray fight and vote for him."[30] Another of Cox's colonels had every reason to join his colleague in petitioning Schenck to transfer them to Virginia; George Crook received his 1848 appointment to West Point from Congressman Schenck.[31]

Only two of these desperately needed infantry regiments reached Pope before Confederate raids disrupted the train network in the Army of Virginia's rear. The other five and their attached artillery and cavalry were diverted to the defenses of Washington and became McClellan's responsibility. They chafed at the delay in marching to the sound of the guns they could hear plainly. "Our division has been lying here for four days ready to march at a minutes notice, and never were men more eager for the fray," wrote a cavalry trooper. "Our trip from Green Meadow [in western Virginia] here was a very hard one and nothing but the dauntless courage of men enlisted in a holy cause could have induced men to bear it so *good Humouredly.* Our Division forms a striking contrast with the troops from the Peninsula Nowhere do I see such healthy looking boys as those [Ohioans] of the Kanawha Division."[32]

Contraband slaves by the thousands comprised the unarmed auxiliary of Pope's army. The attitudes of the Army of Virginia's soldiers toward slavery and slaves accorded to the soldiers' regional origins and increasing radicalization via the vicissitudes of occupation duty and dealing with a hostile civilian population. Many common soldiers in Pope's army gained a growing disgust with slavery as they saw its harsh reality for the first time, yet they retained many of their existing prejudices against the enslaved. Runaway slaves "forced northern soldiers to either oppose slavery or actively support it," writes historian Stephen Tuck.[33]

While most northern whites were indifferent toward slavery and slaves in the antebellum years, men in Pope's army were compelled to make a choice when confronted with thousands of self-emancipated people seeking refuge. Almost three-fourths of those in this study who expressed an opinion on personal encounters with slaves or contrabands were sympathetic to their plight. Yet the majority who expressed compassion for slaves and a desire to destroy slavery were officers, not enlisted men. Of thirty who noted meeting with slaves or contrabands, fourteen were positive, five negative, and eleven neutral in their opinion. Eight of fourteen describing positive interactions with contrabands were officers. Additionally, four-fifths of those whose political affiliations were clear (fourteen of seventeen) were Republicans. Ten of those Republicans were officers. However, the anti-slavery sentiments of Republican generals in the Army of Virginia compared to the Democratic views of McClellan's generals should not be conflated with "racial egalitarianism" or a belief that Americans should enjoy equal rights under the law, regardless of race or enslavement. Many Republican generals were anti-slavery *and* anti-black, desiring the destruction of slavery accompanied with the removal of the "problematic" black population from the United States. This prejudice was due in part to "scientific" convictions that African Americans could never gain equality with whites in intellect or manners. In the 1850s, future Republican general Robert C. Schenck, then a member of the anti-slavery Free Soil Party, wrote that African Americans were "mere animals, little above the brutes."[34]

Regional origin played a role in role in the anti-slavery or racialist tendencies of Union soldiers; many New Englanders in the army wrote of their anti-slavery convictions and sympathy for self-emancipated contrabands, while soldiers from the mid-Atlantic, border, and western states were more ambivalent or vocally racist. Chandra Manning, using a broader source base, has found that enlisted soldiers began championing "the destruction of slavery a full year ahead of the Emancipation Proclamation, well before" the bulk of their officers took such a stand. That split actually widened, according to Manning, between August and December 1861.[35]

A story from a private in the 80th New York illustrates the ambivalence, as well as the ways in which civil war troubled the waters of deep prejudice. "One sees some of the effects of war and slavery, while on picket duty here [in the vicinity of Fredericksburg] that would wring the tears out of any eyes that were half human yes they would make his Satanic Majesty blush for shame," Constant Hanks wrote. "Pencil sketches cant approach anywhere near the truthful horror of" slavery. "Tuesday our Company were picketing out on the outposts where, most of the contrabands come into our lines. An old gray headed negro woman bent

Contrabands crossing the Rappahannock. (Library of Congress)

almost double with age, and leading by the hand was a little nigger female child not more than three years old," and both shoeless and hatless. The elderly woman's daughter, the mother of the toddler, had been sold "to the far southern market because she had been attracted by those stars of hope that glisten in our national flag" and unsuccessfully attempted an escape to Union lines. When their owners threatened to send the grandmother into Richmond's hospitals as a nurse, she took the orphaned girl and struck out for the Union forces at Fredericksburg. "Whether she in her old [age] and the helpless child will be any better off in this selfish world, is a question that God alone can answer," the soldier concluded.[36]

The pair—evocative of stereotypical images of youth and age—traveled for three days, walking at night and hiding in swamps in the daytime to evade Confederate soldiers and the surviving slave patrols, the bane of runaway and holiday reveling slaves in the antebellum period.[37] The soldier found their story believable when he saw "the way they eat our dry bread and drank coffee," after the woman claimed they had not yet eaten that day. "The thought came rushing into my mind, Con[stant,] suppose that was your Mother and little one instead of poor miserable niggers?" This soldier was clearly struggling to push beyond his prejudices to imagine himself and his family in the same situation, much as an evangelical Protestant abolitionist would seek to persuade white northerners to identify with the enslaved. Yet he still called them "niggers," not Americans or fellow Christians. Elsewhere in the letter Hanks admitted that he was a "roughhewn" fellow, so he probably should not be lumped in with sentimental, middle-class evangelical Protestants.[38]

"During that one day some 80 of these poor beings came into our lines, through our company alone," Hanks continued. Many women carried small children, and "some of the women were naked down to the waists one of them had her back all cut to pieces with the whip" as punishment for a previous escape attempt. This scene moved many of the soldier's comrades. "Many of our boys gave all their days rations, thinking it would do the poor wretches more good than it would themselves. I don't know as I was doing right, but it did me good to see the poor buggers eat than it would to eat myself," he noted. "But you will get sick of nigger yarns," the soldier closed his tale, "forgive me this time and I wont write any more nigger chapters."[39] Prejudice clearly remained, or at least the author anticipated his mother's ongoing prejudice.

A member of the 13th Massachusetts who thought it natural to persuade a slave boy to run away from his master still could not envision African Americans as Union soldiers, whatever Congress decided. Walking on the battlefield at Cedar Mountain—still littered with unburied bodies—this soldier came upon the corpses of Union men. "At first I thought them Colored, they were so black and swollen" by the sun, "and I wondered how Negros should be wearing the blue coat of a soldier, but I soon discovered my mistake."[40] If "niggers" were sent "out hear to fight it will raise a rebellion in the army that all the abolitionist[s] this side of hell could not stop," a sergeant wrote home.[41] For these northerners, the war was still a white man's fight.

The attitudes toward slaves of white northerners serving with the Army of Virginia could be complex and inconsistent, changing according to circumstance, though New Englanders were the most consistently anti-slavery. Even among their number it was difficult—as for the Massachusetts sergeant above—to conceive of African Americans as American soldiers (or voters), despite the July 17 Confiscation and Militia Acts passed by the Republican Congress that opened the door to contrabands serving as laborers and even soldiers in Union armies. Volunteer soldiers commanded by officers learning their trade from West Point–trained generals found draconian regulations, drills, and punishments akin to slavery. The authority officers wielded seemed similar to the powers of overseers or masters. The lieutenant colonel of the 2nd Wisconsin was shocked by the powers officers held and sometimes abused. "I never before realized what a perfect slave a soldier is," he wrote; "how much he gives up—and becomes a part of a great machine."[42]

An officer on Pope's staff found the temporary censorship of all outgoing mail from the army in late August unbearable, an unforgiveable breach of the basic rights of all free men. "It is hard enough to be a soldier," wrote this privileged staff officer, son of an influential Illinoisan politician, "but to be compelled to give up those dear rights, which the meanest and lowest citizen can enjoy, and be treated like a slave or hireling, is a little more than I wish or intend to stand." This temporary inconvenience convinced him to "leave the army at my earliest opportunity, giving place to some one more anxious and willing than I am, to be treated like a dog."[43] "Saw one of the boys bucked and gagged [a treatment also meted out to recalcitrant slaves] today, and I thought it was a hard way to punish a boy for being absent from roll call," wrote an English-born soldier in late June.[44]

Many saw beyond their martial trials to sympathize with the plight of the self-emancipated. One journalist noted with compassion the weary tread of contrabands fleeing Lee's army: "poor ragged, flying Negroes, with their families and their worldly all, God help them!" They "touched their hats so obsequiously" that the journalist "felt a nervous impulse to put them upon my steed and take their burdens upon my back. Little sable folk, asleep and ahungered, drawn to that barefoot woman's breast; and the tired boy, weeping as he held to his father's hand. These are the 'wandering Jews' of our day," he wrote, "hated North and South, because they are poor and blind, and do no harm."[45]

Yet earlier, the same journalist, traveling with the Army of Virginia, condemned the "idleness and vice" that "soon characterized the mass" of contrabands arriving within the army's lines at Warrenton. "They were ignorant, degraded, animal beings," he recorded, "and many of them loved rum; it was the last link that bound them to human kind."[46] Increased exposure to the trials of self-emancipated African Americans broadened the reporter's sense of empathy.

What did not change in the summer of 1862 was the magnetic attraction that the Army of Virginia held for the self-emancipated, who sought refuge from former masters, slave patrols, and Confederate troops alike. "Pope's Army is famous for the contrabands it has thousands of them," in stark contrast to the "very few straggling along" behind McClellan's army, noted a Maine lieutenant.[47] "If we stay here a day or two longer we will be surrounded by Negroes," a New Yorker stationed near Fredericksburg wrote. He needed only to raise his eyes to behold "twenty little" African American children, whom he called "Chipmunk[s]."[48] This was all the more remarkable as the slave population was much larger and more densely concentrated in the Tidewater area occupied by McClellan compared to the regions held by Pope. "This talk about arming niggers is all 'bosh,'" a soldier in McClellan's army wrote in mid-July. "We have got to take Richmond before we have got any to arm."[49] Only after McClellan's army retreated from Richmond did more than a trickle of contrabands flock to it.[50] "At Harrisons Landing there was quite a city of them, dwelling in tents. We were here but an hour or two till they were beside us putting up their tents," a Pennsylvanian wrote. "What is to be done with them I do not know," but they seemed "more uncomfortable than they were with their masters."[51]

Confederate governmental sources corroborated these Union accounts. In a report to Virginia's state legislature in late 1863, the auditor of public accounts noted that the loss of commonwealth slaves to Union forces by flight or confiscation was significantly less than anticipated. Only 31,551 slaves, "less than 10 per cent (exclusive of West Virginia) of the slave population," were lost throughout the state.[52]

From these isolated observations, it might seem that runaway slaves found the Republican-led, hard-war policies of the soldiery of the Army of Virginia to be in effect a mobile emancipation community, a military refuge for the self-emancipated. Indeed, Republican-oriented political generals made it army policy to aid the crowds of contrabands that streamed into their lines, even if only justified by strict military necessity rather than idealism. "Negroes on horseback," a German revolutionary-turned-Republican general noted from Sperryville on July 21. "Sigel orders that negroes be confiscated" from their masters "wherever we can get them," the division commander recorded. As an anti-slavery political general, Carl Schurz was only too happy to comply.[53]

Self-emancipated slaves were true camp-followers *and* constituents of the Army of Virginia. By remaining within the army's picket lines, they gained a measure of protection from civilian slave hunters and Confederate soldiers, who would not hesitate to return them to their masters. When the army abandoned its campsites, African Americans scavenged among the trash and treasure left behind. According to one Rhode Islander, "resident and 'contraband' negroes stood ready to pick the camp carcass" of the Army of Virginia for the "camp furniture and every pet thing [that] was cast aside" by the soldiers when Pope's army moved forward to the Rapidan River on August 1.[54]

Even in defeat or retreat Pope's army attracted runaways. "A great many negroes accompanied the Union army in its retreat" from the Rapidan to the Rappahannock River. A New York colonel felt they "manifested the most extravagant and ludicrous joy when they got across," as if by moving away from their former sites of enslavement and toward

Brigadier General Carl Schurz. (From *The Reminiscences of Carl Schurz,* vol. 2, facing p. 348 [New York: McClure, 1907])

Washington they were leaving slavery behind forever.[55] While marching along the Orange and Alexandria Railroad in this same mid-August retreat to the Rappahannock, a Wisconsin soldier observed "hundreds of slaves running away" with the northward-moving Army of Virginia.[56] These fugitives had good reason to keep up with the marching soldiers; Pope's retrograde movement was compelled by the aggressive advance of Lee's Confederate Army, whose soldiers re-enslaved any African American apprehended. There were enough contrabands accompanying the Army of Virginia, a Rhode Island soldier noted—"on foot, on horse or mule, in old broken-down vehicles tied with straps and strings, in all manner of costumes grave and gay"—to significantly slow the army's march.[57]

Contrabands sought work with the Army of Virginia, or were sought out by Pope's soldiers for menial employment. An Irish-born noncommissioned officer in the 6th Wisconsin wrote of the hiring of a contraband named "Jack" as his company's cook and officer's servant while in camp near Fredericksburg. The company commander paid half of Jack's wages while the enlisted men raised the other half, establishing a symbiotic relationship between emancipated and emancipators.[58] Not all instances were so idyllic. A Vermont sharpshooter partnered with a comrade to hire "a big stout nigger to lug our Baggage for us we shall put all our stuff on one knapsack and let the nigger tote it."[59] He also devised other duties for the contraband: "We have got us a big nigger to go out foraging for us we send him out Blackberrying some times he gets a large pail full that lasts us for Berries and milk for a day or two milk we can get any time either buy it or send John the nigger out to milk the cows."[60]

Virginia contained a sizeable population of free blacks, as Pope's soldiers quickly noted.[61] A Rhode Island cavalryman encamped near Culpeper on a mid-August morning walked over to a "free negro's" house with coffee beans and sugar in hand: "She made me a splendid cup of coffee and I had plenty of bread and milk."[62] A spy from the 10th Maine stopped at the house of a free black near Milford on June 25, confirming the intelligence he gathered firsthand before returning to Union lines.[63]

Contrabands were the single most reliable source of military intelligence within the population of northern Virginia for the officers and generals of the Army of Virginia. Current information and actionable intelligence about the enemy was essential for Pope and his headquarters staff as they defended Washington by safeguarding the Shenandoah Valley, western Virginia, and the line of the Rappahannock near Fredericksburg. Pope used any and every means of intelligence gathering he could, up to and including paying spies to infiltrate the Confederate army or capital and obtain news on the intentions and movements of rebel forces. Indeed, Pope's spy network was more effective than McClellan's Allan Pinkerton–led agency on the peninsula.[64] Officers and men of the Army of Virginia found African Americans a vital source of information on the actions and intentions of the Confederate Army. In many cases the intelligence they provided was more useful than that gathered by the official reconnaissance activities of the army's three cavalry brigades or the unofficial scouting done by paid spies. A scouting party from an Indiana cavalry regiment set out from Fredericksburg on July 26 toward Spotsylvania Court House, accompanied by an African American guide. He informed them of a house a few miles from Spotsylvania that flew a rebel flag and stored rebel war materiel.[65] Generally untutored in military matters, slaves seeking to be helpful to their northern liberators could provide inaccurate or exaggerated information, however.

"A contraband from Gordonsville" where the Confederate Army was concentrated in mid-August, "came into camp a few days since. He reports that there are no fortifications at that point. This I am inclined to doubt—though I understand the country is not as favorable for defence as some points they have occupied," one Pennsylvanian wrote to his father.[66] The contraband's intelligence was of key importance at army headquarters, as Pope was keen to take the offensive against the enemy, but defensive works at Gordonsville would render an attack against an enemy force of equal size illogical. Of course, slaves could be used by Confederates and rebel sympathizers among the southern citizenry to deliver misinformation to Union forces, a reality of which northern soldiers were aware. On or about the evening of August 26, a New England sharpshooter wandered between the armies with a teamster as they sought to trace the footsteps of their retreating unit. "We were called on twice in the night by some colored people who were quite anxious to find out whether we were Confederates or Yanks. We told them we were both Yankees and Confeds." He was sure "the owners of these Negroes sent them to find out if we were Yankees so they might inform the rebels to come and capture us. Whether that was so or not, we were not molested," he recorded with relief.[67]

If they might be given to exaggeration in counting Confederate soldiers nearby or estimating the proximity of those forces, enslaved and self-emancipated African Americans were generally eager to volunteer what information they had. They were often the only civilians to welcome Union troops into their communities. A few proved invaluable as active scouts and spies. A staff officer from III Corps noted that one "usual guide" of the cavalry brigade attached to his corps was "a native-born Virginian." The scout seemed to the aide "a sort of Daniel Webster in ebony—a strong, clear-headed man, who had reached a true conception of the real issue in this war, and devoted himself, body and soul, on the right side. Knowing all the roads and by-ways in this section, and brave as a lion, he led our boys with all the cool courage needed in a scout." He "established a comprehensive system of espionage among the people of his own color, and thus brought in much valuable information. The rebels did him the honor to offer fifteen hundred dollars reward for his head, and well they might, for he was worth to the Union cause any two of the best of us [white men]." Clad in a Union military forage cap and a revolver tucked into his shirt, the scout, along with "his brother contrabands," took particular pride in the fact that he was "jet black" in complexion, "no white blood in *his* veins."[68]

Not all members of the Army of Virginia found African Americans to be worthy of sympathy, useful camp servants, or harmless sources of entertainment. Many white northerners who voted the Republican ticket were simultaneously anti-slavery and anti-black, fearing that emancipated slaves would migrate to northern cities and compete with white laborers for work, depressing the wages of white northerners. "It is now about 11 oclock" on a Sunday morning when an Indiana captain wrote his wife and children, "and just at this time you are all probably at your devotions at church and breathing prayers for our safety and welfare . . . and at the same time we are issuing out rations to the men. our Nigger Cook a Contraband we captured the other day with her two little monkey looking young ones, is out in the hot sun cooking our dinner the grease just boiling off her and her two monkeys." The captain—a brigade commissary officer—wished he had a "White Cook" as "it goes against the stomach awfully to see the grease rolling off her face around the hot fire." He speculated on the wisdom of taking "a little Contraband" home to Indiana to nurse his small daughter "and tote up wood and help about the kitchen but they are all so lazy." He heard that Abraham Lincoln intended to "try to colonize all the Niggers and I only hope he will make it" happen, "but the Niggers down here are not worth 3 cents put them where he will." Even those contrabands who were willing to work have to be told "every thing you want done. I have to tell the oldest monkey (about 6 years old) to keep the flies off the table every time I set down. They and their mother lays around on the ground like hogs and only gets up to Cook when told."[69]

A brigade commander in McDowell's Corps held high standards for servants in his employ. When "Leonard," a black contraband, displayed intolerable evidence of having "become very lazy," General Marsena Patrick sent him packing off to Washington. He acted quickly to replace his cook, appropriating his orderlies' chef, and made sure to employ "a white man and soldier" this time.[70] Patrick was in the habit of sending contrabands to Washington and away from the Army of Virginia's camps. On July 22, the general "captured" thirty-five or forty contrabands "and sent them to Washington." He justified the decision—certainly made without the consent of the contrabands—by arguing that they were parasites "on the outskirts of my Brigade, living by stealing and plundering."[71] When one of his orderlies was wounded in battle, Patrick noted that his staff officers found the man "a nice place for him" to recover, "with a *very* neat family of free negroes."[72]

By the first of August Patrick had "established [a] negro quarters where the fugitives can remain a day until sent forward to Washington by rail."[73] Many of the African Americans held in this structure or quarantined areas would have been struck by its similarity to slave quarters, and their treatment in this manner by a Union general as akin to the condescension of a slave master. The next day the "hegira of Negroes" continued. He sent "some 50 or more" slaves belonging to two Fredericksburg-area masters toward the federal capital, pushing them away from the army, where he did not think they belonged. "They came over here in the family coach and loaded" with passengers and their masters' goods.[74] Republican general Rufus King, Patrick's division commander, further ordered him to implement Pope's orders regarding holding local civilians accountable for guerrilla attacks and property damage and to make a list of four citizens of Fredericksburg to be held as hostages. Patrick obeyed these Republican orders, singling out four men to be arrested on the same evening that he sent "35 or 40 Contrabands" to Washington. The hostages would follow the contrabands on the railroad "by the early train, tomorrow."[75]

A soldier in I Corps felt hard labor building an oven under the July sun was work fit only for a slave. "Worked like a nigger all day with nothing to Eat," he groused.[76] A New Englander was displeased by the presence of masses of contrabands with Pope's army. "I have a profound disgust for the darky as do all soldiers," he wrote.[77] "Thair is a grate controversy out hear about the nigger Question at present if thay go to sending them out hear to fight thay will get enough of it for it will raise a rebellion in the army that all the abolitionist this side of hell could not stop," a Pennsylvania NCO wrote. "The Southern Peopel are rebels to the Government but thay are White and God never intended a nigger to put White Peopel Down," but "if thay wood hang a few of the Speculators and leading politicians who are trying to make Presidents instead of Good Generals the War would soon be over without the help of niggers."[78]

Fortunately for self-emancipated slaves, all soldiers did not profess disgust at their company. One staff officer from III Corps witnessed the "exultation" of contrabands employed as teamsters, blacksmiths, or other army laborers when they received, "for the first time in their lives, honest pay for their honest labor," a staple of Republican ideology. The officer commented that he was "satisfied that this is impulse sufficient with them, *as with us*, to induce their best efforts."[79]

"I have at last got a most excellent servant, Charles—(none of the negroes have any last names)," a II Corps staff officer wrote in early August. "His history is a most sad one and he is melancholy, but faithful, honest, and my heart has quite gone out towards him. He stoops so much as almost to be a hunchback. there is nothing prepossessing in his appearance; yet everybody likes him," and he was "a universal favorite" among the other servants. Henry Scott went further than most in sympathetically enquiring about and reflecting on his servant's background. "He was raised near Warrenton and when his master died just before the rebellion broke out," Charles was manumitted and left "land enough to exchange for a good farm in Ohio." The executor of his master's will, however, "was a harsh man; the friends of the deceased disputed the will, kept up a long litigation," and in the meantime, "the slaves were treated with great severity. Charles' wife and child died under it and he was sent off to another country. Then the war broke out, and all prospect of ever getting back his land or its equivalent was lost," excepting a Union victory.[80]

Charles, "being an intelligent blacksmith readily got work and when [rebel General Turner] Ashby came along was picked up by him. He worked for Ashby until the battle of Winchester when he managed to escape and I, being in want of a servant, picked him up." Charles was "weak and sickly," yet the best servant the officer ever had, and Scott cared enough for Charles's health that he "almost exhausted Aunt's stock of ginger in curing his gripes."[81]

A few soldiers took it upon themselves to not merely welcome the self-emancipated but to become active emancipators. A New Yorker who took part in a foraging expedition in late June 1862 made a stunning discovery at the farm of a Mr. Stickles. The soldier conversed with a lad whom he "supposed was the son of the proprietor," only to find that this boy—"whiter than many we had in our regiment, had straight hair, and little or nothing of the negro in his features"—was in fact Stickles's slave. Hearing that the "white" slave wanted freedom but did not dare to run away, the soldiers determined to free him. The boy's appearance alone convinced the New Yorkers that he must be freed, while another slave of a darker skin color had to show the permanent effects of a severe whipping on his back to convince them to help him. When the soldiers succeeded in freeing the boy, they were sure they had "done God's service."[82]

Other members of Pope's army also noted the variety of complexions worn by the contrabands seeking shelter with their units. "There was niggers in some of the groups that came in" through one New York regiment's picket line "that were white as you or I," wrote a soldier at Fredericksburg.[83] On August 2, the chaplain of a Rhode Island cavalry regiment noted that some of his unit's officers stayed overnight at the plantation house of a Mr. Bowen, "whose Union sentiments were like [the biblical] Joseph's coat. A smart mulatto boy, . . . belonged to this lord of the soil, as no one would doubt who saw the two faces. Slavery was a patriarchal institution, with a prodigious tail to it," as evidenced in the "miscegenation" of white masters and black slave women, a "sin" prewar advocates of slavery claimed northern abolitionists promoted yet in fact was widely practiced by southerners.[84]

Some members of the Army of Virginia took the opportunity of witnessing slavery and interacting with teeming crowds of contrabands for the first time to reflect on the "peculiar institution" and the proper place of African Americans. "There are differences of opinion in the army as to the slavery question," a Massachusetts chaplain wrote in July. "Some want emancipation proclaimed. Some, practical and effectual emancipation without proclamations. Some, to leave slavery as it was before the war. The drifting is towards emancipation, mainly to the second position. In that I rather coincide," he declared, "though I want the thing *done* at any rate, as necessary for the country."[85] Regardless of their positions on the necessity of emancipation, the chaplain argued, the men of the Army of Virginia "love their country first and best. If we can accomplish emancipation, it would be a glorious deed for our country. If not now, yet the old Flag must triumph. But, to emancipate, is the way to succeed; and therefore the government needs policy, needs firmness, needs energy. The more I see, the more I believe in the feasibility of emancipation," he wrote. "The difficulties in the way are not unconquerable; I mean, as to adjusting the elements of the new state of society caused thereby. The only obstacle is in the masters, who have so long made men work without wages, that, like all tyrants, they cannot bear to go to work for an *honest* living."[86] The idea of sending the emancipated slaves "back" to Africa as a condition of freedom seemed to the chaplain "a perfect humbug,—unless you colonize the masters, the real encumbrances. To remove the industrious portion of the community is foolish." If "Massachusetts were to expel from its borders its day-laborers, its working farmers, its shoemakers, its blacksmiths,—where would the wealth of Massachusetts be? The blacks are the workmen,—peasant laborers generally, but often mechanics. They do not wish to leave their native land. Why should they? What *right* have we to expel them? Is their race not a native of the soil [of the United States]?"[87]

The climax of the Second Bull Run campaign in late August involved a great deal of hard marching and hard fighting for the men of the Army of Virginia, often under a hot sun and without regular issues of food or access to potable water. Union officers and soldiers thus found themselves worse off than slaves and contrabands in a material sense, perhaps for the first time in their lives. In several instances, African Americans found themselves being begged for food or shelter from weary and beaten Union soldiers. On August 31, a fatigued sharpshooter from New Hampshire awoke, "pulled myself together and thought if I could get something to eat, I might be able to follow after our troops" in their retreat to Centreville and Washington. "I went to a house near by and an old colored woman gave me a part of a hoe cake. I presume that it was part of her own ration. She said that she had two sons with the Yankees and she wanted me to tell de boys that, 'she was [tolerable] well when you see em.'"[88]

The Republican character of the Army of Virginia was on best display in the celebration of the one national holiday Pope's army witnessed, the Fourth of July. Northern Democrats and Republicans alike commemorated Independence Day, none more so than the soldiers and officers of the Army of Virginia. Numerous observers of the festivities on July 4, 1862, noted it as a day when military norms were turned topsy-turvy, with enlisted men taking the role of officers and officers adopting the duties of privates for inspection and dress parade. The celebrations involved alcohol, sanctioned or otherwise.[89]

If Republicans and Democrats fought over which party was the legitimate heir to the legacy of the American Revolution, on the Fourth of July they stood united in the face of a spurious challenge. The union of northern Democrats and Republicans possessed a much stronger claim to a shared revolutionary legacy than Confederates' claims of resistance to tyranny. As several soldiers encamped near Fredericksburg noticed, rebel soldiers seemed not to venerate George Washington to nearly the extent demonstrated by his democratic heirs in the northern states, as demonstrated by the desecration of the grave of Washington's mother. A member of the 7th Wisconsin encamped at Ferry Farm, Washington's birthplace, noted that rebels "have fired at the tombstone" of Washington's mother "three or four times and disfigured it very badly."[90] The Union occupation force left soon after; rebels reoccupied Fredericksburg, and the next time a northern soldier recorded visiting the tomb, the grave was further disfigured. "The monument is not finished," a sharpshooter from

New Hampshire remarked, "and has been shamefully abused by the rebels, who used it for a target. I counted 145 bullet marks on one side of it besides any quantity of shot marks."[91] Seeing how little Confederate Virginians thought of the sacred site, the New Englander found nothing untoward in taking a piece of the monument to send home as a souvenir.

# 6 Make the Traitors Feel the Cost

The partisanship of the Army of Virginia expressed itself perhaps most clearly in its embrace of John Pope's punitive policy toward rebellious citizens. But just as the politicking of officers mixed ideology and ambition, so too did the actions of common soldiers combine the personal with principles. Weary of protecting the property of civilians they suspected of secretly supporting the rebel army and guerilla forces, much less those who did so openly, common soldiers in the Army of Virginia found in Pope's orders license to punish *and* plunder. Radical officers and generals turned a blind eye on nonlethal excesses, and sometimes stretched the general's orders to the limit of plausible interpretation. Conservative commanders aghast at the excesses of petty theft reined in their soldiers. Even Pope expressed disapproval of the worst overreach officially, but this did not prevent enlisted men from continuing to appropriate civilian property when officers were not looking, or chose to look away. The behavior of the men of the Army of Virginia as an occupational force illustrates the challenges to order posed by an army bonded and impelled by retributive zeal.

Plenty of officers and men found in Pope's orders just another form of ammunition to expend in the war effort. An aide to General Franz Sigel "determined to see the matter through—Jackson or ourselves whipped. And if they can keep us supplied with Amm[unitio]n we will fight him forever." If he was later convinced that "General Pope is a perfect brute—gives the most conflicting [tactical] Orders and scarcely knows what he does half the time," he was ready to fight under any general so long as he was ordered to advance on the enemy.[1]

A colonel from Ohio wrote an eloquent letter to his wife about the need to destroy slavery and defeat the Confederacy, as both were deadly enemies to Unionists like him and the men he led. As a Catholic, he had been a gradual emancipationist before the war, believing "that the

Catholic religion was Anti-Slavery, never ceas[ing] until it attained its object. It thus abolished Slavery from every Country where it had power on Earth." He did not glean this position from reading Catholic historians alone; "Protestant historians, with a candor not common to them," concurred in the "heroic and untiring efforts of the Popes through the middle ages" to abolish peonage in Europe. "All history told me, that every country, without exception, that failed in due time to emancipate their slaves was through them brought to utter ruin by insurrections or external war—that the system was a disease—a social, moral, and political evil," and if "no steps were taken for its cure, it inevitably ended in terrible convulsions." With this knowledge, the colonel previously opposed abolitionists "who wished to end it in a day" for the convulsions that sudden and uncompensated emancipation would bring to the southern states. Instead, abolition "should be left to the [white] people who were afflicted by it, to effect the cure gradually," though note the common conceit that those most "afflicted" by slavery were the masters. But he "never dreamed that they, with the light of the past before them, would hurry on the awful Judgment which had overtaken the persistent slave holders of the past."[2]

The southern people said "No" when they should have prepared for gradual emancipation, Hugh Ewing, the colonel from Ohio, was shocked to discover in the secession winter of 1860–61. Instead they proposed to "lay the foundations for [slavery's] perpetuity and future extension," a foundation to be placed "on the smoking ruins of the U.S. Government—that good gift of God to oppressed humanity, which Catholic Arch Bishops tell us is better for the progress and freedom of the Church than that of any other Country on the face of the earth." Having "convulsed the entire nation," Ewing said, "in the name of Almighty God who abhors it, let [slavery] die; and disturb the world no more." Opposing immediate emancipation in the antebellum years to preserve order, this Catholic colonel now fought pro-slavery Confederates as the greatest threat to order in the United States. More personally, this civil war, "this convulsion, the child of Slavery, threatens, every day it lasts, to make you a widow and our children orphans," the officer reminded his wife. He gladly chose abolition as preferable to "a widowed wife and orphan children" if his life was offered up "on the Altar of Slavery." "Slavery has forfeited its right, if it even had any, to the life of any man—especially to mine which it is laboring day and night to destroy. It has already spilt rivers of blood—it has spent enough. I am willing to shed my blood, to preserve our Government to our children and grand children," but he would not make his beloved children orphans "to preserve that system for any body elses children."[3]

A lieutenant in the 107th Pennsylvania told his father that "this war must be conducted on different principals than what it has been or our case will be in danger." He attacked slavery and slaveholders as the root and leadership of the resistance to Union occupation: "Slaveholders must not look for their property or negroes to be protected they must either be for us or against us. They who are loyal must come out and them who are rebels must swear allegiance to the country or be taken as prisoner of war." A week later Pope ordained just this, banishing those who refused the oath from their homes and beyond the army's lines. Northern armies could not prevail on the battlefield "if we alow rebels to run lo[o]se carry all information to the enemy."[4] Enemy intelligence-gathering must be stopped. Pope used this argument to persuade the president that loyalty oaths had to be imposed on Virginia's adult male civilians.[5]

Shortly after the issuance of Pope's string of general orders regarding stringent policies toward disloyal civilians, General Adolph von Steinwehr arrested five civilians in Luray, Virginia. The division commander in Sigel's I Corps threatened to execute one man for each of his murdered by guerrillas unless those responsible were surrendered by their neighbors. The Confederate high command responded immediately, with Robert E. Lee ordering Stonewall Jackson—confronting Pope's forces while Lee faced George McClellan at Richmond—to not simply defeat the "miscreant Pope" but to "destroy" him. Lee warned General Henry Halleck that Pope and his officers would be treated as "robbers and murderers" for executing civilians. Confederate political leaders simultaneously declared the officers of Pope's army outlaws, not meriting treatment as prisoners according to the rules of war if captured.[6]

Spying and guerilla warfare were among the dangers Union soldiers encountered in enemy territory. Officers and men in Pope's army were convinced that they were surrounded by spies, male and female. Spies were caught during the spring campaign in northern Virginia and the Shenandoah Valley, and dealt with in a draconian and summary manner well before the advent of Pope. "We caught a rebel spy in our camp last week, disguised as a newspaper vendor," a Massachusetts soldier wrote in April 1862. "Papers were found in his boots that convicted him beyond doubt, and he was hanged up by the neck, with very little ceremony."[7] The situation had changed little by the time the Army of Virginia formed in June. "Spies were all around us," a Rhode Island chaplain noted on

July 2, "sometimes playing the role of 'Union men' very sharply."[8]

Staff officers were particularly vigilant against local residents spying on units as they marched by. "We are in the house of a big burly Virginian, who is now, I think in communication with the rebels," a staff officer in George Gordon's brigade (Nathaniel Prentiss Banks's corps) wrote on July 10: "I have just given him a pass [to travel through the army's lines], but at the same time sent three men to watch him, and if they notice any suspicious conduct to bring him back 'dead or alive.' In the meantime I shall search his house for rifles, revolvers, etc. which if I think he has," and if he possessed any such weapons, "stick him in jail."[9]

Some southern spies were known well enough to be identified by name. Members of an Indiana cavalry regiment stationed near Fredericksburg were ordered to "hunt for a spy which crossed the river at Ballards farm and had stayed there all night" and left on the morning of August 30: Harrison Hill.[10] A federal provost marshal in Martinsburg sent out a notice that one B. R. Boyd left that place for Front Royal "in [a] buggy [that] has in it many letters going South" and should be interdicted.[11]

A member of the 10th Maine was particularly keen on catching spies to speed the "war of conquest" against the Confederacy: "Punish the rascally spies, farmers, women and children that are constantly passing through our lines and informing the enemy of every movement we make. We lose men every day by guerrillas, or our loss in battle is greater from the information the rebels have of our positions before the fight. If our lives are worth less than" those of traitorous civilians, "let these things go on." The New Englander concluded, "If the enemy's are worth less than ours, the[n] punish for offences. At least be as severe as our enemy." He wanted to teach the people of Virginia "that the Yankees were dangerous beasts, though devoid of horns which some of them think we have. WAR is a great and terrible game. Let the terror be with our enemies and not among ourselves. So I think, and I thought exactly opposite on all these points before I came in contact with the rebels, natives and soldiers."[12]

Worse than spies, from the perspective of common soldiers, were the guerrilla bands, which were more deadly to unwary sentries and small scouting parties. Lonely pickets and guards were quick to attribute sudden outbursts of gunfire to guerrilla activity. A western soldier in Banks's corps on guard duty heard firing on the road to the east. The fire was reported to be an attack by "Gerillas."[13]

"Pope's orders are received with universal satisfaction," particularly insofar as counterinsurgency (or counter-guerrilla policy) was taken seriously. "It seems to indicate that the *miserable policy of mercy* to a gang of assassins is at an end, and hereafter we are to have stern, and unyielding justice," a soldier in the 28th Pennsylvania wrote.[14] Regular army veterans among the volunteer officers had some inkling as to how to deal with guerrillas from their service on the western plains. An Indian fighter for the past decade, Colonel George Crook confronted the rebel "bushwhackers" in western Virginia as if they were his indigenous antebellum foe.[15] Yet Confederate guerrillas could be as frustratingly elusive as Native Americans when defending their own land; "it is impossible to force them to fight unless they want to, for they carry little or no baggage, and can live on little or nothing. When approached they disintegrate and hide in the mountains until all danger is over, when they again reassemble for fresh depredations."[16]

Newly promoted General John Geary led a cavalry scouting force that encountered "a body of Guerillas" near Middletown on July 1 and made a spirited pursuit of the irregulars.[17] "We are in a country of guerrillas. They are continually picking up our men," a staff officer in Banks's II Corps wrote. "At a farm house some five miles off, they urgently pressed two men to stay to tea; they waited some time and then concluded they must go. A little way from the house they were fired on; one shot wounded both of them, another brought down one of the horses; they both got on" the other horse and made their escape. "These men belonged to Gen. Williams' [cavalry] escort. The house surrounded and 15 men taken prisoners; one of them had a pistol, one barrel of which had been discharged and the ball which lodged in the boot of the wounded man just fitted that barrel."[18]

The gun with its empty barrel "would be evidence enough to hang him under Gen. Pope's last order, but he will probably be referred to Gen. Banks who will administer to him the oath of allegiance and let him go," the officer wrote. Ambushes of this nature "are happening all the time here; indeed they have become so common as to cause no excitement except to new comers or the immediate actors."[19] In mid-August, a hundred men of the 110th Pennsylvania guarded the bridge over Hazel Run near Culpepper against guerrillas. "I do not believe one of us slept 10 hours for the last 10 days for it is in such a strong secesh [secessionist] nabourhood about half way between Warrenton and this place," and guerrillas were so active "that it wood not do to be caught napping," a sergeant wrote.[20] Men of the 13th Pennsylvania Reserves—the "Bucktails"—found the warning about being caught napping by guerrillas all too literally true. "We picket all around, and send out Scouts in every direction," a soldier in the 9th Reserves noted, but these precautions were not enough to save a number of Bucktails from ghastly deaths. "Three Bucktails poisoned and one found with the Throat cut, the tail off the Cap in his mouth."[21] Five days later, another Bucktail was "found with his throat cut."[22]

A volunteer officer detailed to Irvin McDowell's corps for the construction and maintenance of bridges and railroad tracks hoped that Pope's authoritarian orders would stave off the menace of guerrilla activity: "We will clean [Virginia's civilians] out as we go, and wont leave them to form guerrilla bands in our rear, to burn bridges and attack our trains, in fact those orders will save us fifty thousand men in Virginia that would have been left to guard Railroads Bridges," and so on.[23] The officer knew firsthand the deleterious effects of irregular warfare on the transportation and supply of the Army of Virginia, as much of his time was spent rebuilding bridges destroyed by Confederate cavalry and guerrillas. Counterinsurgency even featured in recruiting posters. A poster for the 2nd Massachusetts enticed men to join "general pope's army. 'Lynch Law for Guerrillas and No Rebel Property Guarded!' Is the motto of the Second Massachusetts Regiment." After detailing the $1,800 a recruit could earn from pay, state aid to the soldier's family, and bounty for a two-year enlistment, the poster claimed, "This Regiment, although second in number, is second to none in regard to discipline and efficiency," and served in healthy and "delightful" country.[24]

In the politically fractious Army of Virginia, officers showing too much leniency toward pro-secession, or "secesh," southern civilians ran some danger of arrest as suspected spies or guerrillas. "Capt. [John] Mansfield from the Second Wisconsin Regt. who was Provost Marshal of this district has been arrested and sent to Washington for aiding the rebels," an Indiana sergeant wrote. "He was engaged in sending them salt etc. and forwarding their mail."[25] A volunteer nurse working at a hospital in Fredericksburg found additional fault with this Wisconsin captain: "We all were so provoked a few days ago to hear that the Provost Marshal ordered our flag to be taken down from a N.Y. store here because of it discommoding the secesh ladies here by having to go out in the street to avoid walking under it." The nurse noted that the officer's own men disagreed with his policies. "All the Wisconsin boys condem him very much some of them know him personally his name is Mannsfield I think he ought to be arrested by all means. I think it ought to be published in all the papers."[26]

Union soldiers in the Army of Virginia were sometimes compelled by military necessity to destroy U.S. government property, in addition to using, seizing, or destroying the property of Virginia's civilians. This destruction generally occurred when an orderly retreat verged on rout, and supplies that would impede the army's march were consumed by fire rather than left for the enemy. As the troops tasked with the property destruction were most interested in rejoining their retreating units, "collateral damage" in the form of destroyed or damaged civilian buildings resulted if the flames raged out of control beyond the army depot or supply wagon corral. In May, fires set by Banks's retreating troops to destroy military, medical, and sutlers' supplies stored in wagons near Winchester spread to the town, an oversight that drove some of the town's citizens to take up arms against the retreating soldiers.[27]

While the guns boomed near Manassas in late August, Banks's corps was again tasked with destroying army supplies, including in this case railroad stock. A corporal in the 28th Pennsylvania wrote on August 31 that his regiment set fire to "5 1st Class [train] Engines and 148 Freight Cars containing a large amount of valuable Government Property" upon reports that Confederate units were advancing on the station.[28]

Not all interactions between Pope's "brigands" and white Virginians were of a tense or rapacious character. "I had nothing to eat," a sergeant in the 2nd Wisconsin wrote in late July, so he and "another fellow got permission to go to a house a mile distant" from Fredericksburg. "We went got some bread and buttermilk and hoe cakes [and] stayed about a half hour discussing politics with the ladies, though 'secesh.'"[29]

By 1863 at the latest, some northern volunteer soldiers were convinced that thousands of Democrats at home were traitors, organizing secret societies to overthrow the democratically elected Union government or at least undermine the war effort. Jennifer L. Weber has argued that "for the most part, soldiers were silent on the subject of Copperheads well into the fall of 1862."[30] But there are signs that such suspicions already existed in what would become the Union Army of Virginia by late 1861. The provost marshal of Sigel's corps, busily administering the oath of allegiance to Virginian civilians, wished that the "southern sympathizers" in Ohio could be forced to take the oath. "The *draft may reach some of them,*" compelling them to choose loyalty to the Union and home or the Confederacy and exile.[31]

But enlisted men and officers in the Virginia army were increasingly divided over what Pope's punitive orders meant in practice. Some of the 13th Massachusetts's enlisted men, "construing [Pope's] order[s] to mean an indiscriminate plunder of everything that could be found, went out in squads of two or three and took whatever they could lay their hands upon."[32] A soldier from Maine wanted the "senseless, intensely foolish idea that this is a war of 'restoration'" given up as a dead hypothesis. "Nothing of the kind. It is a war of conquest."[33] "The men seem to think they have a right to assume the responsibility of destroying every thing in Virginia," a Pennsylvania officer recorded.[34]

One explanation for some soldiers' resort to petty theft was lack of pay. Corps commander Sigel wrote the army's chief of staff that "it is a matter of great Complaint that a great many of our troops have not received any pay for several months, some of the regiments and batteries have been six months without money. Officers and soldiers who have their families at home receive letters from them daily, that they are in the most deplorable condition which undoubtedly obliges a great many to resort to the most extreme measures."[35] Soldiers on both sides generally took the welfare of their dependents seriously and regularly sent home a portion of their pay. Chaplains or officers going home on leave were a frequent vehicle for the conveyance of enlisted men's money by direct, personal transmission.[36] The alternative was to pay for an express delivery service, but these were not always available to men on an active campaign.

A few enlisted men felt compelled to explain to their family when delays in the delivery of their wages occurred. "We were payed of[f] 2 months pay on the 17th of the month and I Gave the adjutant of our regt 25 Dool[lar]s to take on to you," a sergeant in the 110th Pennsylvania wrote to his wife on June 25. "This morning he gave me the money back and Sayed he had not time to attend to it. When I was payed up at Luray thair Was no Way to Send money back home."[37]

The great disparity in pay between enlisted men and officers could mean that an officer would hire a servant as well as send money home, or at least think nothing of those who did. One of General Geary's clerks sent twenty dollars home to Philadelphia "by Robert, the General's servant. He is a very trustworthy man," the clerk assured his parents. "He lives in Fallon st right back of us."[38] Barely a week after sending his first letter, the clerk was happy to receive confirmation that his parents had received the money by Robert's hand.[39]

A week before he was killed in battle at Cedar Mountain, a captain from Massachusetts sent $120 home, $80 for his wife and $40 for his mother. Ironically, his last letter home dealt mostly with difficulties renegotiating the terms of his life insurance policy. Already sick for weeks, the captain had been advised that the rate of the premium on his life insurance had increased so much as to be illogical to pay. He hoped "that everything may be satisfactorily arranged" for his wife's wellbeing should he fall in battle. "How the deuce do you suppose people live who have only $1500 and have to pay house-rent?" the captain asked his wife.[40] Many did not, and they may have reasoned that if Uncle Sam did not pay on time, then the treasonous southern civilians who kept them from home and family would.

Union soldiers also possessed an elastic definition of what constituted "stealing" when it came to the satisfaction of their hunger. While "Genl. Pope has issued strict orders against stealing sheep and honey and other citizens property, as long as his commissaries fail to issue the regular rations his orders will amount to nothing," a Maine lieutenant noted in July. "A hungry soldier is the most infernal pest that can visit a country and I witness proceedings that make me feel bad, but I have no desire to stop a man from stealing sheep and bacon when his only other resource for life is in hard bread."[41]

A keen-eyed sergeant of the 2nd U.S. Sharpshooters noted the systematic disappearance of Virginia's fruit in mid-July.[42] A month later the sharpshooter was near Culpeper, subsisting "on fresh pork, which we shoot ourselves, and sauce made from peaches, and apples, which are plenty, as our regt. is encamped in an orchard."[43] Another New Englander detailed the lengths—fair and foul—to which soldiers went to obtain savory meals if left in camp for weeks at a time. "We sogers keep a large dairy and have potatoe patches we shall have green corn in a few days now. We didn't get ours planted quite early enough on account of the war," the farming soldier commented, "but our crops here look pretty well now though we are going to have Beef steak new potatoes etc. for dinner[.] for supper last night we had Mackerel for meat and the other things to go with it," however "Butter and such things we have to buy or steal. Bread Sugar and such things are furnished us we have fresh Beef 2 or 3 times a week. Salt Beef and Pork the rest of the time with what Government and Secesh give us you see we manage to live. Some of the boys send their money all home, but I like to live a little better than that when I can."[44]

Line officers, elected from their company's ranks, generally sympathized with the men and their motivations. "The boys work faithfully on Popes order no. 5," a lieutenant in the 22nd New York wrote. "We have had fresh Pork and mutton all the time and to day one of the boys brought us a chicken and some Potatoes. Every one that can steals a horse or mule and I have got one of our boys looking out for one for me."[45]

An officer who turned the other way might receive a share of the spoils.

Other soldiers may have been driven by their experience in August 1862, the first sustained campaign in a near total war. For three weeks, from August 14 to September 4, Union soldiers were under fire, targeted by cannon and exposed to constant artillery duels when not facing massed musketry volleys. The war represented a transition point in combat, when battlefield casualties were caused increasingly by indirect artillery fire rather than by musket balls or short-range cannonballs, a shift complete by the First World War. Union infantrymen were "terrified at the prospect and actuality of [indirect artillery] bombardment"—when death came whirling in at them from long range while not presenting an opportunity to fire back—"and experienced considerable psychological fear and anxiety as a result."[46] The campaign of Pope's army was the first in which Americans experienced daily combat for weeks at a time. "For the last 20 days and nights we have not bin out of the hearing of Cannon firing," a sergeant in the 110th Pennsylvania noted.[47]

Close combat presented a different challenge to morale and a psychologically disturbing experience. "A man in battle is worse than a brute," a Pennsylvania Reserve confessed. "He looses all feeling and cares for nothing at all. I seen a man in our company pin a rebel captain to a tree with his bayonet and then pull it out and run it through him 5 times. He and three other fellows bayoneted 7 men as far as they could." He also witnessed rebels shot in the head at pointblank range.[48] George McClellan's army never faced such constant campaigning with its concomitant threat of death. Even during five months on the peninsula, the Potomac army did not experience twenty consecutive days of combat. "Shell shock" almost undoubtedly contributed to the Virginia army's penchant for looting.[49]

The case should not be made too strongly that the officers and men lost all sense of military discipline or patriotism. Individual courage and small-group cohesion persisted during the Army of Virginia's campaigns. For example, three of the 2nd Massachusetts officers killed at Cedar Mountain were "too sick to march and went up to the battle field in ambulances rushing forth when their regiment was ordered forward," despite being unfit for duty.[50] One of these ill-fated officers wrote his wife a week before his death, admitting that he had been sick for weeks but expressing the hope that "many a sicker man has got well and we must not begin to despair yet by any means. I should have perfect confidence if I had *any* faith in the Government but it is so mixed up with politicians and intrigues of all kinds that one can't hope with any reason of seeing any permanent improvement."[51] He did not express any lack of confidence in the fighting abilities of the men.

Another of these Massachusetts officers whose last decision in life was to choose duty to his men over personal health and safety had been "sick nearly two months . . . and applied for leave, but they told him if he was so sick as that he had better resign."[52] The officer informed his mother that he was hardly in a mood to resign a mere four days before his death in battle. "I shall have to do my marching in the ambulance, at present, for I am quite weak, having averaged nothing but 2 slices of toast a day for the past two weeks, and rather having to force them down. I am going to try a little broth today." Despite his weakness, the captain sent one hundred dollars home and apologized for his scrawl: "I had to write just when [the] spirit moved me, and it is too hot and flies are too troublesome to take much pains."[53] When the officers of the regiment visited the men wounded at Cedar Mountain, they found it "hard to see some of the very best of our men disabled. But their pluck and cheeriness" was heartening.[54]

The real killer of Civil War soldiers was disease. "Two entire regiments from [Christopher] Augur's Division [of Banks's corps] have been sent to hospital," a II Corps staff officer wrote. "In the 60th N.Y. men died 8 or 10 a day. Typhoid fever is what does it. The men are green in that Division; don't know how to cook and like insane men, insist on eating every crabbed apple tree they see."[55] The 60th New York was ravaged by typhoid in July and August.[56] On July 24, the colonel reported that "we had but five captains and two lieutenants fit for duty, and that sickness being very much on the gain among the men, we were not in a condition for active service."[57] On July 26, "the surgeon's record showed one hundred and forty cases of typhus fever. Three died that day." The chaplain spent all day at the regimental hospital.[58] On August 4, "the Medical Directors decided that we must go out of the field at once" and ordered the regiment to move to White Sulphur Springs the next morning. The men of the 60th rested there until August 20, when the offensive advances of the rebel army caught up with the convalescent men, and it was necessary once again to move the regiment, now numbering 525 sick men.[59] The regiment's ordeal robbed Pope of more than five hundred effectives when he needed every fighting man at Cedar Mountain and Second Bull Run.

"War is not a most dangerous game from the enemy's shot but from exposure, disease, carelessness, and home-sickness," an officer from Maine noted. "Homesickness makes more demoralization than anything

I know of, except skedaddling." In his regiment's case, as of July 21, three men had been killed in action, "four or five badly wounded, while 27 have died [of illness] and more than 60 men discharged for disability, the foundation of the latter being in ¾ of the cases, dislike of soldiering, i.e. home-sickness."[60] Fatal accidents and "acts of God" could and did happen as well, of course. "The Guard tent here was struck by lightning yesterday evening, seriously injuring several," a trooper in the 1st (West) Virginia reported on August 7, "besides breaking up a Game of Cards that was in progress at the time."[61]

Prior to germ theory, illness—let alone acts of God—could not be easily combated, but breakdowns in morale caused by homesickness had a remedy: proper discipline, as West Point–trained officers knew. But professional officers and proper discipline were often lacking. Officers without combat commands and those who spent a lot of time at army headquarters viewed the despoiling of the countryside as inevitable, not the willful act of vengeful soldiers. "It is not pleasant to see the change that take place in the country from our occupancy of it," an engineer on Pope's staff observed. The corn "which waved so freshly in the morning breeze shows now but a field of, or fields of stubble. The army is a destroying host! There will be nothing left in the track of our army," he continued, "upon which to subsist man or beast next winter! This is [what] the deluded Virginians have chosen for themselves."[62]

"*The Regt. Officers,* as a general rule, are of the *opinion that property in Rebeldom is, or ought to be, free to all in arms* against them," a West Point–educated brigadier noted in mid-June. Marsena Patrick lumped field and company officers—all state volunteers—together. He relished the opportunity to arrest soldiers for various infractions, a good preface to his future as the Army of the Potomac's provost marshal. Patrick saw the general malaise of McDowell's corps—"our present disordered state"—as due to their "hanging upon the whim of the Comdg. General," and as such "there is very little to be accomplished in the way of discipline and instruction." As a result, "*the men are indifferent and feel that they are acting without an object, or a purpose;* consequently they *behave badly,* strolling over the country, stealing, destroying fruit trees loaded with partially ripened fruit, etc."[63]

Union soldiers stole from their comrades as well, often opportunistically rather than in premeditated acts. An orderly to Pennsylvania Reserve Division commander John Reynolds "liberated" a horse belonging to a Union cavalry regiment that was running free during the Battle of Gaines's Mill. When the captain of the company that owned the horse confronted the orderly, he truthfully claimed that he was on his general's business and rode off. Although caught eventually, the soldier was not seriously reprimanded by the general.[64] In this case, the orderly likely assumed the horse's owner was a battle casualty, so he was appropriating a horse from someone who no longer needed it. Other enlisted men engaged in more blatant thievery.

Membership in a cavalry regiment may have seemed like especial license to plunder, as the ability to jump on a horse and make a quick getaway from the scene of a crime presented a temptation denied to infantrymen. The chaplain of the 2nd Massachusetts Infantry declared an entire regiment of Union cavalry to be full of horse-thieves: "I am better fitted for a march than I was a week ago, when I had lost my horse! He turned up, at last, in the Fifth New York horse-thieves (known *officially* as cavalry). General Gordon lost a horse of his, it was found in, and with great difficulty (ending in the arrest of a captain) procured from, the Fifth New York." When the 2nd's adjutant lost a brace of horses, they were found with the 5th New York.[65] Henry Besancon's twentieth birthday was memorable on at least two counts. First, the upstate New York musician witnessed the second day of Second Bull Run and then his "haversack was stolen containing letters testament hymn book fife eating materials" and all his rations.[66]

On the day the army was formed, the 1st Vermont Cavalry's adjutant requested that Lieutenant A. J. Grover submit "an immediate report" for why he stole "one saddle, one girth, one nose bag, one shirt, two pairs drawers, and one pair stockings."[67] The adjutant also requested a reply from Captain George Conger to the following query: "By what authority are you absent from the regiment?"[68] In keeping with the New England tradition of community governance, the 1st Vermont Cavalry held a "regimental town meeting always in session." As Stephen Z. Starr points out, "every cavalry regiment had its court of public opinion, with its own crude but effective machinery, unknown to the regulations, for enforcing its sentences," a practice shared with volunteer infantry regiments and batteries.[69]

Wounded soldiers were particularly vulnerable to theft by their comrades. A 3rd Wisconsin soldier at Cedar Mountain had a close call when a musket ball tore through his hat, "just clearing the crown." He also suffered a wound to his right hand.[70] His wife asked if he lost anything, and he replied, "Yes, I did, after I got back to Culpepper I had only one shirt and had been wearing it for nearly 2 weeks and left it off till a niger could wash it. I paid her 10 cents, during the washing process I was shirtless and I just got back to the hospital and left it on the seat," and someone "smarter than me stole it." Thieves also took his "knapsack, coffee, sugar, knife, fork and spoon, canteen and tincup so I had nothing" except trousers and an oilcloth blanket. He gave the last item away, putting it "on a wounded and naked man of our regiment and that was the last I saw of it."[71] "The only thing that troubles me now is I have no money," an NCO wounded at Brawner's Farm and comfortably ensconced in a Washington hospital informed his parents. "I had plenty when I left the Reg't but while I was asleep at Manassas somebody stole my pocketbook which contained all the money I had, a silver pen case and gold pen worth three dollars and a half and the very needle case which you gave me when I left home."[72]

Local discipline meted out by New England town meeting–style regimental courts as in the 1st Vermont Cavalry failed to prevent the petty looting of fruit trees and fence rails—civilian property—to feed campfires. But enforcement of basic military discipline required the active efforts of volunteer officers. The colonel of the 1st Rhode Island Cavalry enforced Pope's "severe" orders "modestly, quietly and lawfully." Even so, he told his men, "don't you let me see when you take anything," with "a twinkle of the eye."[73] Other regimental commanders were less lackadaisical in enforcing discipline. A Philadelphia journalist came upon the colonel of the 94th New York encamped near the Rappahannock River. The commanding officer berated his soldiers for plucking green apples (stealing from civilians). "Boy," he said to one, "put down that fruit! Drop it, or I'll blow your head off! Directly you'll double up, pucker, and say that you have the 'di-o-ree,' and require an ambulance. Orderly!" When a sergeant arrived, the colonel ordered him to shoot any man who failed to obey an order to move away from the apple trees. "A few such colonels would marvelously improve the volunteer organization," wrote the journalist, although the colonel seemed more concerned that this minor act of vandalism would hamper his unit's marching discipline than for the civilians' loss.[74]

Despite the many instances of disorder among the troops, and the occasional encouragement to unruly behavior by sympathetic officers, some field officers internalized the ideals of military discipline enough to enforce them, even in the face of jarring battlefield losses. "I have fallen into camp life and its spirit quite easily," a lieutenant colonel of a Massachusetts regiment that suffered heavily at Cedar Mountain wrote. "It is the virtue of duty in the field that it is persistent, inexorable leading. It is the virtue of the military life that it is busy and ardent. Both of these considerations urge themselves on me as I sit down to write in cheerful temper while there are so many reasons for heaviness and sorrow," the officer noted. "Our crippled regiment turns out to its duties and parades as if nothing had happened to it, while its thinned ranks and vacant [officers'] posts tell the story of its trial and losses—of its glory too."[75]

Generals were alarmed by the excesses of private soldiers taking a loose interpretation of Pope's decrees regarding rebel property, and his corps commanders quickly induced Pope to issue clarifying instructions. Patrol guards were accordingly set up to intercept would-be plunderers. A member of the 13th Massachusetts, appointed to one of these patrols with orders to "arrest all found outside the camps without a permit to forage," claimed that this precaution "soon put a stop to all such proceedings."[76] "The men having become much addicted to pillaging," a colonel in the Pennsylvania Reserves noted, "the Division General commanded the order prohibiting the destruction of private property and authorizing the severest penalty on all offenders to be read at the head of each Regiment." Not all of his men accepted the order from on high; while the colonel was reading the order against pillaging, "some of the men stirred up a bumble-bee's nest which created quite a furor. The ord[er]s seem to have done no good. Little pigs, chickens and corn come in as fast as ever."[77] In regard to the order to banish beyond Union lines civilians who failed to take the oath of loyalty, a reporter noticed "frequent evidences of scrupulous humanity on the part of general officers" who refused to enforce the letter of this martial law.[78]

Insubordination spread from the enlisted men to the officers as they sought personal gain from looting, even as they punished disloyal citizens. "Received much insolence from a captain in the Harris light cavalry because I chastised him for allowing his men to plunder," a staff major reported. He nonetheless "drove the [captain's] men from the Garden and barnhouse."[79]

Republican generals in the army tacitly approved of their soldiers' actions when they fell within the parameters of Pope's decrees. Even the most radical of the officers, however, were quick to protect the property of civilians of whose loyalty to the Union the generals were certain. Even General Robert Huston Milroy, the most stridently anti-slavery general in the army, was solicitous of a Unionist living near Culpeper: "My Brigade was for some time encamped on the farm of Mr. Slaughter, considerable forage and subsistence was taken from him for the use of my [men].

I left what forage and subsistence I thought would be necessary for his own use."[80]

After his command moved on, Milroy heard that other brigades had encamped on Slaughter's property and confiscated most of the food and stores the general had left for the family. Thus he wrote his corps headquarters on behalf of the Unionist farmer: "Can you not give Mr. Slaughter an order that will reserve to him what little forage and subsistence he has remaining his own use?" Franz Sigel's staff responded promptly, and the corps provost marshal extended protection to Slaughter's property at Cedar Mountain.[81] As Slaughter was willing to swear an oath of allegiance to the federal government, the protection of his property was in keeping with the policy of Pope's new punitive regime.

Despite their emphasis on the maintenance of order—drilled into cadets at West Point—generals were not immune to flashes of anger that contributed to disorder and exacerbated civil-military relations. Even Democratic generals in Pope's army, deploring the attempt of Republicans to radicalize the war into a social revolution, grew frustrated with disloyal civilians. Political general John Geary was no exception. As a Maryland subaltern later commented, Geary's tendency to suspect "everyone of a desire to shirk duty or make profit out of our countrys ruin" rendered "him exceedingly arbitrary with all evildoers. With the enemy or with a traitorous citizen he has nothing in common. He looks upon them as persons who have forfeited all rights they ever possessed[;] life and property are no longer theirs."[82] While his brigade was encamped near Culpeper, Geary established his headquarters—and lodgings—in a private home nearby. When he mislaid his revolver, Geary flew into a great rage and terrorized the house's female inhabitants, drawing his sword on them and demanding their arrest, until his son—a member of his brigade staff—found the mislaid item.[83]

Union soldiers were not always the offenders when it came to unpleasant incidents, and not all interactions involved the confiscation or petty theft of southern property. Many altercations were of a wholly verbal nature. Union soldiers often managed to dismiss insults or intended insults by Virginians as bad jokes, or turned the humor on the civilians. "For the first time," a Wisconsin lieutenant confessed in early July, "yesterday I saw and had a personal illustration of rudeness of one of the young ladies of the Bon Ton of this 'Burg [Fredericksburg]. I was walking up the walk of the principal street, saw two young ladies coming," and "gave way." One of the women "crowded me into the Gutter and swept by, I had just time to raise my hat and say Thank you my bully 'secesh.'"[84] Yet the backwardness of southern society, the persistence of armed rebellion, and the transformation of fabled southern ladies into socially aggressive rebels excused in Republican minds acts of revenge and thievery by war-weary Union soldiers, whether on personal or political grounds.

# 7 Ambivalent Allies

THE REPUBLICAN PARTISANSHIP of the Army of Virginia is cast into relief by the opposing politics of the Army of the Potomac under General George McClellan. John Pope's rhetoric and harsh policies toward southern civilians directly contradicted the limited war policy of McClellan and other Democratic generals. McClellan fought to return the Union to the status quo antebellum, the sectional compromise that suited the Democratic Party since its Jeffersonian inception. Questioning the loyalty and confiscating the property—including slaves—of purportedly friendly or at least neutral civilians, in this view, threatened to turn the war into an outright revolution with apocalyptic results.[1]

Radical Republicans were equally fervent in their opposition to McClellan, and his failure to take Richmond provided additional ammunition. "The traitors North are worse than the traitors South," declared Joint Committee on the Conduct of the War member Zachariah Chandler, for they were guilty of "stabbing their country in the dark." "The traitors have been denouncing every man who did not sing paeans to 'strategy,'" particularly McClellan's professional West Point strategy, yet "it led to defeat every time."[2]

Mark E. Neely, Jr., finds in Chandler's words "a typical transformation made by the two-party system" in a time of civil war: "The opposition political party became an enemy more to be dreaded than the rebels in arms in Virginia."[3] Journalists joined Radical Republicans in attacking McClellan for indulging the enemy, if not outright treason. George Wilkes of the Republican *Chicago Tribune* published a series of articles critical of McClellan's performance on the peninsula. Wilkes credited the general's "bloodless strategy" as part of an attempt to coax the Confederates to peace talks, and claimed that his sympathy toward southerners "emasculated [McClellan] of a great portion of that vigor and devil which is the first requirement of a fighting general."[4] "Wilkes helped establish the narrative from which McClellan's military reputation never recovered," as Neely has observed.[5]

The warring politics of the two armies—and signs that the Army of Virginia, although soon to be absorbed into the Army of the Potomac, was the truer harbinger of the future—are highlighted by the experiences of two groups that joined the Army of Virginia shortly prior to the Second Battle of Bull Run: the IX Army Corps, commanded by Ambrose E. Burnside, and the III and V Corps of McClellan's Army of the Potomac.

The Union's IX Army Corps was transferred from North Carolina, where in a series of skirmishes Burnside's forces, then really a strong division rather than an army corps, defeated seriously outmatched enemy units.[6] "The strategy Burnside devised during the campaign was adequate, but only that; he had needed no brilliance, so heavily did he outnumber his enemy," Burnside's biographer has noted.[7]

Burnside's corps was more demographically representative of the loyal states of the Union than any corps in McClellan's army. Of the fourteen infantry regiments to reach Pope's army by the time battle was joined at Manassas, no fewer than four were raised outside New England and the mid-Atlantic, with two regiments from Ohio and one each from Maryland and Michigan. This was not the case while the IX Corps campaigned in North Carolina, when all but one of its infantry regiments was organized on the eastern seaboard.

By September 1862, the IX Corps numbered four divisions—reinforced to such strength in no small part due to the friendship between its commander and the restored McClellan; it had contained only two divisions when it campaigned in North Carolina. A third division under Isaac Stevens joined it from garrison duty in South Carolina before the corps reinforced Pope.[8] The fourth division, sent to reinforce the Army of Virginia from western Virginia in August (only two regiments arrived in time for Second Bull Run), was under Oberlin-educated Jacob Cox and gave the corps its western representation; all seven of its regiments were from Ohio. In one of those Buckeye regiments, the 23rd, served two future presidents of the United States: Rutherford Hayes and William McKinley.[9] This Kanawha Division might have been attached to Franz Sigel's I Corps, as both forces previously served together in western Virginia, or sent to reinforce Nathaniel Prentiss Banks's II Corps, eviscerated at Cedar Mountain. The restoration of McClellan to the Union Army command enabled him to augment Burnside's force by adding Cox's Ohioans to IX Corps.

General in Chief Henry Halleck marked two of the corps' generals—

both affiliated with the Democratic Party during the antebellum years—as replacements for McClellan by summer 1862. They were Burnside and division leader Isaac Ingalls Stevens. While John Pope was busy waging a war of words against the white population of Virginia from his Washington headquarters, President Abraham Lincoln offered one of McClellan's closest friends the chance to take the mantle from the discredited McClellan. "Sometime between July 23 and 27 Lincoln offered command of the Army of the Potomac to Burnside," according to James M. McPherson. Burnside's "success in North Carolina had impressed the president."[10] "I have been informed that Burnside has been twice urged to take the command of the Army of the Potomac but always refuses to supercede McClellan," a Pennsylvania Reserves brigade commander wrote. The general believed "the thing will soon be done without consulting either of them for the more I see the more I am satisfied that McClellan is irretrievably gone, and has lost the greatest chance any man ever had on this continent" of ending the rebellion, and perhaps gaining the White House.[11] Burnside (accurately) claimed he was unfit for such a responsibility, and likely warned McClellan of the danger of being shelved by the president.[12]

Burnside was a West Point graduate and a friend of McClellan. Burnside's victorious campaign in North Carolina made him a darling of politicians of all stripes, but radicals found little to praise in his attitude or policy toward the contrabands flocking to his force's lines. After taking New Bern, North Carolina, Burnside found himself distributing rations to the town's needy, including formerly wealthy planters whose Confederate scrip was now worthless, "and negroes who refuse to acknowledge any debt of servitude." As he notified the War Department, "nine-tenths of the depredations of the 14th [of March], after the enemy fled from the town, were committed by the negroes before our troops reached the city. They are now a source of very great anxiety to us."[13]

These were hardly the words of a man decisively committed to the extirpation of slavery and the freedom of African Americans. Indeed, Burnside seemed keen to have the War Department tell him how to handle so politically sensitive a topic. Burnside was aware of McClellan's contempt for John Pope. While the two generals watched the Army of the Potomac's five corps cross the Chickahominy River on August 17, McClellan commented on the appearance of his legions. "Look at them, Burn," McClellan mused. "Did you ever see finer men? Oh; I want to see these men beside of Pope's." Burnside, never the quickest wit, apparently missed his friend's invidious comparison of the Potomac and

Virginia armies.[14] That was probably just as well, as he was tasked by Halleck with acting as the go-between to effect the speedy unification of the armies. From his headquarters at Fredericksburg, Burnside was to exercise authority over each of McClellan's corps in turn to expedite their union with the Army of Virginia.[15]

A West Point graduate, Isaac Stevens served as the governor of Washington Territory during the secession crisis. Traveling east to Washington, D.C., in hopes of a brigadier's star, Stevens was disappointed despite interviews with Lincoln and Irvin McDowell, and had to settle for a regimental command, for which he was indebted to the Republican governor of New York.[16] Stevens had been a Stephen Douglas Democrat in the 1860 election, and apparently for a few years before. One of his West Point colleagues, even more politically conservative than Stevens, scornfully dismissed him as on a slippery slope toward radicalism: "If he isn't a black republican" in 1858, he "will be" by 1860.[17] Stevens tired of the generalship of George McClellan much earlier than any of his West Point colleagues in the Army of the Potomac though. "I am glad to leave McClellan's army," Stevens told his son when transferred to Annapolis in mid-October 1861. "I am rejoiced to get out of that army. I tell you that army under McClellan is doomed to disaster."[18]

While occupying coastal North Carolina for the first half of 1862, the officers and men of IX Corps witnessed more white southern intransigence and self-emancipatory efforts by African Americans than their future colleagues in the Potomac and Virginia armies. The aftermath of the force's first significant battle, a skirmish near New Bern that established their foothold shortly after landing in North Carolina, demonstrated the intractable secessionist sentiment of Confederate civilians, particularly women. A company commander in the 48th Pennsylvania tried to engage a white woman resident of New Bern in polite conversation shortly after the battle. She belligerently "remarked that she Could blow Abe Linkons Brains out with a pistol."[19] A few months later, a pro-Confederate woman came upon Massachusetts soldiers digging a grave to bury a comrade and recommended that they dig it deeper. "They asked why? She said that the journey to hell might be shorter."[20] A slave-owning woman swore at northern soldiers for aiding and abetting her slaves in running away. One of their officers replied that "it sounded very strange to a northerner to hear such language from a lady."[21]

The woman had some cause to turn the air blue with invective though; freedom-seeking slaves flocked to Burnside's camps. "Stealing in from every direction by land & sea—in squads from 6 to 30 each—they come and dump themselves by the side of the fence and 'wait orders from Mr. Burnside,'" one Union soldier wrote.[22] They were the only friendly North Carolinians, however. "The slaves alone seemed rejoiced at our coming, and looked upon our victorious banners as signs of their approaching millennium," a New Jersey colonel wrote.[23]

Yet many northern soldiers, including some of the most anti-slavery among them, found evidence to reinforce their preexisting racial prejudices, even as they employed self-emancipated African Americans as cooks and servants. A captain in the 27th Massachusetts devoted in theory "to destroy[ing] from off the face of the country every vestige of this enormous crime" of slavery was appalled by African Americans in person. He wrote of a "great buck nigger, very black & very fragrant, bare feet, tattered shirt & knotted hair," using a stick with a rug tied to one end to fan a lieutenant on a stiflingly hot day. While acknowledging that "the flies are really tormenting & the heat is intolerable [he would] rather endure both, than to have one of those confounded dirty niggers anywhere within twenty feet of me. As a class they are lazy, filthy, ragged, dishonest & confounded stupid." He knew of "exceptional cases," and if he "could find a decent bright mulatto boy I would take him & bring him home with me but the boys learn mischief & wickedness so early that a respectable specimen is as scarce as hens teeth."[24]

Union soldiers pursued sexual relations with black women, with or without their consent. "Many black women, who came into [Union camps] ostensibly to sell pies and cakes, often ended up dispensing sexual favors," Judkin Browning has noted. This "interaction began immediately after the troops arrived" in North Carolina.[25] By May one soldier was commenting ruefully, "Some [enlisted men] have been seen promenading the streets with Negro wenches." It was not uncommon for officers to take up with contraband women and order noncommissioned officers to ensure their privacy while occupied in their tents.[26]

Until Burnside's men joined the Army of Virginia at Fredericksburg in August, the soldiers of the corps also were blissfully unaware of "the accursed jealousy towards brother soldiers which was rampant in Virginia," one regimental historian contends. "Like a happy family, a spirit of mutual confidence and concord had prevailed among them, and generally a gratifying cordiality, and even affection existed between officers and men." The veteran of the 21st Massachusetts credited "the magnanimous and open-hearted spirit with which our general administered his command." All was to change upon arrival in northern Virginia, where proximity to Washington meant swarms of journalists eager for printable quotations from generals and political intrigue permeated the army camps. "Nearness to Washington and army jealousy" were the twin evils that Burnside's corps was exposed to upon joining the Army of Virginia.[27] There was nothing unique in this observation; men in the Army of Virginia and members of the two corps of the Army of the Potomac that joined Pope in mid-August also condemned the interference of politicians in military matters and the internecine jealousies of generals.

On August 9, Burnside sent two staff officers to Fredericksburg to liaise with McDowell's corps, the previous garrison of the strategic city on the Rappahannock River. Their general was particularly concerned about Pope's punitive orders toward the recalcitrant civilian population of northern Virginia, and whether his subordinates carried out the letter of his decrees or merely paid lip-service. Burnside's aides evidently made a beeline for the tent of West Point General Marsena Patrick, circumventing the division headquarters of Republican political general and military amateur Rufus King. "Gen. Burnside holds about the same views upon the treatment of these people" of Fredericksburg "that I do," Patrick confided in his diary. Patrick followed his orders precisely, in proper obedience to the military chain of command, but did not see Pope's orders as an excuse to plunder or otherwise terrorize the citizens of Fredericksburg. "Stevens is pursuing my course, thus far, precisely," which encouraged Patrick to live up to the standards of a West Point–educated professional soldier, obeying commands he detested to the letter, but no further.[28]

Burnside stayed in Fredericksburg when the divisions of Jesse Lee Reno and Isaac Stevens marched forward to join Pope's forces. General Reno assumed command of the IX Corps divisions released to active duty with the Army of Virginia.[29] McClellan's dilatory efforts to reinforce Pope—the longer he took to dispatch his corps to Pope, the longer he possessed the semblance of an army to command—complicated Burnside's task.

Burnside was in any case peculiarly suited to aid in uniting two forces whose commanding generals were barely on speaking terms. A close friend of McClellan's, he alone of the Potomac general's clique bore Pope no ill will, and was naive about higher echelon civil-military politics. "I do not think it was the impression with the officers generally that General Pope, notwithstanding he was a talented officer, was fully up to the task of conducting so large a campaign," Burnside wrote in response to Pope's July 14 proclamation.[30] Burnside certainly did McClellanite Fitz John Porter no favors, moreover, when he forwarded Porter's caustic epistolary critiques of Pope's command style on to Halleck, which only inflamed an already charged military crisis.[31]

The common soldiers of Burnside's corps, though, took up the practices of the Army of Virginia with a will, particularly confiscation of southern property. "August the 15th we moved forward and camped near the battlefield of Cedar Mountain. We had then become a part of General Pope's army," a 21st Massachusetts man recalled, "and we immediately took advantage of Pope's General Order No. 10, which allowed the army to live off of the country." Yet "the land was not overflowing with milk and honey; the cows, what there were of them, were kept milked pretty dry," but sheep, pork, and bread could be found, and were duly appropriated.[32]

Another member of the 21st took Pope's order to live off the enemy's country as "legalizing private pillage," and the men "had their full share of chickens, sheep, and green corn." When the brigade to which the 21st belonged "captured" a flock of sheep, the unit historian's company took thirteen for their share.[33] By openly distributing the spoils of confiscation, all who partook were equally culpable. "This is as handsome a country as I ever saw," poet Walt Whitman's brother wrote. "We find plenty of forage in the shape of Beef, Chicken, eggs, potatoes, and the way the cattle and sheep have suffered since we have been here is a caution to secesh farmers." At farms that encompassed sheep and a sheep dog, the men "take the dog and make him catch as many sheep as they want, and bring them in and cook them, and you may be sure the yankees get some tall cussing from the farmers."[34]

Liberal foraging practices were necessary by the time Burnside's divisions joined Pope's army; rebel cavalry raids had reduced the flow of supplies from Washington to a trickle. Easy campaigning in North Carolina, one of the war's strategic backwaters, had left the men ill-prepared for the strenuous marching and fighting in summertime Virginia that John Pope asked for and received from an obliging Robert E. Lee. "During the rapid marching [under Pope] our commissariat had become sadly demoralized, and had it not been for the privilege we had of subsisting off the inhabitants, we would have been in a starving condition," a New Yorker recalled. "Pope believed in compelling the country through which we passed to contribute to our support, so we managed to subsist without serious trouble."[35]

If Burnside's corps merged with the Army of Virginia relatively smoothly, in action and beliefs, a more difficult assimilation could have been expected for two corps of McClellan's Army of the Potomac, the III and V Corps. But change was already afoot by the time McClellan's two forward corps joined the Army of Virginia.

The III and V Corps were the least- and most-professionally led units, respectively, of the Army of the Potomac. Fitz John Porter's V Corps contained the largest single contingent of regular troops in any part of the Union Army, in two brigades of George Sykes's division.[36] All eight division and brigade commanders were West Point graduates. By contrast, III Corps, albeit led by West Pointer Samuel Heintzelman, was full of volunteer soldiers commanded by volunteer officers.[37] Only two of the corps' eight division and brigade commanders graduated from West Point, with an entire division composed of amateur brigade commanders led by the wealthy military adventurer Philip Kearny.[38] Worse still from a West Point professional's perspective, four of the six brigade commanders were political generals, appointed more for their electoral influence than for their military experience; the most infamous was New York's Daniel Sickles.[39]

The Army of the Potomac's III Corps comprised thirty-one infantry regiments and two artillery batteries. Only four of the regiments originated from beyond the mid-Atlantic and New England regions; 87.1 percent were northeastern. The corps contained some of the most homogenous brigades in either army, with the Excelsior Brigade's five regiments entirely from New York and another coming mostly from New Jersey.[40]

The chief of III Corps, Pennsylvania's Samuel Heintzelman, did not attain high command due to political influence but also did not fit in with McClellan's West Point coterie. Heintzelman owed his appointment to West Point to the patronage of future president James Buchanan, then a representative from Lancaster.[41] Heintzelman's family name and Pennsylvania Dutch origins made him a prominent German American general. He kept detailed journals over the long decades of his army service, and his entries provide valuable insights into peacetime soldiering and internal army politics.[42]

Although by no means an out-and-out abolitionist, in the 1840s Heintzelman attended the anti-slavery Free Soil Party's meetings as well as lectures by radical abolitionists Lucretia Mott and Frederick Douglass.[43] He was one of the first Union generals to oppose slavery and the rights of slaveholders, and to maintain that secession nullified the Fugitive Slave Law. In the fall of 1861, he refused to return self-emancipated slaves who took refuge in his unit's camps to their erstwhile owners, claiming that he "refused to be either a slave catcher or a slave driver."[44]

By the time the Army of the Potomac embarked on the Peninsula Campaign, Heintzelman was persona non grata in McClellan's inner circle because of his meetings with Radical Republicans Zachariah Chandler, Benjamin Franklin Wade, and Vice President Hannibal Hamlin. In the course of these surreptitious meetings, the anti-slavery politicians broached the possibility of raising a command for him independent of McClellan's army. When word reached McClellan, Heintzelman's stock dropped in the West Point cabal.[45] Matters were not helped by the fact that Heintzelman was one of the four corps commanders promoted by White House fiat over McClellan's head, or that he had opposed McClellan's proposed campaign to capture Richmond via an amphibious landing on the peninsula.

Heintzelman's two division commanders (Philip Kearny and Joseph Hooker) rank among the most aggressive combat commanders in either the Potomac or Virginia army. Philip Kearny was one of several generals to participate in the Peninsula Campaign to emerge thoroughly disgusted with McClellan's generalship. As early as May 14, after the first major battle of the campaign near Williamsburg, Kearny—then a brigade commander—expressed his frustration with McClellan. "Is it not a cruel thing that after all my zeal and activity under nearly insuperable obstacles in arriving, after positively saving Hooker's Division, which had become completely demoralized, after exposing myself," the general wrote, "only to have my first fruit of victory swindled away by that most untrustworthy of men and officers, McClellan."[46]

Two weeks later Kearny explained this new frustration with the army commander: "The fact is this: McClellan has changed his nature. I do not say that he has any equal, or competitor, (he has so cautiously kept strong men away from him)."[47] Weeks after the Seven Days Battles were over, and with them McClellan's best chance to capture Richmond, Kearny's opinion of his commander had only darkened. "I look on McClellan with horror, as the thief of my military reputation. I regard him, as in the past, a traitor, as well as utterly incapable. I consider him as the doomed of ill fortune," Kearny wrote. "The only salvation I can see is the hope, that my Division will be ordered to join Pope."[48]

He received his wish, and his division joined Pope's army. On August 12, while awaiting the ships to send his force northward, Kearny wrote his wife regarding a letter voicing his support for the use of unarmed African Americans in the war effort that Cortlandt Parker, a political ally, had published in a northern newspaper. Even though he professed to "*dislike* extremely" to write a letter for public consumption, "still it must be done, for I foresee that inasmuch as the Northern gentlemen stand aloof from the dangers of war, and the Northerners are absolute *cowards,* not all but certainly the generality, that our *existence* in the North depends on our having a good regular force, even niggers."[49]

Kearny's last surviving letter to his wife is poignant in its hope for a glorious victory with Pope's army. "I fear lest you are very uneasy amidst all this marching and battling. Gen'l Pope is quite active in his measures, and that suits me. As usual, the hardest fighting has been done by men," Kearny asserted, "and they are terribly reduced. We have lost all our best officers—and the men, though in high spirits, seem a little disgusted at having to fight for other people. Yesterday, I held my own position, and everyone else's that gave way, which they all did."[50] A common soldier marching into battle on August 30 saw "Genl. Kearney leaning on a cannon carelessly writing with a pencil," probably penning that last letter to his wife, the picture of a martial man at home on the battlefield.[51] "Kearney is dead! Let the nation mourn! To us it seems to *crown* all recent disasters," the chaplain of an Excelsior Brigade regiment wrote in early September. "Phil Kearney and Joe Hooker were the men who, yoked, could move anything. They were the complements of each other."[52]

Joseph Hooker, Heintzelman's other division commander, actively cultivated relationships with influential Republicans by the summer of 1862. As late as April, however, Hooker had allowed slaveholders to enter his units' camps to apprehend runaway slaves, earning condemnation from Senator Charles Sumner and the radical Joint Committee on the Conduct of the War. "What the hell do they expect an officer to do?" he complained to a Democratic friend in May.[53]

Hooker soon realized that the politically expedient thing to do was hide behind the political convictions of his New England soldiers when slave catchers came calling. "Yes, I have seen the order [of McClellan's to arrest runaways], and yonder is the Massachusetts camp," Hooker told one party of owners. "And if your slaves are there and choose to go with you, and the Massachusetts boys are content, I have no objections. But if they refuse and a row occurs over there, I fear you will get into the guardhouse—the same as any other marauders." When the Virginians protested and demanded that he aid them, Hooker replied, "I am a Brigadier General United States Volunteers, and no nigger catcher. I was born and bred in New England."[54]

Hooker demonstrated increasing political acumen, sounding more and more radical to fit in with the radical politicians who seemed to be gaining ascendancy in Washington, and cultivating a rapport with important journalists. The day before the Battle of Antietam, Hooker would admit George W. Smalley to his staff as a volunteer aide. A reporter for the influential, Republican *New York Tribune,* Smalley was an asset to a politically conscious general.[55] The general's military reputation was also growing in the wake of the Peninsula Campaign, where he had acquired the nickname "Fighting Joe" from a misinterpreted dispatch sent by a war correspondent.[56] Hooker was keen to demonstrate the superiority of his military genius over McClellan's, boasting to Charles A. Page of the *Tribune:* "McClellan knows that *I* am a better general than he ever dared hope to be."[57] "Hooker's military genius and accomplishments together with his bravery and good looks," gushed a newspaper in California, "ought to secure for him one of the noblest and handsomest of the loyal daughters of the land."[58]

Hooker lived up to his fighting reputation almost immediately. Barely twenty-four hours after joining Pope's Army of Virginia, Hooker's division struck the rearguard of Stonewall Jackson's force as it fell back after looting Manassas Junction and hurried it along. Two days later, one of Hooker's brigades was the only unit to pierce Jackson's defensive line of trenches, formed by an unfinished railroad, by means of a spirited bayonet charge. Hooker had good reason for discontentment with his role in the battle, however, as his brigades were allocated to other commanders and sent into battle piecemeal.[59] Pope still made use of Hooker at Second Bull Run, placing him in command of Rufus King's division in Irvin McDowell's corps when King was incapacitated by epilepsy and his successor was wounded. Hooker thus added to his combat reputation amid a debacle.

With Kearny and Isaac Stevens dead, and Pope and McDowell discredited, President Lincoln asked Secretary of the Navy Gideon Welles who should take command of the Army of the Potomac if not McClellan. Welles mentioned Hooker. The president agreed, to a point: "I think as much as you or any other man of Hooker, but—I fear he gets excited."[60] From his Minnesota exile, where he had been sent to suppress a Sioux uprising following the August defeat at Manassas, Pope extolled Hooker and warned Halleck not to allow McClellan to sack him. "The Praetorian faction in the Army of the Potomac is now seeking to remove every officer of distinction from that army who is not in their interests," Pope wrote. "Hooker is by his rising reputation, and known hostility to them and their purposes is becoming dangerous. He will be gotten rid of in some way. Do not allow such transparent intrigue to induce you to consent. You will find him a true man and one of incalculable use to you with that Army."[61]

One of Kearny's brigade commanders was the son of James Birney, a prominent Kentucky transplant to Ohio and abolitionist. David Bell Birney noted early on in the Peninsula Campaign that black slaves were essential to the Confederate war effort: "Negroes are building their fortifications" near Yorktown, "doing all the work that they can do better than soldiers. We have the negrophobia and avoid them. Gen. [John E.] Wool corps gives them a ration a day but is afraid to make them useful." Birney further granted the potential for African Americans to contribute to the preservation of the Union: "Much talking has demented us on the subject of Negroes. Instead of philosophy why not take the negro and work him in the war, why not let a negro shoot a secessionist if they are to be shot. It will have to be permitted."[62]

Birney thus went beyond the logic of some of the more "liberal" Army of the Potomac soldiers who preferred to arm slaves if that meant that African Americans would stop bullets otherwise meant for white soldiers. "Man proposes but God disposes and I have a pure abiding faith that the latter will lead us as a Nation through the ordeal and punishment for our forgetfulness of the Christian philosophy of Justice or to do unto others as etc etc.," Birney wrote. "We require punishment for our craven submission to the great crime of slavery." Added to his humanitarian and religious concern for the nearly 4 million slaves, Birney also believed that once the government crushed the rebellion it should take "our immense Army and Navy [and] take Hayti and Mexico under our wing," but not to aid their inhabitants. Rather these new annexations were to provide new homes "for our colored free population, and drive Europe into proper respect for the Monroe Doctrine."[63]

Three months later, Birney confessed his bewilderment at the current state of the Army of the Potomac. "We strange to say conquered each day [we fought the enemy], and to enemy's surprise left our wounded and dead to insects vermin and rebels and retreated. . . . This fine army is as dispirited as the army after Bull Run," Birney continued. "It has lost confidence and must have new leaders, new plans. Pope seems a blessing, a leader to die under, a true man." Birney wished that the army had advanced overland via Fredericksburg. "Swamp malaria has decimated our troops. We have lost more by fatigue exposure in trenches picketing swamps than we would have in twenty battles."[64]

"Pope is said to be a braggart but still enterprising and a fighting man,"

Birney confided in his friend. Yet he acknowledged that many West Point graduates in the Army of the Potomac disparaged Pope. "His reputation and [Ulysses S.] Grants were low in the [antebellum] army. But that is a small matter—and is more against his social than belligerent status. The old army was not a fighting one, did more *club* duty than sword and musket. But still the education of West Point has been the hearth and nucleus of both armies." Birney joined his division commander in expressing a desire to "withdraw and get into Another Army."[65] "I trust this army will be reorganized," Birney penned around August 1, "and under a new order of things we may retrace our footsteps to that city—the Mecca to which for weary months we have turned our footsteps in vain." Birney saw in the reorganization of the army, moreover, an opportunity for promotion and a larger command: "I expect five more regiments to be added given to me and a Division [command]. I of course prefer a larger command, it is human nature. But must try and keep my brigade as a nucleus."[66] His brigade was an all-Pennsylvanian unit, and Birney was keen to retain the command of men from his home state and thus attention from state newspapers.

The Army of the Potomac's V Corps was the epitome of McClellan's desire for a professional core of regular units for his army and his "praetorian" guard, in Pope's pejorative phrasing.[67] The ten regiments in the division led by George Sykes represented the largest concentration of regular troops in any Union army. There were in V Corps twenty-nine infantry regiments and five artillery batteries during the campaign with Pope. Three of the twenty volunteer regiments hailed from Michigan, and none came from the border states; 85 percent of the corps' volunteer infantry units were organized in New England or the mid-Atlantic states.[68] Only the III and VI corps under McClellan's ally William Franklin were more northeastern in representation, with all of Franklin's regiments hailing from the mid-Atlantic or New England.[69]

McClellan's esteem for this corps and its commander is demonstrated by the fact that when the Pennsylvania Reserve Division was transferred from McDowell's corps to the peninsula in June, McClellan assigned it to V Corps. This made V Corps the strongest of McClellan's corps at the beginning of the Seven Days Battles and the only army corps to contain three divisions instead of two.[70] Nevertheless, V Corps joined Pope's army in less than fighting trim and paid for it heavily. "The V Corps sustained more than half the total killed, and nearly half the wounded and missing, of the entire Army of the Potomac" during the Seven Days Battles.[71]

Fitz John Porter of V Corps was McClellan's most trusted lieutenant. By January 1862, Porter had established himself as an enemy of the radical-dominated Joint Committee on the Conduct of the War. Alone among the division commanders summoned to testify before the committee while McClellan was ill with typhoid fever, Porter "told the committee to mind its own business."[72] If any general officer merited commendation for his conduct in the Army of the Potomac at the corps level during the Seven Days Battles, it was Porter. While McClellan was ill or miles away from the fighting during the Peninsula Campaign, Porter coordinated the Union defensive stands and fighting retreats in late June and early July.[73]

The officers and men of McClellan's army were fully aware of the political warfare in Washington. "The feeling that is springing up now between the conservative men and the radical Republicans is I think getting very intense," wrote one of Porter's brigade commanders in July, "and I fear old Abe trembles at the prospect much as old Buck [James Buchanan] did in his day." This New Yorker knew which side he supported and thought that the president should "discard the New England and Greely Abolitionists entirely; this would remove the cause for resistance from the minds of the masses South, and we would crush out the Secession Leaders." He favored "allowing the Southern people their constitutional rights" as he was "fighting for the Union," and its preservation could not be attained without reconciliation with the rebels.[74]

The Army of the Potomac was no stranger to internecine political warfare during the summer of 1862, much of it involving recriminations after the lost battles before Richmond. "I learned last evening that you had requested one of [V Corps's generals' aides] to say to the Genl. that I had not been on the field" during the Seven Days Battles, colonel of sharpshooters Hiram Berdan wrote to his second-in-command. "Et tu Brutus? I can understand that you might have made a remark of this kind under the excitement of being wounded and not knowing the exertions I had been making during the day to get something for the men to eat and as to the state of my health," which was so poor that "I did not have the strength to stand up."[75]

Berdan's lieutenant colonel, William Ripley, wrote his reply, "bolstered up in my bed which I have not left since I arrived at home. . . . As I was leaving the field, barely able to sit my horse, some person rode up to me and asked if I was wounded. He then enquired for the Regt and I informed him that it was out of Am[munition] and had long since gone to the rear." The man then "enquired particularly for you and . . . I replied, perhaps with some sign of bitterness, that I had not seen you since morning, that you left the Regt as soon as the men were posted on some errand and had not returned during the day to my knowledge."[76]

Every account in which Pope's men commented on the Army of the Potomac's battles before Richmond indicated a hope that the men of McClellan's army would emerge victorious. "We have been waiting for weeks in ancious suspense hoping to hear of the fall of Richmond," a trooper in the 1st (West) Virginia Cavalry noted on July 5, "but yesterday the humiliating rumours of a repulse reached us. Ten thousand more brave spirits gone from the Union ranks, . . . Ten thousand more homes draped in mourning, and yet the lenient course pursued in dealing with treason."[77] The men of the Potomac army expressed greater ambivalence in their assessment of the officers and men of the Army of Virginia.

"A citizen was shot last night at his own house by a trooper" from one of Pope's cavalry brigades noted a Michigan soldier. "He was a notorious rebel and some justify the act while others are in favor of shooting the soldier at once. Much drunkenness and shooting both on the part of citizens and soldiers are reported at Alexandria."[78] A colonel from McClellan's army recounted the same incident but was much more certain as to what should be done with the perpetrator. "A citizen, a peaceable man, was murdered in cold blood within a mile of our camp by a cavalry man. I never before, regretted quite so much that I did not have power to order a summary execution, for I wanted to shoot the villain who had dared to blow out the brains, of an unarmed man," and to do so "right in the presence of his family," Orlando Poe wrote. "The discipline of this army bears no comparison with that of the Army of the Potomac, and unless the authorities are very careful the army will degenerate into a band of thieves and robbers."[79]

Admiration for slaves and contrabands was much less evident in the Army of the Potomac than in Pope's army. "The negroes everywhere exhibit the greatest evidence of joy," a Pennsylvanian traveling down the Rappahannock River to reinforce McClellan's army wrote, "waving handkerchiefs and throwing up their arms. They are poor deluded creatures, that do not know what they are rejoiced about"; however, they "have a vague idea that this war is going to benefit them in some way. It may a few. But I am inclined to think that it will be an injury to most of them although it may benefit their posterity and the civilization and religion of the world in general."[80]

After dismissing the debate in civilian circles about arming African Americans in regiments to fight for the Union, a soldier in the 5th New

York went on to say, "besides they can only be used to dig and cook and such duties to any advantage. Let the nigger question take care of itself, put down the rebellion by any means and at any cost."[81] "Let the niggers be sent *here,* to use the pick and shovel in the broiling sun as we are now doing, and we will take up a soldier's tool—the gun, and bayonet," a New Yorker in Heintzelman's III Corps wrote.[82] A tiny minority of the Potomac army, estimated by a sergeant in the Irish Brigade to be "one in one thousand," were vocally anti-slavery.[83] A Yale student who dropped out of school to join a New York cavalry unit emphatically volunteered "to free the slave," not "to get a living or to escape the penalties of [crime]," and was tempted to desert an army that did not live up to "the spirit of Liberty."[84]

Even so, growing doubts about the reason for their defeat nagged McClellan's men after the failure to take Richmond, except for those McClellan diehards who bought the story that the Confederates held an overwhelming numerical superiority. Many of those doubts centered on their commander's view that southern civilians and their property needed to be protected, even when they supported the rebels. By early August, huddled at Harrison's Landing for a month while McClellan looked for excuses to keep his peninsula scheme alive, officers and men knew what their counterparts in Pope's army had learned in the Shenandoah during the spring: the vast majority of Virginia's white men were clearly secessionists. "The theory that the Union animal exists at the south is too ridiculous, every man, except in niggerless East Tennessee and West Virginia, is venomously secesh, and will be so till we lay the axe at the roots," a soldier from Massachusetts wrote. "The most pro-slavery of our officers here is a little sore over the idea of the guarding of the property" of vocally secessionist civilians.[85]

Glenn David Brasher's study of the interactions of McClellan's army with slaves during the campaign against Richmond notes that many Union soldiers came to accept that fugitive slaves should replace them in doing the hard work of digging trenches or latrines and building bridges. He does not, however, establish the growth of anti-slavery sentiment among many units. Brasher uses at least one unit history written at the end of the war, not a contemporary source. The men of that unit—the Pennsylvania division on loan from Pope—were depicted by their historian as more than happy for slaves to do the dirty work and frustrated that McClellan would not allow contrabands to labor in their place.[86]

New England soldiers in McClellan's army, as in the Army of Virginia, were most active in protecting fugitives from their masters and readily agreed that emancipation must become a war aim. Soldiers from the mid-Atlantic and western states were—like the fighting historian above—often deeply prejudiced. Brasher neglects to mention this important demographic fact, or to provide a regional breakdown of McClellan's units' shifting views regarding slavery. As for McClellan himself, he dared to tell the president, when Lincoln visited the melancholy army in early July, that it was imperative to resist demands for emancipation.[87] Despite battlefield defeats and the fact that only contrabands could be trusted among Virginia's civilians, McClellan remained dead set against the revolution he feared must follow emancipation. This fear of Republican revolution—a revolution that would be hastened by a Union victory courtesy of Pope—filtered down from McClellan to his most trusted Democratic lieutenants; therefore they failed to act with alacrity to reinforce Pope's army in northern Virginia.

The personal animosity between John Pope and George McClellan extended to their personal staffs. "The fact is, General, we have no friend in this man McClellan," one of General Robert Schenck's staff officers warned. Donn Piatt was a devoted Republican and had accompanied Schenck in stumping for Abraham Lincoln in southern Illinois in 1860. McClellan therefore had little to gain by befriending Schenck or his staff. "McClellan was selected by the old remnant of the Democratic Party to make a president of and understanding that you may clearly see the fact of his opposition and his reason for it. He hates [William] Rosecrans, Banks, [Benjamin] Butler, McDowell and you." The policy of McClellan and his political allies "is to protect slavery until they can restore the Union."[88]

The critical views of headquarters staff officers toward the other army commander extended to the common soldiers of the other army. A private in the 5th New Jersey of Heintzelman's corps noted that members of Pope's staff observed his regiment crossing Bull Run on August 29. The staff officers, seated high and dry on their horses, "thinking perhaps that we were not crossing enough to suit them or were shirking our duty, told us that if we did not cross they would shoot us, at the same time pulling out a revolver." One of the soldiers, dripping from the crossing, "told the officer, that if he shot any one he would be shot himself, at the same time bringing his piece down for action, informing him at the same time that we belonged to the Army of the Potomac, and we were not used to running away or be shot down either."[89]

Colonel Alexander S. Webb of McClellan's staff arrived at Pope's headquarters on September 1 "quite hungry," and Pope's chief of staff, George D. Ruggles, invited his fellow staff officer to breakfast. "Pretty soon [Webb] saw Pope call Ruggles aside and begin to scold at him. He thought from Pope's manner that he was displeased at Ruggles and so he took up his hat and bid them good morning." Ruggles confirmed the colonel's fears: "The truth is, Webb, that General Pope don't like my asking you to breakfast. He says that he won't have any of General McClellan's staff at his table." "Pretty small for Pope," commented a member of Fitz John Porter's staff.[90]

Shortly after the Second Battle of Bull Run, McClellan exulted in a letter to his wife that "my enemies are crushed, silent, and disarmed."[91] He referred not to Lee and Jackson but to Pope and McDowell. McClellan's triumph was short-lived. The shifting attitudes occurring even within his own former corps hinted at the coming changes in the political atmosphere, and ultimately of government policy, of which Pope's Army of Virginia was an undeniable harbinger.

# Epilogue

THE FOG OF war ruins the best-laid plans, and the Republicans' first army was repulsed in its bid to fulfill radical ambitions. Veterans of First Bull Run relived their worst memories on August 28–30, 1862. Irvin McDowell again hurried here and there, paying attention to details better left to lieutenants. James Ricketts personally supervised the withdrawal of two cannon on the road to Centreville, Virginia, daring the Confederates to take these guns as they had overrun his battery the year before on Henry House Hill.[1] In the wake of John Pope's defeat at Second Manassas, Radical Republicans assailed anew the conservative leadership of the Army of the Potomac, starting with George McClellan. "All this has been brought about by *West Pointers*—Soulless, brainless, Selfish Villains who having made their *Profession*—Care nothing for the country, so they can be hoisted into high places," thundered a Republican general.[2]

The failure of McClellan to reinforce his colleague in a timely fashion certainly provided the radicals with new ammunition. "McClellan ought to be shot!" Secretary of the Treasury Salmon P. Chase exclaimed. Abraham Lincoln admitted that McClellan had behaved badly—"shocking" and "atrocious" were the words he used—toward Pope.[3] Yet with the Union armies in Washington demoralized and the Confederate Army invading Maryland, Lincoln had little choice but to allow McClellan to assume command of both the Virginia and Potomac armies and give chase. McClellan's army absorbed the Army of Virginia's three corps, and McClellan wasted little time in removing Nathaniel Prentiss Banks and McDowell and leaving Franz Sigel's corps behind before pursuing Robert E. Lee. The reinforced Army of the Potomac followed Lee into Maryland, eager to avenge the latest defeat at Manassas. "I hear the rebels are in Pensylvania," a sergeant in the 110th Pennsylvania wrote, "and if thay are I suppose thay will destroy everything befor them." He hoped "thay only go far enough for us to get in behind them for the men sware that if thay get at them in thair own State thay will not take eney prisoners and as they have raised the black flag before we will keep them to it."[4]

Pope and McDowell lost their posts and never again held major field commands. Pope was exiled to Minnesota to suppress a major uprising by the Sioux nation. His sympathy for the plight of slaves did not extend to Native Americans, and he set out to "exterminate" the Sioux.[5] McDowell waited in limbo for two years before being sent to California.

In consuming the Army of the Virginia though, the Army of the Potomac also digested a spreading anti-slavery sentiment and the conviction that white southern civilians must be treated harshly if the war was to be won. Crossing from slave-owning and disloyal Virginia into slave-owning but loyal Maryland in pursuit of Lee's army, a trooper in the 1st Maine Cavalry was more convinced than ever that slavery had caused the war. He contrasted the "squalid poverty" of Virginia with the "well-to-do farmers" of the North, and predicted that Maryland would "bloom and become the land flowing with milk and honey" once the "accursed institution," the South's "great sin," was eradicated.[6] "This nation has trusted too much to McClellan & [Henry] Halleck," a private in the 16th Connecticut—a new regiment assigned to IX Corps—wrote a week after the death of the Army of Virginia. One of the 300,000 recruits called up while the Army of Virginia looked eagerly for reinforcements, he was convinced that emancipation was essential: "We *must* free the blacks or perish as a nation. I have long held this view and have been sneered at & called an abolitionist, but I am content to wait. I think I'm *right.*" After all, "we have got to fight *now* to save our northern states from invasion!" Only two months before, the Union Army had been at the gates of Richmond. "I honestly think it is because the nation has disregarded God's voice we've not let the enslaved blacks go free when we had the power. Many if not most of our Gens are profane, wicked men—and as a nation we have been proud and corrupt. Are we not now receiving a just rebuke? It certainly seems so to me. *Conquer* the rebels first, effectually *subdue* them; let their slaves go free and *then* talk about *Union.*"[7]

McClellan did not lose his commission or his command; his tactical victory at Antietam in mid-September earned him a reprieve, but the radicals demanded a scapegoat. McClellan's chief lieutenant, Fitz John Porter, was hauled before the Joint Committee on the Conduct of the War, found guilty of disobeying Pope's commands at Manassas, and cashiered.[8] Lincoln used McClellan's moment of triumph at Antietam to his advantage. The general's greatest and last victory was the catalyst for publication of the preliminary emancipation proclamation. McClellan deplored it.[9] Porter, about to be delivered up to the radicals, dismissed it as "the absurd proclamation of a political coward," which "caused disgust, and expressions of disloyalty, to the views of the administration" in the Potomac army.[10]

The radical triumvirate of Salmon Chase, Charles Sumner, and Thaddeus Stevens wrote the final chapter of McClellan's active military career when they presented Lincoln with an ultimatum in November. Unless the general was shelved, an open revolt would be staged when Congress resumed and appropriations necessary for the war effort would be withheld. Lincoln removed McClellan after the 1862 elections.[11]

The rank and file of the Army of Virginia chose various ways to remember John Pope, their army, and its campaign in later years. One New Englander applied a revisionist slant, discussing Lee's attempt to "bag" the Army of Virginia rather than the more widely understood effort by Pope to "bag" the Confederates. "And in time to come," the memoirist wrote, "the unbiased historian will give to Pope and the little army he commanded a proud place in the galaxy of gallant deeds performed. For three weeks Popes little army held the victorious legions of Lee at bay." While admitting that Second Bull Run was "a most disastrous defeat for the union army," he also claimed "it was not near so bad as McClellan defeat before Richmond" but received different popular response because of McClellan's "hold on the army." If Pope was guilty of issuing bombastic proclamations, McClellan "would suffer defeat, and then issue a pompous order claiming a victory, and poor fools, the privates would throw up their caps and hurrah and believe every word of it."[12] Members of the Potomac army were far blunter in their assessment of Pope and his generals. "Pope, Sigel, [John] Fremont and the whole batch of political Generals are objects of honest terror to every soldier in the Union army," a Vermont captain wrote in September.[13]

One of Pope's staff officers penned a fitting epitaph to the final campaign of the Army of Virginia. "The campaign has been matter of greater controversy than any others in our history: and such it still remains," Colonel Thomas C. H. Smith of Ohio wrote. "This is because its political environment largely,—perhaps decisively—affected its fortunes, and rendered it the turning point in the political and military conduct of the war. From its period indeed dates the real formation of the two great parties, into one or the other of whose channels [the multitude of] previously varying and tumultuary currents of opinion merged and took definite course, and which for a generation succeeding divided the vote between them." Smith identified the questions surrounding "the campaign, its necessity, its plan, its facts, its management, [which] took shape from its very inception and to a remarkable degree, as party questions, and were regarded one way or the other according as the proclivity was towards the support of the government. I say remarkable, because these questions were by their nature purely military, and should have been passed upon accordingly."[14]

A III Corps staff officer from New York, working for a brigade commander and so likely closer to the experience of the common soldier than Colonel Smith at army headquarters, wrote a no less poignant memoir. Its publication within a year of the Army of Virginia's demise ensured a much larger audience and greater influence in shaping the memory of the Army of Virginia than Smith's account, which sits in an Ohio archive. Captain George Freeman Noyes observed, "In calmly reviewing the results of the late campaign, I confess that, though there was much to regret, there seemed little of which to be ashamed."[15]

The Lincoln administration "had proposed to the Army of Virginia one specific object, viz., by a strong demonstration, threatening Richmond from the right, to extricate the Army of the Potomac from its dangerous position on the Peninsula. This object it fully accomplished, and M'Clellan was thus enabled to withdraw his forces without losing a man," Noyes wrote. "Pursued by the whole rebel army, and compelled to fall back by disparity in numbers," the army under Pope "contested every point, giving ample time for the Army of the Potomac to come up, join forces, and overthrow the enemy."[16]

The captain realized that the failed campaign was fated to be the subject of debate for decades to come but was confident that "history" would be kind to the Army of Virginia. "Before the impartial tribunal of the future, in the days when all personal animosity has subsided; when the investigations of congressional committees, courts-martial, and courts of inquiry have crystallized into history," Noyes felt "sure that the verdict of guilty of neglect of duty will not be entered up against the Army of Virginia. Half-fed for days, often exhausted by fighting, long marching, and want of sleep, I have yet to learn that they were found wanting in courage and patience in the hour of trial."[17]

The former corps of the Army of Virginia made key battlefield contributions several times before the year was out. A week after Second Manassas, soldiers in the 27th Indiana of Banks's old corps found a copy of Lee's invasion plans and tactics for the capture of Harpers Ferry, plans which enabled the reinstated McClellan to catch the Army of Northern

Virginia divided and ripe for defeat in detail. Barely a fortnight after Second Bull Run, the Army of the Potomac and the assimilated units of the Army of Virginia attacked Lee's forces at South Mountain's passes and then at the Maryland village of Sharpsburg. At South Mountain the westerners of John Gibbon's unit earned the sobriquet "Iron Brigade" for their successful uphill assault under heavy fire. McDowell's and Banks' corps launched the determined dawn attacks near Antietam Creek, cracking Lee's line in John Miller's cornfield.[18] McClellan's partisans claimed that I Corps, now commanded by Joseph Hooker in place of the unpopular McDowell, only needed new leadership to show their true mettle. "What a difference it makes whether men have confidence in their commander or not," one III Corps colonel observed.[19]

Unlike Antietam, the last major battle in Virginia in 1862 was a disaster for the Union forces except for those units formerly part of Pope's army. At Fredericksburg the Pennsylvania Reserve Division was the only unit in Ambrose Burnside's 118,000-strong army to pierce the Army of Northern Virginia's defensive position. While II and V Corps battered themselves bloody against James Longstreet's prepared defenses on Marye's Heights, I Corps assaulted Stonewall Jackson's wing. The Pennsylvania Reserves found a hole in Jackson's line and briefly broke through.[20]

Ten months after Second Bull Run, the three corps of McDowell, Sigel, and Banks—now the Army of the Potomac's I, XI, and XII Corps—were the first major Union forces to arrive at Gettysburg, a small Pennsylvania town. They rushed there under the command of John Reynolds, responding to the summons of cavalry division commander John Buford. On July 1, 1863, the Union I and XI Corps sacrificed themselves—the I in a rather more combat-effective manner than the XI—north of the town. Their battle with half of Lee's army purchased enough time for the rest of the Army of the Potomac, helmed for less than a week by Pennsylvanian George Meade, to arrive on the heights south of Gettysburg.[21] The Iron Brigade of westerners led the honor roll of I Corps, suffering 60 percent casualties in the division commanded by the anti-slavery Republican James Wadsworth.[22]

German Americans still commanded the bulk of Sigel's old I—now XI—Corps including Carl Schurz, Wladimir Krzyzanowski, Alexander Schimmelfennig, and Adolph von Steinwehr, though led by abolitionist Oliver Howard of Maine. The heavily "Dutch" XI Corps marched to Gettysburg under the cloud of having been routed by Stonewall Jackson's devastating flank attack—Jackson's last—at Chancellorsville, and two months later in Pennsylvania the corps was again broken by an attack that lapped around its right flank. Nativists within the Army of the Potomac did not allow these back-to-back disasters to fade away, and the contributions of the German Americans of Sigel's corps in 1862 were forgotten.[23]

Political generals once more made their mark on the battlefield, although the most egregious case was III Corps—still disproportionately led by politicians rather than West Pointers—under New York Democrat Daniel Sickles, who on July 2, 1863, jeopardized the entire army by a unilateral advance in defiance of Meade's orders. V Corps of volunteers, regulars, and Pennsylvania Reserves arrived on the crest or vicinity of Little Round Top in the nick of time to save the day on the Union left. While V Corps strove to restore the situation on the opposite side of the battlefield, XII Corps (previously Banks's) battled to hold the right wing, its two divisions commanded by Army of Virginia veterans John Geary and Alpheus Williams.

There is little question of the battlefield courage of the men of the Army of Virginia. But an equally significant battle fought by John Pope and his troops was one of policy and ideas. While conservative politicians approved of the limited war aims of the conservative West Point graduates who helmed the Army of the Potomac, the Army of Virginia presented Republican politicians—particularly those of the radical stripe—with an opportunity to strike at the heart of the rebellion. The goals of political radicals and political generals meshed with frustrated citizen-soldiers tired of protecting the property of their Confederate foes. The failure of the Virginia and Potomac armies to give Abraham Lincoln the military victory necessary to issue the Emancipation Proclamation forced Radical Republicans to await the advent of a more successful western general to end the war. Yet the conservative policies of George McClellan ensured that the war lasted long enough for most northern politicians, soldiers, and civilians to eventually accept that to save the Union, slavery would have to be destroyed.

Pope well understood the symbiotic relationship between soldiers and citizens in a democratic society. In an 1873 speech to western veterans, he argued that "a common sympathy and a common interest" between military personnel and civilians was essential to the fulfillment of their "hopes and aspirations," with political engagement an essential link.[24] The complication-ridden birth and violent death of Pope's army presents an understudied chapter in the political radicalization of an over-studied war. A war begun by southern planters to protect the future of slavery was transformed by western generals and northern radicals into a revolution to remake the Confederacy in the North's image, subject to the friction and abrasion of Clausewitzian war as politics by other means.

# Notes

## Abbreviations

| | |
|---|---|
| CHS | Chicago Historical Society |
| CWM | Civil War Miscellaneous |
| DU | David M. Rubenstein Rare Book and Manuscript Library, Duke University |
| HSP | Historical Society of Pennsylvania |
| IHS | Indiana Historical Society |
| LC | Library of Congress |
| MHS | Massachusetts Historical Society |
| MUO | Miami University of Ohio |
| OHS | Ohio Historical Society |
| *OR* | *War of the Rebellion* |
| WHS | Wisconsin Historical Society (formerly State Historical Society of Wisconsin) |
| UM | William L. Clements Library, University of Michigan |
| USAMHI | U.S. Army Military History Institute |
| UVA | Alderman Library, University of Virginia |

## Introduction

1. David Bell Birney to George I. Gross, July 24, 1862, Folder 1, David Bell Birney Papers, USAMHI.

2. Sanger, *Statutes at Large,* 270; Shannon, *The Organization and Administration of the Union Army,* 1:158–60; Wiley, *The Life of Billy Yank*, 24.

3. www.virginiaplaces.org/population/pop1860numbers.html.

4. Paret, "The New Military History."

5. John J. Hennessy wrote the definitive history of the second Manassas campaign, *Return to Bull Run.*

6. Brasher, *The Peninsula Campaign and the Necessity of Emancipation;* Slotkin, *The Long Road to Antietam*; Woodward, *Marching Masters.*

7. Recent examples of army studies include Russel Beatie's three-volume history of the Army of the Potomac; Daniel, *Days of Glory;* Glatthaar, *General Lee's Army*; Prokopowicz, *All for the Regiment*; and Woodworth, *Nothing but Victory.*

8. Hyde, *Following the Greek Cross;* Powell, *The Fifth Army Corps*; Walker, *History of the Second Army Corps in the Army of the Potomac.* Recent studies include Armstrong, *Unfurl Those Colors*, and Kreiser, *Defeating Lee.*

9. See the University of North Carolina Press volumes edited by Gary W. Gallagher, including *The Antietam Campaign; The Richmond Campaign of 1862;* and *The Shenandoah Valley Campaign of 1862.*

10. Examples of similar organizational studies in the modern European context at a macro- (or societal-) level include Cobb, *The People's Armies;* Craig, *The Politics of the Prussian Army*; and Taylor, *Politics and the Russian Army.* A study in line with this project in its micro- (or army-) level scale is Lynn, *The Bayonets of the Republic.*

11. Glenn David Brasher makes a limited case for the growth of antislavery sentiment and policy in the Army of the Potomac in *The Peninsula Campaign and the Necessity of Emancipation.*

12. McPherson, *The Struggle for Equality,* 72–74, 94–97, 106–22.

13. Nash, *Stormy Petrel.*

14. Miller, *Lincoln's Abolitionist General,* chaps. 3–4. For Frémont, see Chaffin, *Pathfinder*, chap. 26.

15. Shanks, *Vindication of Major General John C. Frémont.*

16. Daniel and Bock, *Island No. 10.*

17. Goss, *The War within the Union High Command.*

18. Rafuse, *McClellan's War.*

19. Joyner, "Robert Cumming Schenck"; Trefousse, *Carl Schurz;* Pula, *The Memoirs of Wladimir Krzyzanowski*; Nathaniel C. McLean Papers, LC; Paulus, *Papers of General Robert Huston Milroy*; Noyalas, "*My Will Is Absolute Law.*"

20. Williams, *Lincoln and the Radicals,* 70.

21. Randolph B. Marcy to Mary Ellen Marcy, November 15, 26, 1856, George B. McClellan Papers, LC.

22. Democrats in the upper echelons of the army included McClellan and Marcy at headquarters; William Franklin and Fitz John Porter (corps commanders); Darius Couch, Joseph Hooker, John Peck, John Sedgwick, Henry Slocum, and William Smith (division commanders); and Hiram Berry, William Burns, N. J. T. Dana, William Emory, William French, Willis Gorman, Cuvier Grover, Winfield Hancock, Thomas Meagher, Henry Naglee, Daniel Sickles, and George Stoneman (brigadiers). Corps commander Erasmus Keyes and division commander Israel Richardson were

Republicans, and brigade commander John Martindale helped found the Republican Party.

23. Abraham Lincoln to Carl Schurz, November 10, 24, 1862, Lincoln Papers, LC; Lincoln to John F. Seymour, n.d., in Fehrenbacher and Fehrenbacher, *Recollected Words of Abraham Lincoln,* 400.

24. Julian, *Speeches on Political Questions,* 202–4.

25. Burton, *Melting Pot Soldiers,* chap. 5; Efford, *German Immigrants, Race, and Citizenship in the Civil War Era*, chap. 2; Kamphoefner and Helbich, *Germans in the Civil War*; Kaufmann, *The Germans in the American Civil War*.

26. Focusing on snapshots of the officer corps in 1830 and 1860, William B. Skelton found northern officers outnumbered southerners at both moments, but the percentage of southerners had increased by 1860 and were overrepresented relative to national demographics—thanks in part to the Constitution's three-fifths clause, which counted slaves toward southern states' representation in Congress, thus affecting the proportion of southerners receiving appointments to West Point. Officers hailing from the western states were underrepresented in both antebellum years. The religious affiliations of antebellum regular officers reveal their generally elite social origins. In 1830, 37.3% of officers were identified as Episcopalians, growing to 41% by 1860, while only 3.9% of the general population was Episcopal. Congregationalists and Presbyterians lost ground to Episcopalians in the officer corps between 1830 and 1860. The Episcopal Church was dominant in the elite, slaveholding circles of the southern states. The growing numbers of Episcopalians in the officer corps suggested increasing ties to the denomination whose members had the most to lose from the abolition of slavery. See Skelton, *An American Profession of Arms,* 155–56, 162–63. On antebellum religious affiliation, see Irons, *The Origins of Proslavery Christianity*, 100–102, 161–63; Najar, *Evangelizing the South*, 90–92; and Rable, *God's Almost Chosen Peoples*, 14–15, 59–60, 325.

27. William Augustus Brand to *Union County Gazette,* ca. July 31, 1862, in *Union County Gazette*, August 11, 1862; Thackery, *A Light and Uncertain Hold*, 84; Warren Hapgood Freeman to his father, July 29, 1862, in Freeman and Freeman, *Letters from Two Brothers Serving in the War*, 43–45; Loyd G. Harris to Otis, June 18, 1862, Loyd G. Harris Letters, WHS.

28. Townsend, *Rustics in Rebellion,* 220.

## 1. The Origins of the Army of Virginia

1. Gary W. Gallagher, "Introduction," in Ayers, Gallagher, and Torget, *Crucible of the Civil War,* 1–8.

2. Brewer, *The Confederate Negro,* 3.

3. Samuel S. Halsey to Joseph J. Halsey, May 16, 1861, Morton-

Halsey Papers, UVA, quoted in Sutherland, *Seasons of War*, 44.

4. Samuel S. Halsey to Joseph J. Halsey, May 20, 1861, Morton-Halsey Papers, UVA, quoted in Sutherland, *Seasons of War*, 44.

5. Sears, *To the Gates of Richmond*, chap. 7.

6. Cozzens, *Shenandoah 1862*.

7. James Abraham to William Abraham, July 5, 1862, James Abraham Letters, HSP.

8. Alpheus S. Williams to his daughter, May 17, 1862, in Quaife, *From the Cannon's Mouth*, 75.

9. William Blackstone Williams to Moses Williams, June 17, 1862, Moses Williams Papers, MHS.

10. Beatie, *Army of the Potomac: McClellan Takes Command*, 214–17.

11. Beatie, *Army of the Potomac: McClellan Takes Command*, 214–15; Sperber, *Rhineland Radicals*, 407, 423–24.

12. Rea, *War Record and Personal Experiences of Walter Raleigh Robbins*, 36.

13. Townsend, *Rustics in Rebellion*, 202–3.

14. John Porter Hatch to his father, June 29, 1862, John Porter Hatch Papers, LC. "Dutch" is an American misnomer for "Deutsch" and therefore indicates the German language or an immigrant from the German states, not a Dutch-speaking immigrant from the Netherlands.

15. Matthias M. Bechter to unknown, August 3, 1862, Matthias M. Bechter Papers, CWM Collection, USAMHI.

16. Lonn, *Foreigners in the Union Army and Navy*, 658–59.

17. Efford, *German Immigrants, Race, and Citizenship in the Civil War Era*, chap. 3; Honeck, *We Are the Revolutionists*, chap. 5.

18. Richard S. Ewell to Robert L. Dabney, June 16, 1862, in *OR*, Series 1, 12 (part 1):783; Krick, *Conquering the Valley*, 274.

19. Richard S. Ewell to Joseph E. Johnston, April 8, 1862, Benjamin Stoddart and Richard Stoddart Ewell Papers, DU.

20. "Fremont's Army in Rockingham," *Rockingham Register*, n.d., in M. J. Solomon's Scrapbook, DU; Krick, *Conquering the Valley*, 488–89.

21. Welton, *"My Heart Is So Rebellious,"* 150–51.

22. William Roberts, Jr., to his parents, March 17, 1862, William Roberts, Jr., Papers, HSP.

23. Hadley, "An Indiana Soldier in Love and War," 215.

24. Kent, *Three Years with Company K*, 67–68.

25. George T. Spaulding to Fida Spaulding, May 27, 1862, George T. Spaulding Papers, WHS.

26. Andrew J. Torget, "Unions of Slavery: Slavery, Politics, and Secession in the Valley of Virginia," in Ayers, Gallagher, and Torget, *Crucible of the Civil War*, 29.

27. Charles E. Gardner, "My Experiences in the First Maine Cavalry," 7, Charles E. Gardner Papers, *Civil War Times Illustrated* Collection, USAMHI.

28. Henry S. Graham's 1861 map of the enslaved population of Vir-

ginia from the 1860 census is available online at www.loc.gov/resource/g3881e.cw1047000.

29. Grimsley, *The Hard Hand of War,* chap. 4.

30. Horace Currier to Edwin Currier, December 19, 1861, Horace Currier Papers, WHS.

31. Henry Falls Young to his father, July 5, 1862, Henry Falls Young Papers, WHS.

32. Noyes, *The Bivouac and the Battle-Field,* 63.

33. Alpheus S. Williams to his daughter, June 22, 1862, in Quaife, *From the Cannon's Mouth,* 99.

34. Lauramann H. Russell to Serena Russell, June 13, 1862, Lauramann Howe Russell Papers, DU.

35. Gardner, "My Experiences in the First Maine Cavalry," 7, Gardner Papers, *Civil War Times Illustrated* Collection, USAMHI.

36. Nathan B. Webb Diary, May 30, 1862, Nathan Webb Diaries, UM.

37. Samuel J. Nasmith to his wife and children, June 12, 1862, Samuel J. Nasmith Letters, WHS.

38. Ryan, *Women in Public,* 143; Ryan, *Civic Wars*, 167.

39. Samuel J. Nasmith to Jary Nasmith, June 20, 1862, Samuel J. Nasmith Letters, WHS.

40. George T. Spaulding to Fida Spaulding, May 27, 1862, George T. Spaulding Papers, WHS.

41. Ida Powell Dulany Journal, March 19, 1862, in Mackall, Meserve, and Sasscer, *In the Shadow of the Enemy,* 73–74.

42. Ida Powell Dulany Journal, March 20, 1862, in Mackall, Meserve, and Sasscer, *In the Shadow of the Enemy,* 74.

43. Ida Powell Dulany Journal, March 20, 1862, in Mackall, Meserve, and Sasscer, *In the Shadow of the Enemy,* 74–75.

44. Susan Caldwell to Lycurgus Caldwell, May 14, 1862, in Welton, *"My Heart Is So Rebellious,"* 116.

45. *OR,* Series 3, 2:2–3, 29, 44, 109; Shannon, *The Organization and Administration of the Union Army*, 1:270.

46. Neely, *The Union Divided,* 71.

47. Work, *Lincoln's Political Generals.*

48. Rafuse, *McClellan's War.*

49. McPherson, *Battle Cry of Freedom,* 500.

50. Skelton, *An American Profession of Arms,* chap. 10.

51. Carmen and Luthin, *Lincoln and the Patronage.*

52. Goodwin, *Team of Rivals.*

53. Quoted in James M. McPherson, "A. Lincoln, Commander in Chief," in Foner, *Our Lincoln,* 23.

54. *New-Yorker Criminalzeitung und Belletristiches Journal,* August 8, 1862, quoted in Keller, *Chancellorsville and the Germans*, 41.

55. Ulric Dahlgren to John A. B. Dahlgren, June 29, 1862, John A. B. Dahlgren Papers, LC.

56. John C. Frémont Proclamation, August 30, 1861, in *OR*, Series 1,

3:466–67; John C. Frémont to Abraham Lincoln, September 8, 1861, in *OR*, Series 1, 3:477.

57. Tap, *Over Lincoln's Shoulder,* chap. 3.

58. Dicey, *Spectator of America,* 165–66.

59. James Abraham to William Abraham, June 20, 1862, James Abraham Letters, HSP.

60. John C. Frémont to Thaddeus Stevens, April 28, 1862, Thaddeus Stevens Papers, LC.

61. Jones, *Civil War Command and Strategy,* 18.

62. James Abraham to William Abraham, June 20, 1862, James Abraham Letters, HSP.

63. Robert H. Milroy to Mary Milroy, July 4, 1862, in Paulus, *Papers of General Robert Huston Milroy,* 1:54.

64. Robert C. Schenck to Sally Schenck, n.d., Robert C. Schenck Papers, MUO.

65. Robert C. Schenck to Lilly Schenck, June 30, 1862, Schenck Papers, MUO.

66. Engle, *Yankee Dutchman.*

67. Stephen D. Engle, "Yankee Dutchmen: Germans, the Union and the Construction of a Wartime Identity," in Ural, *Civil War Citizens,* 29; Gerteis, *Civil War St. Louis,* 73–76, 90–92.

68. John S. Carlisle to Salmon P. Chase, August 18, 1861, Abraham Lincoln Papers, LC.

69. Charles Sumner to Abraham Lincoln, September 1861, Abraham Lincoln Papers, LC; Engle, "Yankee Dutchmen," in Ural, *Civil War Citizens,* 36.

70. Townsend, *Rustics in Rebellion,* 202.

71. Harrington, *Fighting Politician;* Hollandsworth, *Pretense of Glory.*

72. William Wallace to Sarah Wallace, April 19, 1862, May 18, 1862, William Wallace Papers, WHS.

73. Townsend, *Rustics in Rebellion,* 203.

74. Nathaniel Prentiss Banks to Mary Theodosia Palmer Banks, June 27, 1862, Nathaniel Prentiss Banks Papers, LC.

75. Nathaniel Prentiss Banks Diary, May 20, 1862, Nathaniel Prentiss Banks Papers, LC.

76. Nathaniel Prentiss Banks Diary, July 9, 1862, Nathaniel Prentiss Banks Papers, LC.

77. Davis, *Battle at Bull Run;* McDonald, *"We Shall Meet Again."*

78. Beatie, *Army of the Potomac: Birth of Command,* 201–2; Gienapp, *Abraham Lincoln and Civil War America,* 86–87.

79. Russell, *My Diary North and South,* 2:187–89.

80. Beatie, *Army of the Potomac: McClellan Takes Command,* 566–67.

81. Ward, *The Slaves' War,* 39–40.

82. Beatie, *Army of the Potomac: McClellan Takes Command,* 403–4, 419, 429.

83. Snell, *From First to Last.*

84. Notes on Interview with President Lincoln, January 10–13, 1862,

Irvin McDowell Collection, CHS.

85. Beatie, *Army of the Potomac: McClellan Takes Command,* 110, 179–81.

86. Mahood, *General Wadsworth,* chap. 8; Joseph C. Willard Diary, August 30, 1862, Willard Family Papers, LC.

87. Joseph C. Willard Diary, July 16, 1862, Willard Family Papers, LC.

88. Townsend, *Rustics in Rebellion,* 206.

89. George Washington Partridge, Jr., to Cordelia Howe and Phebe Holdridge, June 23, 1862, in Whitehouse, *Letters from the Iron Brigade,* 35.

90. Joseph C. Willard Diary, August 18, 19, 30, 1862, Willard Family Papers, LC.

## 2. John Pope Takes Command

1. Cozzens, *General John Pope;* Schutz and Trenerry, *Abandoned by Lincoln.*

2. Bradley and Dahlen, *From Conciliation to Conquest,* 45; Schutz and Trenerry, *Abandoned by Lincoln*, 57–60.

3. Cozzens, *General John Pope,* 30–31; Special Orders 60, February 27, 1861, Samuel Peter Heintzelman Papers, LC. Major Heintzelman would have served as an officer of the court, as noted in Thompson, *Civil War to the Bloody End*, 110.

4. Bradley and Dahlen, *From Conciliation to Conquest,* 130; Yates and Pickering, *Richard Yates*, 156–59.

5. Mountcastle, *Punitive War,* 24; Etcheson, *Bleeding Kansas*; Harrold, *Border War*, chap. 8.

6. John Basil Turchin, "First Steps in War: Organizing a New Regiment and Taking It to the Field," *National Tribune,* August 2, 1888, quoted in Bradley and Dahlen, *From Conciliation to Conquest,* 46.

7. John Pope to the people of northern Missouri, July 21, 1861, in *OR*, Series 1, 3:403–4.

8. Mountcastle, *Punitive War,* 25–26.

9. Fellman, *Inside War,* 159.

10. John Pope to John C. Frémont, August 25, 1861, in *OR,* Series 1, 3:456–57.

11. Orders No. 3, August 2, 1861, in *OR,* Series 1, 3:420–21.

12. Mountcastle, *Punitive War,* 27.

13. Mountcastle, *Punitive War,* 29–31; Daniel and Bock, *Island No. 10.*

14. Williams, *Lincoln and His Generals,* 120.

15. Cyrus Clay Carpenter to Susan Kate Burkholder, July 4, August 4, 1862, Cyrus Clay Carpenter Papers, State Historical Society of Iowa, Des Moines; Throne, *Cyrus Clay Carpenter and Iowa Politics*, 60.

16. Randall and Pease, *The Diary of Orville Hickman Browning,* 1:552; Clara Pope to John Pope, June 26, 1862, Fitz John Porter Papers, LC; Tap, *Over Lincoln's Shoulder*, 127.

17. John Pope to the officers and soldiers of the Army of Virginia, July 14, 1862, in *OR,* Series 1, 12 (part 3):473–74.

18. Pope to Army of Virginia, July 14, 1862, in *OR,* Series 1, 12 (part 3):474.

19. Hennessy, *Return to Bull Run,* 12–13; Cozzens, *General John Pope*, 84–86.

20. Rufus R. Dawes to Mary Beman Gates, July 1, 1862, in Dawes, *Service with the Sixth Wisconsin Volunteers,* 51.

21. Richard Cary to Helen Cary, June 28, 1862, Richard Cary Letters, MHS.

22. James T. Miller to Robert E. Miller, July 26, 1862, Miller Brothers Letters, James S. Schoff Collection, UM.

23. Samuel J. V. B. Gilpin Diary, July 16, 1862, E[benezer] N. Gilpin Papers, LC.

24. Charles S. Curtis Diary, June 29, 1862, Curtis Family Papers, WHS.

25. Julian Wisner Hinkley Diary, June 29, 1862, Julian Wisner Hinkley Papers, WHS.

26. Julian Wisner Hinkley to R. W. Wells, July 27, 1862, Julian Wisner Hinkley Papers, WHS.

27. John Mead Gould Diary, July 25, 1862, in Jordan, *The Civil War Journals of John Mead Gould,* 161.

28. Richard Chapman Goodwin to Lucy Goodwin, July 19, 1862, Goodwin Family Papers, MHS.

29. Samuel V. List to Theodore and Susan List, August 9, 1862, Samuel V. List Collection, IHS.

30. Prokopowicz, *All for the Regiment,* 86–87.

31. Horace Currier to Edwin Currier, March 12, 1862, Horace Currier Papers, WHS.

32. Warren H. Freeman to his father, May 18, 1862, in Freeman and Freeman, *Letters from Two Brothers Serving in the War,* 29.

33. Warren H. Freeman to his father, May 23, 1862, in Freeman and Freeman, *Letters from Two Brothers Serving in the War,* 30–31.

34. Charles S. Curtis Diary, July 13, 24, 1862, Curtis Family Papers, WHS.

35. Richard Cary to Helen Cary, July 14, 1862, Richard Cary Letters, MHS; Charles S. Curtis to "Folks at Home," July 21, 1862, Curtis Family Papers, WHS; John Oppell Foering Diary, July 14, 16, 1862, John Oppell Foering Papers, HSP.

36. Charles Fessenden Morse to unknown, July 18, 1862, in Morse, *Letters Written during the Civil War,* 72.

37. Richard Chapman Goodman to Lucy Goodwin, July 19, 1862, Goodwin Family Papers, MHS.

38. George Hyer Brayton Diary, June 28, 1862, WHS.

39. Julian Wisner Hinkley Diary, July 13, 1862, WHS.

40. Alonzo H. Quint to unknown, July 16, 1862, in Quint, *The Potomac and the Rapidan,* 168.

41. Charles F. Morse to unknown, July 12, 1862, in Morse, *Letters Written during the Civil War,* 71–72.

42. Noyes, *The Bivouac and the Battle-Field,* 99.

43. Charles E. Davis Diary, June 7, 1862, in Davis, *Three Years in the Army,* 81.

44. Davis, *Three Years in the Army,* 127.

45. Warren H. Freeman to his father, May 18, 1862, in Freeman and Freeman, *Letters from Two Brothers Serving in the War,* 29–30.

46. Warren H. Freeman to his father, n.d., in Freeman and Freeman, *Letters from Two Brothers Serving in the War,* 30–31.

47. George Washington Partridge, Jr., to Cordelia Howe and Phebe Holdridge, June 23, 1862, in Whitehouse, *Letters from the Iron Brigade,* 35.

48. Nathaniel Prentiss Banks Diary, July 9, 1862, Nathaniel Prentiss Banks Papers, LC.

49. Oscar B. Lane Diary, July 15, 1862, Lane Family Papers, DU.

50. Speed Butler to William Butler, August 4, 1862, William Butler Papers, CHS.

51. Noyes, *The Bivouac and the Battle-Field,* 135.

52. Richard Chapman Goodwin to Lucy Goodwin, August 5, 1862, Goodwin Family Papers, MHS.

53. John Buford, Personnel Return, June 1862, Union Staff Officers' Files, Record Group 94, National Archives, Washington, D.C.; Longacre, *General John Buford,* 83.

54. Bradley and Dahlen, *From Conciliation to Conquest,* 131; Warner, *Generals in Blue*, 54.

55. Kent, *Three Years with Company K,* 102.

56. Starr, *The Union Cavalry in the American Civil War,* 1:289–90, 303–4.

57. Warner, *Generals in Blue,* 405–6.

58. Sutherland, "Abraham Lincoln, John Pope, and the Origins of Total War."

59. Sutherland, *A Savage Conflict,* 20–23, 97–98; Mountcastle, *Punitive War*. For Virginians' responses to Pope's policies, see Ash, *When the Yankees Came*, chap. 2.

60. Jones, *The Right Hand of Command,* chap. 1.

61. Jones, *The Right Hand of Command,* 15–22, 26.

62. Carl Schurz Diary, July 1, 1862, Carl Schurz Papers, LC.

63. Guy Weatherly Collection of McParlin Family Papers, Maryland State Archives.

64. Eby, *A Virginia Yankee in the Civil War,* 68.

65. Cozzens, *General John Pope,* 23, 89; Robert E. Lee to Mildred Lee, July 28, 1862, in Dowdey and Manarin, *The Wartime Papers of R. E. Lee*, 240.

66. Curry, *Four Years in the Saddle,* 376.

67. Turner, *Victory Rode the Rails,* 148–60.

68. Turner, *Victory Rode the Rails,* 161, 196–202.

69. T. A. Meysenburg to Hubert Dilger, July 22, 1862, Hubert Dilger Papers, DU. See also Lowery, *The Story of Battery I.*

70. Longacre, *The Man behind the Guns;* Henry J. Hunt Papers, LC.

71. Ulric Dahlgren to John Adolphus Bernard Dahlgren, June 29, 1862, John Adolphus Bernard Dahlgren Papers, LC.

72. Ulric Dahlgren to John Adolphus Bernard Dahlgren, August 26, 1862, John Adolphus Bernard Dahlgren Papers, LC.

73. Townsend, *Rustics in Rebellion,* 192.

74. Townsend, *Rustics in Rebellion,* 191.

75. John Navarre Macomb to Ann Minerva Macomb, July 12, 15, 1862, Rodgers Family Papers, LC.

76. Foner, *Fiery Trial,* 217.

77. Hennessy, *Return to Bull Run,* 15–16; Cozzens, *General John Pope*, 88.

78. Henry W. Halleck to George B. McClellan, August 6, 1862, in *OR,* Series 1, 12 (part 2):9–11; *New York Daily Tribune*, July 19, 1862.

79. John Pope to Abraham Lincoln, July 23, 1862, in *OR,* Series 2, 4:270.

80. Schutz and Trenerry, *Abandoned by Lincoln,* 93; *Report of the Joint Committee on the Conduct of the War*, 1:276–81; Tap, *Over Lincoln's Shoulder, 127.*

81. McPherson, *The Struggle for Equality,* 71–81.

82. Williams, *Lincoln and the Radicals;* Trefousse, *The Radical Republicans*; David Donald, "Devils Facing Zionwards," in McWhiney, *Grant, Lee, Lincoln and the Radicals*, 72–91.

83. Niven, *Salmon P. Chase.*

84. McClure, Lamphier, and Kreger, *"Spur up Your Pegasus,"* 181–85, 192–94, 200–202, 231–33, 242, 256–57.

85. Dell, *Lincoln and the War Democrats,* 53; Thomas and Hyman, *Stanton*, 260.

86. Donald, *Inside Lincoln's Cabinet,* 97.

87. Daniel, *Days of Glory,* 97, 228; Bradley and Dahlen, *From Conciliation to Conquest*, 157.

88. Salmon P. Chase to Irvin McDowell, June 3, 1862, Salmon P. Chase Papers, CHS.

89. Salmon P. Chase to "Bryant," September 4, 1862, quoted in Schuckers, *The Life and Public Services of Salmon Portland Chase,* 450–51.

90. William T. Sherman to Salmon P. Chase, August 11, 1862, Salmon P. Chase Papers, HSP.

91. Niven, *Salmon P. Chase,* chaps. 3–5.

92. Margarethe Schurz to Salmon P. Chase, May 29, 1862, Salmon P. Chase Papers, LC; Trefousse, *Carl Schurz,* 83, 99, 117.

93. Trefousse, *Carl Schurz,* 117.

94. Williams, "The Attack upon West Point during the Civil War." On West Point officers' impact on the way the Civil War was fought, see Hsieh, *West Pointers and the Civil War.*

95. *Congressional Globe,* 37th Congress, Session 2, 83.

96. *New York Tribune,* July 23, 1862.

97. Hoffer, *The Caning of Charles Sumner.*

98. Pierce, *Memoir and Letters of Charles Sumner,* 4:142–43.

99. Trefousse, *Thaddeus Stevens,* 124.

100. Basler, *The Collected Works of Abraham Lincoln,* 5:370–75. For Stevens's response, see Thaddeus Stevens to Salmon P. Chase, August 25, 1862; Chase to Stevens, August 31, 1862, in Warden, *An Account of the Private and Public Services of Salmon Portland Chase,* 457.

101. Kendall, *Letters Exposing the Mismanagement of Public Affairs by Abraham Lincoln.*

102. Trefousse, *The Radical Republicans,* 193.

103. Phillip Shaw Paludan, "War Is the Health of the Party: Republicans in the American Civil War," in Engs and Miller, *The Birth of the Grand Old Party,* 60–80; Bogue, *The Congressman's Civil War*; Bogue, *The Earnest Men.*

104. Sanger, *Statutes at Large,* 589–92; Siddali, *From Property to Person*, 225–29.

105. Foner, *Fiery Trial,* 215.

106. Sanger, *Statutes at Large,* 597–600.

107. Foner, *Fiery Trial,* 214.

108. *Chicago Tribune,* July 14, 1862; Foner, *Fiery Trial*, 215.

109. Ambrose, *Halleck;* Marszalek, *Commander of All Lincoln's Armies.*

110. George B. McClellan to Samuel L. M. Barlow, July 23, 1862; George B. McClellan to Ellen McClellan, July 20, 1862, in Sears, *The Civil War Papers of George B. McClellan,* 368–69.

111. McPherson, *Tried by War,* 111.

112. Beatie, *Army of the Potomac: McClellan Takes Command,* 140.

113. Edwin Stanton to Charles A. Dana, January 24, 1862, Charles A. Dana Papers, LC.

114. Hedrick, *Lincoln's War Cabinet,* 237.

115. Miller, *Second Only to Grant,* 166–68.

116. Eby, *A Virginia Yankee in the Civil War,* 64–65.

117. Eby, *A Virginia Yankee in the Civil War,* 68.

118. Grimsley, *The Hard Hand of War.*

119. James Abraham to William Abraham, July 5, 1862, James Abraham Letters, HSP. James Abraham clearly read his Shakespeare.

120. Manning, *What This Cruel War Was Over,* chap. 2.

121. James J. Gillette to his mother, June 16, 1862, James Jenkins Gillette Papers, LC.

122. Richard Cary to Helen Cary, June 28, 1862, Richard Cary Letters, MHS.

123. Aldous, *The Civil War Letters of Albert E. Higley,* 169, quoted in Hennessy, *Return to Bull Run,* 12.

124. Harrison White to unknown, July 31, 1862, George Hay Stuart Collection, LC.

125. Hiram Huntington to his father, July 24, 1862, Schoff Civil War Collection, UM.

126. George Alexander Hussey (83rd New York) to George Tuttle Hussey, June 13, 1862, Schoff Collection, UM; Edwin B. Quiner, "Correspondence of Wisconsin Volunteers," Wisconsin Miscellaneous Pamphlets, vol. 7, 84, WHS.

127. General Order No. 13, July 25, 1862, in *OR,* Series 1, 12 (part 3):509.

128. John F. Sosman to his sister, July 28, 1862, Sosman Family Papers, Western Reserve Historical Society, Cleveland.

129. Solomon Hamrick to A. D. Hamrick, July 28, 1862, Solomon Simpson Hamrick Papers, IHS.

130. Letter of George Breck, *Rochester Union and Advertiser,* July 31, 1862; *New York Tribune*, August 4, 1862.

131. Gould, *History of the First-Tenth-Twenty-Ninth Maine Regiment,* 162.

132. Samuel V. List to Theodore and Susan List, July 29, 1862, Samuel V. List Collection, IHS.

133. Sparks, *Inside Lincoln's Army,* 110.

134. Dawes, *Service with the Sixth Wisconsin Volunteers,* 51.

135. Robert E. Lee to Mildred Lee, July 28, 1862, in Dowdey and Manarin, *The Wartime Papers of R. E. Lee*, 240; Robert E. Lee to Jefferson Davis, July 26, 1862, in Freeman, *Lee's Dispatches*, 38–40.

136. Jackson, *Life and Letters of General Thomas J. Jackson,* 310–13.

137. Fitz John Porter to J. C. G. Kennedy, July 17, 1862, Fitz John Porter Papers, MHS, quoted in Hennessy, *Return to Bull Run,* 13.

## 3. An Army of Brigades

1. Sears, *To the Gates of Richmond,* 209.

2. Beatie, *Army of the Potomac: Birth of Command,* chap. 24.

3. Prokopowicz, *All for the Regiment.*

4. Daniel, *Days of Glory,* 29.

5. Reardon, *With a Sword in One Hand and Jomini in the Other,* chaps. 2–3.

6. Rothenberg, *The Art of Warfare in the Age of Napoleon,* 30, 99–118.

7. Rafuse, *McClellan's War,* 191–92.

8. Hsieh, *West Pointers and the Civil War,* 159.

9. Hardin, *History of the Twelfth Regiment, Pennsylvania Reserve Volunteer Corps,* 95.

10. Eugene Powell, History of 66th Ohio (n.p., n.d.), chap. 4, 66th Ohio Volunteer Infantry Records, OHS.

11. Robert C. Schenck to Lilly Schenck, July 13, 1862, Robert C. Schenck Papers, MUO.

12. Starr, *The Union Cavalry in the American Civil War,* 1:289.

13. John Navarre Macomb to Ann Minerva Rodgers Macomb, August

4, 1862, Rodgers Family Papers, LC.

14. George D. Ruggles to Nathaniel Prentiss Banks, August 17, 1862, Nathaniel Prentiss Banks Papers, LC.

15. Starr, *The Union Cavalry in the American Civil War,* 1:289–90.

16. John H. Bevan to his sister, July 5, 1862, John H. Bevan Papers, CWM Collection, USAMHI.

17. Rea, *War Record and Personal Experiences of Walter Raleigh Robbins,* 37–38. Bayard's 2nd New York captured young John S. Mosby, a future Confederate guerrilla leader, in mid-July; see Ramage, *Gray Ghost,* 51.

18. Starr, *The Union Cavalry in the American Civil War,* 1:50.

19. McClellan, *European Cavalry;* McClellan, *Regulations and Instructions.*

20. McClellan, *Regulations and Instructions,* 13.

21. Schurz, *Reminiscences of Carl Schurz,* 2:230–31; Starr, *The Union Cavalry in the American Civil War*, 1:60.

22. Starr, *The Union Cavalry in the American Civil War,* 1:262–63.

23. John Porter Hatch to his father, March 17, 1862, John Porter Hatch Papers, LC.

24. John Porter Hatch to his father, April 1, 1862, John Porter Hatch Papers, LC.

25. John Porter Hatch to his father, April 1, 1862, John Porter Hatch Papers, LC.

26. Nathaniel P. Banks to Edwin M. Stanton, June 1862, in *OR,* Series 1, 12 (part 1):548.

27. Starr, *The Union Cavalry in the American Civil War,* 1:282.

28. Nathaniel P. Banks to Lorenzo Thomas, April 6, 1862, in *OR,* Series 1, 12 (part 3): 49–50.

29. John Porter Hatch to his father, June 4, 1862, John Porter Hatch Papers, LC.

30. Lyman C. Holford Diary, September 11, 1862, LC.

31. John Porter Hatch to Eliza Hatch[?], June 19, 1862, John Porter Hatch Papers, LC.

32. John Porter Hatch to his father, June 29, 1862, John Porter Hatch Papers, LC.

33. John Porter Hatch to his father, July 28, 1862, John Porter Hatch Papers, LC.

34. John Pope to Nathaniel P. Banks, July 19, 1862, in *OR,* Series 1, 12 (part 3):484; Starr, *The Union Cavalry in the American Civil War,* 1:291.

35. John Pope to Nathaniel P. Banks and Banks to Pope, July 21, 1862, in *OR,* Series 1, 12 (part 3):488–91; Starr, *The Union Cavalry in the American Civil War*, 1:291–92.

36. John Porter Hatch to his father, August 2, 1862, John Porter Hatch Papers, LC.

37. Longacre, *General John Buford,* chap. 2; Starr, *The Union Cavalry in the American Civil War,* 1:292–93.

38. *New York Times,* August 8, 1862; Longacre, *General John Buford,* 87–88.

39. Oakey, *History of the Second Massachusetts,* 10.

40. Charles H. Town to Samuel W. Crawford, in *OR,* Series 1, 12 (part 1): 815–16; Starr, *The Union Cavalry in the American Civil War,* 1:284–85.

41. Ordnance invoice, June 22, 1862, John F. B. Mitchell Civil War Papers folder, Nina C. Mitchell Papers, DU.

42. Anonymous [member of 3rd Indiana Cavalry] Diary, August 10, 21, 1862, Civil War Diary, CHS.

43. Starr, *The Union Cavalry in the American Civil War,* 1:294–301.

44. John Beardsley to Franz Sigel, September 13, 1862, in *OR,* Series 1, 12 (part 2):270–72; Starr, *The Union Cavalry in the American Civil War*, 1:302.

45. Walter W. Smith to Edna L. Smith, July 13, 1862, Walter Wallace Smith Papers, DU.

46. John Pope to George W. Cullum, January 27, 1863, in *OR,* Series 1, 12 (part 2):45; John Pope to Henry W. Halleck, September 1, 1862, in *OR*, Series 1, 12 (part 2):80–82; Starr, *The Union Cavalry in the American Civil War*, 1:302.

47. Longacre, *General John Buford,* 94; Starr, *The Union Cavalry in the American Civil War*, 1:297.

48. Rhodes, *History of the Cavalry of the Army of the Potomac,* 17–22.

49. John Mead Gould to "folks at home," July 21, 1862, John Mead Gould Papers, DU.

50. John Porter Hatch to his father, August 9, 1862, John Porter Hatch Papers, LC.

51. Hennessy, *Return to Bull Run,* 198.

52. Hennessy, *Return to Bull Run,* 454; Lusk, *War Letters of William Thompson Lusk*, 181; Eby, *A Virginia Yankee in the Civil War*, 100.

53. John D. Vautier Diary, March 24, 1862, John D. Vautier Papers, USAMHI.

54. William E. Doubleday to Zachariah Chandler, July 5, October 8, December 8, 1861, Zachariah Chandler Papers, LC.

55. John Mead Gould to "folks at home," July 21, 1862, John Mead Gould Papers, DU.

56. Richard Cary to Helen Cary, July 16, 1862, Richard Cary Letters, MHS.

57. Oscar B. Lane Diary, July 12, 1862, Lane Family Papers, DU.

58. John Mead Gould to "folks at home," September 8, 1862, John Mead Gould Papers, DU.

59. Glatthaar, *General Lee's Army,* 157.

60. Nichols, *Toward Gettysburg,* 76–77.

61. Nolan, *The Iron Brigade,* 51–54.

62. Speed Butler to William Butler, August 4, 1862, William Butler Papers, CHS.

63. William Wallace to Sarah Wallace, August 4, 1862, William Wallace Papers, WHS.

64. William R. Ray Diary, August 13, 1862, in Herdegen and Murphy, *Four Years with the Iron Brigade,* 130.

65. George Hyer Brayton Diary, August 14, 1862, WHS.

66. William R. Ray Diary, August 15, 1862, in Herdegen and Murphy, *Four Years with the Iron Brigade,* 130.

67. George Whitefield Reed to "Dear sir," August 4, 1862, Worthington B. Williams Family Papers, IHS.

68. Gaff, *Brave Men's Tears,* 157–61; Hennessy, *Return to Bull Run,* 187–90.

69. Samuel V. List to Theodore and Susan List, July 29, 1862, Samuel V. List Collection, IHS.

70. *Union County Gazette,* August 11, 1862, quoted in Thackery, *A Light and Uncertain Hold*, 84.

71. Robert Schenck to Lilly Schenck, July 13, 1862, Schenck Papers, MUO.

72. Robert Schenck to Lilly Schenck, July 15, 1862, Schenck Papers, MUO.

73. Walter H. Freeman to his father, April 7, 1862, in Freeman and Freeman, *Letters from Two Brothers Serving in the War,* 21.

74. Sypher, *History of the Pennsylvania Reserve Corps.*

75. Charles W. Fuller to his sister, July 20, 1862, Caleb F. Fuller Papers, WHS.

76. Mills, *Chronicles of the Twenty-First Regiment New York State Volunteers,* 196.

77. George Hyer Brayton Diary, July 16, 1862, WHS.

78. George Fairfield Diary, July 17, 19, 21, 22, 1862, George Fairfield Diaries, WHS.

79. Lucius Fairchild to Sarah Fairchild, July 20, 1862, Lucius Fairchild Papers, WHS.

80. Oscar Ladley to his mother and sisters, August 8, 1862, in Becker and Thomas, *Hearth and Knapsack,* 37.

81. George Whitfield Reed to unknown, August 4, 1862, Box 1, Folder 8, Worthington B. Williams Family Papers, IHS.

82. Joseph C. Willard Diary, August 16, 1862, Willard Family Papers, LC.

83. Oscar Ladley to his mother and sisters, August 8, 1862, in Becker and Thomas, *Hearth and Knapsack,* 37–38.

84. Krick, *Stonewall Jackson at Cedar Mountain,* 232–35, 259–62.

85. Robert E. Lee to Jefferson Davis, August 30, 1862, in Dowdey and Manarin, *The Wartime Papers of R. E. Lee,* 267; Nolan, *Lee Considered*, 89.

86. Samuel J. V. B. Gilpin Diary, July 16, 1862, E[benezer] N. Gilpin Papers, LC.

87. Krick, *Stonewall Jackson at Cedar Mountain,* chaps. 6–10.

88. Hennessy, *Return to Bull Run,* chaps. 3–6.
89. Hennessy, *Return to Bull Run,* chaps. 9–16.
90. Hennessy, *Return to Bull Run,* chaps. 17–24.

## 4. Generals, Officers, and Citizen-Soldiers

1. Beatie, *Army of the Potomac: McClellan Takes Command,* 152.
2. Shannon, *The Organization and Administration of the Union Army,* 1:153–60.
3. Doubleday, *Reminiscences of Forts Sumter and Moultrie,* 32; Skelton, *An American Profession of Arms*, 353–58.
4. Patrick and Doubleday quoted in Raus, *Banners South,* 131–32; Nichols, *Toward Gettysburg*, 74; John Reynolds to his sisters, August 15, 1862, Box 8, Reynolds Family Papers, Franklin and Marshall College, Lancaster, Penn.
5. Skelton, *An American Profession of Arms,* 157–58, 232.
6. Skelton, *An American Profession of Arms,* 292.
7. William B. Williams to Moses Williams, July 27, 1862, Moses Williams Papers, MHS.
8. James S. Robinson to L. T. Hunt, August 16, 1862, James S. Robinson Papers, OHS.
9. Robert Huston Milroy to Mary Milroy, August 15, 1862, Robert H. Milroy Collection, Jasper County Public Library, Rensselaer, Ind., quoted in Noyalas, *"My Will Is Absolute Law,"* 62.
10. Henry Falls Young to his father, July 5, 1862, Henry Falls Young Papers, WHS.
11. Lorenzo Thomas and Ethan Allen Hitchcock to James S. Wadsworth, April 2, 1862, in *OR,* Series 1, 12 (part 1):228–29; Hattaway and Jones, *How the North Won*, 174.
12. Work, *Lincoln's Political Generals,* 4.
13. Hsieh, *West Pointers and the Civil War,* 142–47; Rafuse, *McClellan's War*, 191–92, 210–13.
14. Townsend, *Rustics in Rebellion,* 235.
15. *Missouri Democrat,* January 21, 1857; Bilotta, *Race and the Rise of the Republican Party*, 241.
16. Townsend, *Rustics in Rebellion,* 235–36.
17. James Jenkins Gillette to his mother, ca. October 1862, James Gillette Papers, *Civil War Times Illustrated* Collection, USAMHI.
18. Weisberger, *Reporters for the Union,* 196, 202.
19. Fahrney, *Horace Greeley and the Tribune in the Civil War,* 101. I am indebted to historian Wayne Wei-Siang Hsieh for this reference.
20. Hsieh, *West Pointers and the Civil War,* 157.
21. John Navarre Macomb to Ann Minerva Rodgers Macomb, August 4, 1862, Rodgers Family Papers, LC.
22. Marsena Rudolph Patrick Diary, July 20, 1862, Marsena Rudolph Patrick Papers, LC.

23. Marsena Rudolph Patrick Diary, July 21, 1862, Marsena Rudolph Patrick Papers, LC.

24. Rhodes, "Newspapers as Historical Sources"; Fermer, *James Gordon Bennett and the New York Herald,* 5.

25. *New York Tribune,* June 27, 1862.

26. Gene Murray, "Abraham Lincoln's Relationship with James Gordon Bennett and Horace Greeley during the Civil War," in Sachsman, Rushing, and Morris, *Words at War,* 276. Lincoln's response on August 22, in a letter to the *National Intelligencer*, was unmistakable in its pragmatism, if also unsatisfying to African Americans and abolitionists. "My paramount object in this struggle is to save the Union," Lincoln argued, "and is not either to save or destroy Slavery. If I could save the Union without freeing *any* slave, I would do it; and if I could save it by freeing *all* the slaves, I would do it; and if I could do it by freeing some and leaving others alone, I would also do that" (quoted in Murray, "Abraham Lincoln's Relationship," 276). Lincoln chose not to make public at this time that he had informed his cabinet of a plan to issue a preliminary emancipation proclamation but had been persuaded to wait for a significant Union battlefield victory. See Foner, *Fiery Trial*, 219.

27. Fermer, *James Gordon Bennett and the New York Herald,* 218–20; Abraham Lincoln to James Gordon Bennett, May 21, 1862, in Basler, *The Collected Works of Abraham Lincoln,* 5:225.

28. *New York Herald,* July 4, 6, 7, 1862; Fermer, *James Gordon Bennett and the New York Herald*, 218.

29. Andrews, *The North Reports the Civil War,* 265.

30. George Alfred Townsend Scrapbooks, George Alfred Townsend Papers, privately held; Andrews, *The North Reports the Civil War,* 265.

31. Townsend, *Rustics in Rebellion,* 191–92.

32. Andrews, *The North Reports the Civil War,* 267; Crozier, *Yankee Reporters*, 254–57.

33. Andrews, *The North Reports the Civil War,* 266.

34. Smalley, "Chapters in Journalism"; Henry W. Halleck to John Pope, August 19, 1862, in *OR,* Series 1, 12 (part 3):602; Andrews, *The North Reports the Civil War*, 267.

35. Crozier, *Yankee Reporters,* 254.

36. *Chicago Tribune,* August 28, 1862; Andrews, *The North Reports the Civil War*, 268.

37. Charles Walker Diary, June 28, 1862, WHS.

38. Nathaniel Rollins Diary, June 28, 1862, Nathaniel Rollins Papers, WHS.

39. George Fairfield Diary, June 28, 1862, George Fairfield Diaries, WHS.

40. Frank M. Bull Diary, June 28, 1862, WHS; George Hyer Brayton Diary, June 28, 1862, WHS.

41. Robert C. Schenck to Lilly Schenck, July 13, 1862, Robert C. Schenck Papers, MUO.

42. Hugh Ewing to Robert C. Schenck, July 4, 1862, Robert C.

Schenck Papers, MUO.

43. Frederic Denison Diary, July 6, 1862, in Denison, *Sabres and Spurs,* 102.

44. Frederic Denison Diary, July 1, 1862, in Denison, *Sabres and Spurs,* 101.

45. Denison, *Sabres and Spurs,* 103.

46. H. G. Ayer Diary, July 9, 1862, DU.

47. Alfred N. Duffie to 1st Rhode Island Regiment of Cavalry, July 27, 1862, in Denison, *Sabres and Spurs,* 109.

48. James B. Post to Carrie Post, July 25, 1862, James B. Post Papers, CWM Collection, USAMHI.

49. James B. Post to Carrie Post, August 21, 1862, James B. Post Papers, CWM Collection, USAMHI.

50. James B. Post to Carrie Post, July 25, 1862, James B. Post Papers, CWM Collection, USAMHI.

51. James B. Post to Carrie Post, August 8, 1862, James B. Post Papers, CWM Collection, USAMHI.

52. James B. Post to Carrie Post, August 21, 1862, James B. Post Papers, CWM Collection, USAMHI.

53. William Roberts, Jr., to William Roberts, Sr., July 8, 1862, William Roberts, Jr., Papers, HSP; Robert E. Erwin to his mother, July 14, 1862, Robert E. Erwin Letters, CWM Collection, USAMHI.

54. Bates, *Martial Deeds of Pennsylvania,* 859; Thackery, *A Light and Uncertain Hold,* 99.

55. Blair, *A Politician Goes to War,* ix, xv.

56. Solomon S. Hamrick to A. D. Hamrick, July 16, 1862, Solomon Simpson Hamrick Papers, IHS; Jones, *Giants in the Cornfield,* 47–52.

57. William Wallace to Sarah Wallace, May 10, 1862, William Wallace Papers, WHS.

58. Josiah C. Williams to Worthington B. Williams, July 4, 1862, Worthington B. Williams Family Papers, IHS.

59. Henry Bruce Scott to Lizzie Scott, July 10, 1862, Henry Bruce Scott Papers, MHS.

60. Henry Bruce Scott to Lizzie Scott, August 3, 1862, Henry Bruce Scott Papers, MHS.

61. Silbey, *The American Political Nation,* chap. 5.

62. James L. Converse to Mary Converse and children, July 4, 1862, James L. Converse Papers, CHS.

63. Nathaniel Rollins Diary, August 11, 1862, Nathaniel Rollins Papers, WHS.

64. Jones, *The Right Hand of Command,* chap. 2.

65. Joseph C. Willard Diary, August 3, 7, 12, 1862, Willard Family Papers, LC.

66. Henry Bruce Scott to Lizzie Scott, June 19, 1862, Henry Bruce Scott Papers, MHS.

67. John A. Andrew to Nathaniel Prentiss Banks, May 28, 1862, Na-

thaniel Prentiss Banks Papers, LC.

68. Nathaniel Prentiss Banks to Mary Theodosia Palmer Banks, July 22, 1862, Nathaniel Prentiss Banks Papers, LC.

69. R. Morris Copeland to Nathaniel Prentiss Banks, August 13, 1862, Nathaniel Prentiss Banks Papers, LC.

70. Copeland, *Country Life*.

71. Nathaniel Prentiss Banks to Alfred C. Hill, June 22, 1862, Nathaniel Prentiss Banks Papers, CHS.

72. Orestes A. Brownson to Nathaniel Prentiss Banks, July 31, 1862, Nathaniel Prentiss Banks Papers, LC.

73. Edward P. Brownson to Nathaniel Prentiss Banks, August 13, 1862, Nathaniel Prentiss Banks Papers, LC.

74. Edward P. Brownson to Nathaniel Prentiss Banks, September 1, 1862, Nathaniel Prentiss Banks Papers, LC.

75. Alpheus S. Williams to his daughter, August 17, 1862, in Quaife, *From the Cannon's Mouth,* 102–3; William D. Wilkins, "My Libby Prison Diary: Aug 12 to Sept 26th, 1862," August 12, 1862, William D. Wilkins Papers, *Civil War Times Illustrated* Collection, USAMHI.

76. Miller, *Arguing about Slavery,* chap. 4; Remini, *The House*, chap. 6.

77. Miller, *Arguing about Slavery,* 44.

78. Miller, *Arguing about Slavery,* 46.

79. Wallace B. Hoyt to his parents, July 26, 1862, Wallace B. Hoyt Letters, OHS.

80. John Oppell Foering Diary, June 30, 1862, John Oppell Foering Papers, HSP.

81. Dicey, *Spectator of America,* 140.

82. James J. Gillette to his father, July 6, 1862, James Jenkins Gillette Papers, LC.

83. Benjamin Roher to his wife, August 19, 1862, Benjamin Roher Papers, Lewis Leigh Collection, USAMHI.

84. John S. Copley to "Friend Robert," August 20, 1862, John S. Copley Papers, Firestone Library, Princeton University, Princeton, N.J.

85. Robert K. Beecham to his mother, July 27, 1862, Robert K. Beecham Letters, WHS.

86. Cornelius Wheeler to his father, June 25, 1862, Cornelius Wheeler Papers, WHS.

87. Cornelius Wheeler to his father, June 30, 1862, Cornelius Wheeler Papers, WHS.

88. Cornelius Wheeler to his father, July 22, 1862, Cornelius Wheeler Papers, WHS.

89. Cornelius Wheeler to his father, August 14, 1862, Cornelius Wheeler Papers, WHS.

90. Cornelius Wheeler to his father, September 19, 1862, Cornelius Wheeler Papers, WHS.

91. Charles S. Curtis Diary, February 7, 1862, Curtis Family Papers, WHS.

92. Charles S. Curtis Diary, July 9, 1862, Curtis Family Papers, WHS.

93. See Beatie, *Army of the Potomac: McClellan Takes Command,* 122, 573.

94. John Charles Frémont Reminiscences, n.d., Frémont Family Papers, Bancroft Library, University of California, Berkeley.

95. Herr and Spence, *The Letters of Jessie Benton Frémont,* 264–69; Beatie, *Army of the Potomac: McClellan Takes Command*, 122–23.

96. Jessie Benton Frémont to Dorothea Lynde Dix, ca. 1862, Frémont Family Papers, Bancroft Library, University of California, Berkeley.

97. Margarethe Schurz to Salmon P. Chase, n.d., Salmon P. Chase Papers, LC.

98. Edward S. Bragg to Cornelia Bragg, June 22, 1862, Box 1, Edward S. Bragg Papers, WHS.

99. Halttunen, *Confidence Men and Painted Women;* Cott, *The Bonds of Womanhood.*

100. Hugh Boyle Ewing to Henrietta Ewing, August 10, 1862, Hugh Boyle Ewing Papers, OHS.

101. Hugh Boyle Ewing to Henrietta Ewing, August 10, 1862, Hugh Boyle Ewing Papers, OHS.

102. Fanny Lawrence Ricketts Diary, July 25–December 17, 1861, Manassas National Battlefield Park, Manassas, Va.

103. John D. Vautier Diary, August 30, 1862, John D. Vautier Papers, USAMHI.

104. John Navarre Macomb to Ann Minerva Rodgers Macomb, September 4, 1862, Rodgers Family Papers, LC.

105. Oates, *A Woman of Valor;* Pryor, *Clara Barton.*

106. Clara Barton to Stephen Barton, Jr., March 1, 1862, Clara Barton Papers, LC.

107. Oates, *A Woman of Valor,* 32–49.

108. Oates, *A Woman of Valor,* 52–53.

109. Clara Barton to Soldiers' Relief Society of Hightstown, August 1862, Clara Barton Papers, LC; letter printed in *Bordentown Register,* September 12, 1862.

110. James L. Dunn to his wife, August 15, 1862, James L. Dunn Papers, UVA, quoted in Oates, *A Woman of Valor,* 63.

111. Duncan, *The Medical Department of the United States in the Civil War,* 34; Leech, *Reveille in Washington*, 189–92; Oates, *A Woman of Valor*, 66.

112. James L. Dunn to his wife, September 6, 1862, James L. Dunn Papers, UVA; Dunn to his wife, newspaper clipping, Clara Barton Papers, LC.

113. Gilmore Jordan to Harriet Jordan, August 17, 1862, McLaughlin-Jordan Family Papers, IHS.

114. Mitchell, *The Vacant Chair,* chap. 6.

115. Samuel J. Nasmith to his wife, June 12, 1862, Samuel J. Nasmith Letters, WHS.

116. Edward Bragg to Cornelia Bragg, June 22, 1862, Edward S.

Bragg Papers, WHS; Henry Hall to his sister, August 10, 1862, Henry C. Hall Papers, DU.

117. Enoch T. Baker to Sarah A. Baker, July 27, 1862, Enoch T. Baker Papers, HSP.

## 5. Constituents in a Republican Army

1. The brigades of Thomas Meagher (Irish), William Burns (Philadelphia), Daniel Sickles (Excelsior), Joseph Carr, Gouverneur Warren, and George Taylor; see Burton, *Extraordinary Circumstances,* 410–14.

2. Less than 10% (11 of 126) of the Army of the Potomac's infantry force in June were composed of border and western regiments. Included in this count were the II, III, IV, V, and VI Corps. If one adds the 28 infantry regiments of the IX Corps—16 of which fought at Second Bull Run—to the tally, the paucity of non-northeastern regiments (19 of 154) remains, improved to only 12%. Finally, one could double-count the Pennsylvania Reserve Division's thirteen regiments, which served on the peninsula before returning to McDowell's corps. The Army of the Potomac's tally of non-northeastern regiments then drops back to 11% (19 of 167) when combined with the IX Corps, or, lowest of all, just under 8% (11 of 139) without the IX Corps.

3. Historical Census Browser, UVA, http://mapserver.lib.virginia.edu/index.html. Not included are the 3,892,411 free residents of the following states and territories: California, Illinois, Iowa, Kansas, Kentucky, Nebraska, Nevada, and Oregon. The total free population in the states and territories that remained in the Union (and Virginia) was 21,910,184 in 1860.

4. The free population of Virginia in 1860 was 1,105,453 out of a total population of 1,596,318, with 376,688 credited to western Virginia by Boyd B. Stutler in *West Virginia in the Civil War,* vi. By 1870, West Virginia stood at 442,014 residents, compared with 1,225,163 in Virginia.

5. Hennessy, *Return to Bull Run,* 551–56.

6. Burton, *Extraordinary Circumstances,* 387.

7. Richard Cary to Helen Cary, July 14, 1862, Richard Cary Letters, MHS.

8. George Whitfield Reed to unknown, August 4, 1862, Box 1, Folder 8, Worthington B. Williams Family Papers, IHS.

9. Speed Butler to William Butler, August 4, 1862, Folder 4, William Butler Papers, CHS.

10. Charles Simeon Curtis to "Folks at Home," July 21, 1862, Curtis Family Papers, WHS.

11. Daniel D. Jones to John Jordan, Jr., August 7, 1862, Daniel D. Jones Papers, HSP.

12. Daniel D. Jones to John Jordan, Jr., August 11, 1862, Daniel D. Jones Papers, HSP.

13. Hennessy, *Return to Bull Run,* 89–92.

14. Current, *Lincoln's Loyalists,* 15; Ambler, *Francis H. Pierpont,* 74–76, 117–30.

15. Current, *Lincoln's Loyalists,* 18.

16. Kaufmann, *The Germans in the American Civil War,* 97.

17. Dicey, *Spectator of America,* 149.

18. Dicey, *Spectator of America,* 149.

19. Kaufmann, *The Germans in the American Civil War,* 180.

20. Bacarella, *Lincoln's Foreign Legion;* Mahin, *The Blessed Place of Freedom.*

21. Jacob J. Frank Diary, July 5, 1862, LC.

22. Dicey, *Spectator of America,* 149.

23. Dicey, *Spectator of America,* 165.

24. Dicey, *Spectator of America,* 165.

25. Gjerde, *The Minds of the West,* 25.

26. Moe, *The Last Full Measure.*

27. Hurt, *The Ohio Frontier,* 375.

28. Jacob D. Cox to John Pope, n.d., quoted in Cozzens, *General John Pope,* 82.

29. James Abraham to friends, August 19, 1862, James Abraham Letters, HSP.

30. Hugh Ewing to Robert C. Schenck, July 4, 1862, Robert C. Schenck Papers, MUO; Hugh Boyle Ewing to Henrietta Ewing, July 9, 1862, Hugh Boyle Ewing Papers, OHS.

31. L. M. V. Kennon, "Biography of George Crook, 1830–1863," Box 1, Crook-Kennon Papers, USAMHI; Magid, *George Crook,* 20–21.

32. James Abraham to friends, September 2, 1862, James Abraham Letters, HSP.

33. Tuck, *We Ain't What We Ought to Be,* 18.

34. Robert C. Schenck to "Dear Daughters," September 30, 1851, Robert C. Schenck Papers, Rutherford B. Hayes Library, Fremont, Ohio; Bilotta, *Race and the Rise of the Republican Party,* 143. For the origins, demographics, and key ideological interests of the Republican Party, see Gienapp, *The Origins of the Republican Party.*

35. Manning, *What This Cruel War Was Over,* 45.

36. Constant C. Hanks to his mother, August 8, 1862, Constant C. Hanks Letters, DU.

37. Hadden, *Slave Patrols,* chaps. 5–6.

38. Constant C. Hanks to his mother, August 8, 1862, Constant C. Hanks Letters, DU; Halttunen, *Confidence Men and Painted Women,* 96–99, 165.

39. Constant C. Hanks to his mother, August 8, 1862, Constant C. Hanks Letters, DU.

40. Kent, *Three Years with Company K,* 89.

41. Enoch T. Baker to Sarah A. Baker, July 27, 1862, Enoch T. Baker Papers, HSP.

42. Lucius Fairchild to Sarah Fairchild, July 7, 1862, Lucius Fairchild Papers, WHS.

43. Speed Butler to William Butler, August 21, 1862, William Butler Papers, CHS; Ramold, *Baring the Iron Hand.*

44. Charles Walker Diary, June 28, 1862, WHS.

45. Townsend, *Rustics in Rebellion,* 205–6.

46. Townsend, *Rustics in Rebellion,* 199.

47. John Mead Gould Journal, September 2, 1862, in Jordan, *The Civil War Journals of John Mead Gould,* 184.

48. Julius Broadbent to his father, April 21, 1862; Broadbent to "Emogene," July 20, 1862, Julius Broadbent Papers, CWM Collection, USAMHI.

49. Charles Brandegee to Elisha Brandegee, July 18, 1862, Charles Brandegee Letters, CWM Collection, USAMHI.

50. Brasher, *The Peninsula Campaign and the Necessity of Emancipation,* 186, 219–21.

51. James S. Colwell to Annie Colwell, August 23, 1862, James S. Colwell Papers, CWM Collection, USAMHI.

52. See J. M. Bennett, "Communication from the Auditor of Public Accounts, Virginia State Library, Richmond, Virginia," in *Documents of the Senate, 1863–1864,* No. 19, cited in Brewer, *The Confederate Negro*, 15.

53. Carl Schurz Diary, July 21, 1862, Container 175, Carl Schurz Papers, LC.

54. Denison, *Sabres and Spurs,* 112–13.

55. Gates, *The "Ulster Guard" and the War of the Rebellion,* 241.

56. Peter C. Earnhardt Diary, August 19, 1862, DU.

57. Denison, *Sabres and Spurs,* 131.

58. Beaudot and Herdegen, *An Irishman in the Iron Brigade,* 39.

59. Walter W. Smith to Edna L. Smith, July 13, 1862, Walter Wallace Smith Papers, DU.

60. Walter W. Smith to his family, July 28, 1862, Walter Wallace Smith Papers, DU.

61. Ely, *Israel on the Appomattox,* chaps. 1, 8.

62. H. G. Ayer Diary, August 17, 1862, DU.

63. J. S. Fillebrown to Samuel W. Crawford, June 26, 1862, John Mead Gould Papers, DU.

64. Fishel, *The Secret War for the Union,* chap. 8.

65. Anonymous (member of 3rd Indiana Cavalry, Co. E or F) Diary, July 26, 1862, Civil War Diary, CHS.

66. Ario Pardee, Jr., to his father, August 18, 1862, Ario Pardee Letters, Pardee-Robison Collection, USAMHI.

67. White, *The Civil War Diary of Wyman S. White,* 85.

68. Noyes, *The Bivouac and the Battle-Field,* 47.

69. Gilmore Jordan to Harriet Jordan, August 17, 1862, McLaughlin-Jordan Family Papers, IHS.

70. Marsena Rudolph Patrick Diary, July 11, 1862, Marsena Rudolph Patrick Papers, LC.

71. Marsena Rudolph Patrick Diary, July 22, 1862, Marsena Rudolph Patrick Papers, LC.

72. Marsena Rudolph Patrick Diary, September 1, 1862, Marsena Rudolph Patrick Papers, LC.

73. Marsena Rudolph Patrick Diary, August 1, 1862, Marsena Rudolph Patrick Papers, LC.

74. Marsena Rudolph Patrick Diary, August 2, 1862, Marsena Rudolph Patrick Papers, LC.

75. Marsena Rudolph Patrick, Diary, July 22, 1862, Marsena Rudolph Patrick Papers, LC.

76. Jacob J. Frank Diary, July 26, 1862, LC.

77. John Mead Gould Journal, September 2, 1862, in Jordan, *The Civil War Journals of John Mead Gould,* 184.

78. Enoch T. Baker to Sarah A. Baker, July 27, 1862, Enoch T. Baker Papers, HSP.

79. Noyes, *The Bivouac and the Battle-Field,* 44; Foner, *Free Soil, Free Labor, Free Men.*

80. Henry Bruce Scott to Lizzie Scott, August 3, 1862, Henry Bruce Scott Papers, MHS.

81. Henry Bruce Scott to Lizzie Scott, August 3, 1862, Henry Bruce Scott Papers, MHS.

82. Eddy, *History of the Sixtieth Regiment New York,* 119–21.

83. Constant C. Hanks to his mother, August 8, 1862, Constant C. Hanks Letters, DU.

84. Denison, *Sabres and Spurs,* 115.

85. Alonzo H. Quint to unknown, July 16, 1862, in Quint, *The Potomac and the Rapidan,* 169.

86. Alonzo H. Quint to unknown, July 16, 1862, in Quint, *The Potomac and the Rapidan,* 170.

87. Alonzo H. Quint to unknown, July 16, 1862, in Quint, *The Potomac and the Rapidan,* 170.

88. White, *The Civil War Diary of Wyman S. White,* 87.

89. Oscar B. Lane Diary, July 3, 1862, Lane Family Papers, DU.

90. Horace Currier to Edwin Currier, May 18, 1862, Horace Currier Papers, WHS.

91. Amos S. Abbott Diary, July 5, 1862, Amos S. Abbott Papers, USAMHI.

## 6. Make the Traitors Feel the Cost

1. Ulric Dahlgren to John A. B. Dahlgren, August 26, 1862, John Adolphus Bernard Dahlgren Papers, LC.

2. Hugh Boyle Ewing to Henrietta Ewing, August 10, 1862, Hugh Boyle Ewing Papers, OHS.

3. Hugh Boyle Ewing to Henrietta Ewing, August 10, 1862, Hugh Boyle Ewing Papers, OHS.

4. James A. Carman to his father, July 18, 1862, James Carman Papers, CWM Collection, USAMHI.

5. *OR,* Series 2, 4:270–71.

6. Sutherland, *Seasons of War,* 121; Dowdey and Manarin, *The Wartime Papers of R. E. Lee,* 239–40, 949; Lonn, *Foreigners in the Union Army and Navy,* 194; *OR,* Series 1, 12 (part 3):576; *New York Herald,* July 29, 1862.

7. Warren Hapgood Freeman to his father, April 13, 1862, in Freeman and Freeman, *Letters from Two Brothers Serving in the War,* 23.

8. Denison, *Sabres and Spurs,* 101–2.

9. Henry Bruce Scott to Lizzie Scott, July 10, 1862, Henry Bruce Scott Papers, MHS.

10. Anonymous Diary, August 30, 1862, Civil War Diary, CHS.

11. John R. Floyd to Julius White or Colonel Swinney, telegraph received August 27, 1862, Charles F. Gunther Papers, CHS.

12. John Mead Gould Diary, July 14, 1862, in Jordan, *The Civil War Journals of John Mead Gould,* 157.

13. Peter C. Earnhardt Diary, July 21, 1862, DU.

14. William Roberts, Jr., to his father, August 1, 1862, William Roberts, Jr., Papers, HSP.

15. Magid, *George Crook,* 119–20; Kempfer, *The Salem Light Guard,* 38.

16. George Crook Autobiography, Manuscript B, 32, Crook-Kennon Papers, USAMHI; George Crook to G. M. Bascom, April 16, 1862, in *OR,* Series 1, 12 (part 3):84; Magid, *George Crook,* 121.

17. John Oppell Foering Diary, July 1, 1862, John Oppell Foering Papers, HSP.

18. Henry Bruce Scott to Lizzie Scott, July 27, 1862, Henry Bruce Scott Papers, MHS.

19. Henry Bruce Scott to Lizzie Scott, July 27, 1862, Henry Bruce Scott Papers, MHS.

20. Enoch T. Baker to Sarah A. Baker, August 16, 1862, Enoch T. Baker Papers, HSP.

21. Jacob L. Elsesser Diary, April 16, 1862, George Washington Hall Papers, LC.

22. Jacob L. Elsesser Diary, April 21, 1862, George Washington Hall Papers, LC.

23. Henry Falls Young to his father, July 26, 1862, Henry Falls Young Papers, WHS.

24. Capt. C. R. Mudge and Lieut. A. D. Sawyer, 2nd Massachusetts Regiment, recruitment advertisement, Office at Coolidge House, Bowdoin Square, Boston, n.d., in Billings, *Hardtack and Coffee,* 37.

25. Thomas H. Benton to his father, July 26, 1862, Thomas H. Benton Letters, Wiley Sword Collection, USAMHI.

26. Bell Robison to her mother, July 14, 1862, Bell Robison Letters,

Pardee-Robison Collection, USAMHI.

27. George T. Spaulding to his wife, May 26, 1862, George T. Spaulding Papers, WHS.

28. John Oppell Foering Diary, August 31, 1862, John Oppell Foering Papers, HSP.

29. Alured Larke to Tom Larke, July 29, 1862, Alured Larke Papers, WHS.

30. Weber, *Copperheads,* 61.

31. James S. Robinson to L. T. Hunt, August 16, 1862, James S. Robinson Papers, OHS.

32. Kent, *Three Years with Company K,* 82.

33. John Mead Gould Diary, July 14, 1862, in Jordan, *The Civil War Journals of John Mead Gould,* 157.

34. Robert Taggart Diary, August 26, 1862, Robert Taggart Papers, Pennsylvania State Archives, Harrisburg.

35. Franz Sigel to George D. Ruggles, August 7, 1862, Franz Sigel Papers, CHS.

36. James L. Converse to Mary Converse, August 2, 1862, James L. Converse Papers, CHS; Denison, *Sabres and Spurs,* 100; Eddy, *History of the Sixtieth Regiment New York*, 112; Alonzo H. Quint to unknown, September 10, 1862, in Quint, *The Potomac and the Rapidan*, 202–3.

37. Enoch T. Baker to Sarah A. Baker, June 25, 1862, Enoch T. Baker Papers, HSP.

38. William Roberts, Jr., to William Roberts, Sr., July 24, 1862, William Roberts, Jr., Papers, HSP.

39. William Roberts, Jr., to William Roberts, Sr., August 1, 1862, William Roberts, Jr., Papers, HSP.

40. Richard Cary to Helen Cary, August 2, 1862, Richard Cary Letters, MHS.

41. John Mead Gould to W. E. Gould, July 13, 1862, John Mead Gould Papers, DU.

42. Darius Starr to Daniel Starr, July 12, 1862, Darius Starr Papers, DU.

43. Darius Starr to his mother, August 18, 1862, Darius Starr Papers, DU.

44. Walter W. Smith to his family, July 28, 1862, Walter Wallace Smith Papers, DU.

45. Frederick Ranger to his wife, August 14, 1862, Frederick Ranger Papers, CWM Collection, USAMHI.

46. Dean, *Shook over Hell,* 63, 65.

47. Enoch T. Baker to Sarah A. Baker, September 4, 1862, Enoch T. Baker Papers, HSP; George Fairfield Diary, August 21–28, 1862, WHS; Samuel V. List Diary, August 22–28, 1862, IHS; James M. Perry Diary, August 21–24, 1862, WHS.

48. Samuel Selen Kapp to his parents, July 31, 1862, Samuel S. Kapp Family Papers, HSP.

49. Dean, *Shook over Hell,* chaps. 5, 7.

50. Wilder Dwight to Elizabeth A. Dwight, August 15, 1862, Dwight

Family Papers, MHS.

51. Richard Cary to Helen Cary, August 2, 1862, Richard Cary Letters, MHS.

52. Henry Bruce Scott to Lizzie Scott, August 7, 1862, Henry Bruce Scott Papers, MHS.

53. Richard Chapman Goodwin to Lucy N. Goodwin, August 5, 1862, Goodwin Family Papers, MHS.

54. Wilder Dwight to Elizabeth A. Dwight, August 15, 1862, Dwight Family Papers, MHS.

55. Henry Bruce Scott to Lizzie Scott, August 7, 1862, Henry Bruce Scott Papers, MHS.

56. Eddy, *History of the Sixtieth Regiment New York,* 125.

57. Eddy, *History of the Sixtieth Regiment New York,* 142.

58. Eddy, *History of the Sixtieth Regiment New York,* 143.

59. Eddy, *History of the Sixtieth Regiment New York,* 160–62.

60. John Mead Gould to "folks at home," July 21, 1862, John Mead Gould Papers, DU.

61. James Abraham to William Abraham, August 7, 1862, James Abraham Letters, HSP.

62. John Navarre Macomb to Ann Minerva Rodgers Macomb, August 17, 1862, Rodgers Family Papers, LC.

63. Marsena Rudolph Patrick Diary, June 18, 1862, Marsena Rudolph Patrick Papers, LC.

64. Charles Henry Veil, "An Old Boy's Personal Recollections and Reminiscences of the Civil War," 28, Charles Henry Veil Memoirs, CWM Collection, USAMHI.

65. Alonzo H. Quint to unknown, July 16, 1862, in Quint, *The Potomac and the Rapidan,* 168.

66. Henry Besancon Diary, August 30, 1862, Henry Besancon Diaries, DU.

67. Edgar Pitkin to A. J. Grover, June 26, 1862, in First Vermont Volunteer Cavalry, Regimental and Company Order and Letter Books, Record Group 94, National Archives, Washington, D.C.; Starr, *The Union Cavalry in the American Civil War,* 1:147.

68. Edgar Pitkin to George E. Conger, June 26, 1862, 1st Vermont Volunteer Cavalry, Regimental and Company Order and Letter Books, Record Group 94, National Archives, Washington, D.C.; Starr, *The Union Cavalry in the American Civil War,* 1:147.

69. Benedict, *Vermont in the Civil War,* 2:535; Starr, *The Union Cavalry in the American Civil War*, 1:149.

70. William Wallace to Sarah Wallace, August 10, 1862, William Wallace Papers, WHS.

71. William Wallace to Sarah Wallace, September 1, 1862, William Wallace Papers, WHS.

72. William Henry Church to his parents, September 2, 1862, William Henry Church Papers, WHS.

73. Denison, *Sabre and Spurs,* 114–15.

74. Townsend, *Rustics in Rebellion,* 208.

75. Wilder Dwight to Elizabeth A. Dwight, August 15, 1862, Dwight Family Papers, MHS.

76. Kent, *Three Years with Company K,* 82–83.

77. Robert Taggart Diary, August 26, 1862, Robert Taggart Papers, Pennsylvania State Archives.

78. Townsend, *Rustics in Rebellion,* 213.

79. Joseph C. Willard Diary, August 24, 1862, Willard Family Papers, LC.

80. Robert Huston Milroy to T. A. Meysenberg, August 4, 1862, Robert Huston Milroy Letter, CHS.

81. Robert Huston Milroy to T. A. Meysenberg, August 4, 1862, Robert Huston Milroy Letter, CHS; J. S. Marshall to Meysenberg, August 6, 1862, written on back of Milroy letter, CHS.

82. James Jenkins Gillette to his mother, ca. October, 1862, James Gillette Papers, USAMHI.

83. Sutherland, *Seasons of War,* 145.

84. Loyd G. Harris to Harriet Harris, July 2, 1862, Loyd G. Harris Papers, WHS.

## 7. Ambivalent Allies

1. Rafuse, *McClellan's War,* chap. 5.

2. *New York Evening Post,* August 6, 1862.

3. Neely, *The Union Divided,* 74.

4. *Chicago Tribune*, August 4, 1862; Wilkes, *McClellan*, 3, 10.

5. Neely, *The Union Divided,* 71.

6. Woodbury, *Major General Ambrose E. Burnside,* 104.

7. Marvel, *Burnside,* 96. See also Woodbury, *Major General Ambrose E. Burnside*, 104.

8. Marvel, *Burnside,* 98.

9. Marvel, *Burnside,* 112.

10. McPherson, *Tried by War,* 113.

11. George Gordon Meade to Margaret Meade, August 16, 1862, Roll 2, George Gordon Meade Collection, LC.

12. Marvel, *Burnside,* 105.

13. Ambrose E. Burnside to Edwin M. Stanton, March, 21, 1862, in *OR*, Series 1, 9:199–200; Marvel, *Burnside*, 77–78.

14. Marvel, *Burnside,* 105.

15. Marvel, *Burnside,* 103.

16. Stevens, *The Life of Isaac Ingalls Stevens,* 2:320; Dell, *Lincoln and the War Democrats*, 64.

17. Edward O. C. Ord to Placidus Ord, July 7, 1858, Placidus Ord Papers, A. Murray Preston Collection (privately held); Cresap, *Appomattox Commander,* 59.

18. Stevens, *The Life of Isaac Ingalls Stevens,* 2:338–41; Beatie, *Army of the Potomac: McClellan Takes Command,* 21–22.

19. Priest, *From New Bern to Fredericksburg,* 13.

20. I. N. Roberts to Ebenezer Hunt, May 24, 1862, Ebenezer Hunt Papers, MHS.

21. Daniel Read Larned to Henry Howe, March 20, 1862, Daniel Read Larned Papers, LC.

22. Daniel Read Larned to Henry Howe, March 28, 1862, Daniel Read Larned Papers, LC.

23. Charles A. Heckman to Charles S. Olden, March 15, 1862, in Drake, *The History of the Ninth New Jersey Veteran Volunteers,* 65–66.

24. William Augustus Walker to his sister, July 11, 1862, in Silber and Sievens, *Yankee Correspondence,* 61.

25. Browning, *Shifting Loyalties,* 132.

26. James Rumley Diary, May 1862, in Browning, *The Southern Mind under Union Rule,* 37.

27. Walcutt, *History of the Twenty-First Regiment Massachusetts Volunteers,* 124.

28. Marsena Rudolph Patrick Diary, August 9, 1862, Marsena Rudolph Patrick Papers, LC.

29. Hennessy, *Return to Bull Run,* 39–40; Woodbury, *Major General Ambrose E. Burnside,* 105.

30. Ambrose E. Burnside testimony at Fitz John Porter court-martial, December 31, 1862, in *OR,* Series 1, 12 (part 2, Supplement):1005; Cozzens, *General John Pope,* 86.

31. Hennessy, *Return to Bull Run,* 231.

32. Stone, *Personal Recollections of the Civil War,* 57.

33. Walcutt, *History of the Twenty-First Regiment Massachusetts Volunteers,* 128.

34. George Washington Whitman to his mother, August 17, 1862, in Loving, *Civil War Letters of George Washington Whitman,* 60–61.

35. Todd, *The Seventy-Ninth Highlanders,* 189.

36. Powell, *The Fifth Army Corps.*

37. Shreve, *The Story of the Third Army Corps Union.*

38. DePeyster, *Personal and Military History of Philip Kearny;* Werstein, *Kearny, the Magnificent.*

39. Keneally, *American Scoundrel;* Swanberg, *Sickles the Incredible.*

40. Hennessy, *Return to Bull Run,* 557–58.

41. Thompson, *Civil War to the Bloody End,* 3.

42. Samuel Peter Heintzelman Journals, Samuel Peter Heintzelman Papers, LC.

43. Thompson, *Civil War to the Bloody End,* 18, 31.

44. Samuel Peter Heintzelman Journal, October 31, November 7, December 9, 16, 31, 1861, Samuel Peter Heintzelman Papers, LC; Thompson, *Civil War to the Bloody End,* 141.

45. Samuel Peter Heintzelman Journal, December 16, 1861, Samuel

Peter Heintzelman Papers, LC; Thompson, *Civil War to the Bloody End,* 143–44.

46. Philip Kearny to Cortlandt Parker, May 14, 1862, Philip Kearny Papers, LC.

47. Philip Kearny to Cortlandt Parker, May 27, 1862, Philip Kearny Papers, LC.

48. Philip Kearny to Cortlandt Parker, July 31, 1862, Philip Kearny Papers, LC.

49. Philip Kearny to Agnes Kearny, August 12, 1862, Philip Kearny Papers, LC.

50. Philip Kearny to Agnes Kearny, August 30, 1862, Philip Kearny Papers, LC.

51. John D. Vautier Diary, August 30, 1862, John D. Vautier Papers, USAMHI.

52. Joseph Hopkins Twichell to his father, September 5, 1862, in Messent and Courtney, *The Civil War Letters of Joseph Hopkins Twichell,* 177.

53. Joseph Hooker to J. W. Nesmith, May 4, 1862, J. W. Nesmith Papers, Oregon Historical Society, Portland, quoted in Hebert, *Fighting Joe Hooker,* 64.

54. Rusling, *Men and Things I Saw in Civil War Days,* 61–62.

55. Smalley, *Anglo-American Memories,* 146–47.

56. Hebert, *Fighting Joe Hooker,* 90–91.

57. Starr, *Bohemian Brigade,* 194.

58. *Alta California,* June 29, 1862, quoted in Hebert, *Fighting Joe Hooker*, 118.

59. Hebert, *Fighting Joe Hooker,* 121, 123.

60. Welles, *Diary of Gideon Welles,* 1:229–30.

61. John Pope to Henry W. Halleck, September 30, 1862, John Pope Papers, CHS.

62. David Bell Birney to George I. Gross, April 13, 1862, David Bell Birney Papers, USAMHI.

63. David Bell Birney to George I. Gross, April 30, 1862, David Bell Birney Papers, USAMHI.

64. David Bell Birney to George I. Gross, July 24, 1862, David Bell Birney Papers, USAMHI.

65. David Bell Birney to George I. Gross, July 30, 1862, David Bell Birney Papers, USAMHI.

66. David Bell Birney to George I. Gross, August 1[?], 1862, David Bell Birney Papers, USAMHI.

67. John Pope to Henry W. Halleck, September 30, 1862, John Pope Papers, CHS.

68. Hennessy, *Return to Bull Run,* 558–59.

69. Burton, *Extraordinary Circumstances,* 414.

70. Burton, *Extraordinary Circumstances,* 410–14.

71. Burton, *Extraordinary Circumstances,* 387.

72. Beatie, *Army of the Potomac: McClellan Takes Command,* 415; *Report of the Joint Committee on the Conduct of the War*, 1:171–73.

73. Burton, *Extraordinary Circumstances,* 366–67, 390; Jermann, *Fitz-John Porter.*

74. Gouverneur Kemble Warren to W. J. Warren, July 20, 1862, Gouverneur Kemble Warren Papers, New York State Library, Albany; Jordan, *"Happiness Is Not My Companion,"* 48–49.

75. Hiram Berdan to William Y. W. Ripley, July 14, 1862, William Young Ripley Papers, DU.

76. William Y. W. Ripley to Hiram Berdan, July 21, 1862, William Young Ripley Papers, DU.

77. James Abraham to William Abraham, July 5, 1862, James Abraham Letters, HSP.

78. Charles B. Haydon Journal, August 26, 1862, in Sears, *For Country, Cause, and Leader,* 277.

79. Orlando M. Poe to Nelly Poe, August 25, 1862, O. M. Poe Papers, LC.

80. James S. Colwell to Annie Colwell, June 11, 1862, James S. Colwell Papers, CWM Collection, USAMHI.

81. Charles Brandegee to Elisha Brandegee, July 18, 1862, Charles Brandgee Letters, CWM Collection, USAMHI.

82. Felix Brannigan to his sister, July 16, 1862, Felix Brannigan Papers, LC.

83. William T. Pippey to A. H. and B. Y., July 31, 1862, William T. Pippey Papers, DU.

84. Uriah N. Parmelee to his mother, September 8, 1862, Samuel S. and Uriah N. Parmelee Papers, DU.

85. John W. Ames to his father, August 7, 1862, John W. Ames Papers, USAMHI.

86. Brasher, *The Peninsula Campaign and the Necessity of Emancipation,* 173–74, 194; Sypher, *History of the Pennsylvania Reserve Corps,* 156–57, 193.

87. Brasher, *The Peninsula Campaign and the Necessity of Emancipation,* 203.

88. Donn Piatt to Robert C. Schenck, July 17, 1862, Robert C. Schenck Papers, MUO.

89. Donald, *Gone for a Soldier,* 134.

90. Stephen Minot Weld to unknown, ca. September 1, 1862, in Weld, *War Diary and Letters of Stephen Minot Weld,* 133.

91. George B. McClellan to Mary Ellen Marcy McClellan, September 7, 1862, George B. McClellan Papers, LC; James M. McPherson, "My Enemies Are Crushed: McClellan and Lincoln," in Waugh and Gallagher, *Wars within a War,* 52.

## Epilogue

1. Joseph C. Willard Diary, August 30, September 1, 1862, Willard Family Papers, LC.

2. Robert Huston Milroy to Mary Milroy, September 1862, in Paulus, *Papers of General Robert Huston Milroy,* 1:122.

3. Nevins, *Ordeal of the Union,* 6:185–86.

4. Enoch T. Baker to Sarah A. Baker, September 9, 1862, Enoch T. Baker Papers, HSP.

5. Ellis, *General Pope and U.S. Indian Policy;* Wingerd, *North Country*, chap. 11.

6. Nathan B. Webb Diary, September 9, 1862, Nathan Webb Diaries, UM; Jimerson, *The Private Civil War,* 159.

7. Robert H. Kellogg to his father, September 10, 1862, Robert Hale Kellogg Letters, Connecticut Historical Society, Hartford, quoted in Silber and Sievens, *Yankee Correspondence,* 69–70.

8. Eisenschiml, *The Celebrated Case of Fitz John Porter.*

9. McPherson, *Crossroads of Freedom,* 138–41.

10. Fitz John Porter to Manton Marble, September 30, 1862, Manton Marble Papers, LC.

11. Williams, *Lincoln and the Radicals,* 189–90.

12. Kent, *Three Years with Company K,* 112.

13. William Thompson Lusk to Horace Barnard, September 28, 1862, in Lusk, *War Letters of William Thompson Lusk,* 286.

14. T. C. H. Smith, "Memoir and Review of Pope's Campaign in Virginia, July, August, September, 1862: By an Officer on the Staff of the Commanding General" (n.p., n.d.), preface, Thomas C. H. Smith Papers, OHS.

15. George Freeman Noyes Diary, September 3, 1862, in Noyes, *The Bivouac and the Battle-Field,* 149.

16. George Freeman Noyes, September 3, 1862, in Noyes, *The Bivouac and the Battle-Field,* 149.

17. George Freeman Noyes, September 3, 1862, in Noyes, *The Bivouac and the Battle-Field,* 149.

18. Priest, *Antietam,* chap. 3.

19. Orlando M. Poe to Nelly Poe, September 16, 1862, Orlando Metcalfe Poe Papers, LC. Poe idolized Hooker, formerly a division commander in his corps, as Poe admitted in this letter. The *Richmond Enquirer* called Hooker a "second edition of the braggart Pope" on January 27, 1863.

20. Rable, *Fredericksburg! Fredericksburg!* chap. 13.

21. Pfanz, *Gettysburg.*

22. Nolan, *The Iron Brigade,* chap. 12.

23. Keller, *Chancellorsville and the Germans,* chap. 4; D. Scott Hartwig, "The Campaign and Battle of Gettysburg," in Valuska and Keller, *Damn Dutch*, 74–112.

24. John Pope, address to veterans of the Army of the Tennessee, October 16, 1873, quoted in Weigley, *Towards an American Army,* 160–61.

# Bibliography


Adams, Michael C. C. *Our Masters the Rebels: A Speculation on Union Military Failure in the East, 1861–1865*. Cambridge, Mass.: Harvard University Press, 1978.

Aldous, Joan F., ed. *The Civil War Letters of Albert E. Higley*. Glens Falls, N.Y.: J. F. Aldous, 1986.

Ambler, Charles H. *Francis H. Pierpont, Union War Governor of Virginia and Father of West Virginia*. Chapel Hill: University of North Carolina Press, 1937.

Ambrose, Stephen E. *Halleck: Lincoln's Chief of Staff*. Baton Rouge: Louisiana State University Press, 1962.

Anderson, Paul Christopher. *Blood Image: Turner Ashby in the Civil War and the Southern Mind*. Baton Rouge: Louisiana State University Press, 2002.

Andrews, J. Cutler. *The North Reports the Civil War*. Pittsburgh: University of Pittsburgh Press, 1955.

Armstrong, Marion V., Jr. *Unfurl Those Colors: McClellan, Sumner, and the Second Army Corps in the Antietam Campaign*. 2nd ed. Tuscaloosa: University of Alabama Press, 2008.

Ash, Stephen V. *When the Yankees Came: Conflict and Chaos in the Occupied South, 1861–1865*. Chapel Hill: University of North Carolina Press, 1999.

Ayers, Edward L., Gary W. Gallagher, and Andrew J. Torget, eds. *Crucible of the Civil War: Virginia from Secession to Commemoration*. Charlottesville: University of Virginia Press, 2006.

Bacarella, Michael. *Lincoln's Foreign Legion: The 39th New York Infantry, the Garibaldi Guard*. Shippensburg, Penn.: White Mane, 1997.

Barber, Raymond G., and Gary E. Swinson, eds. *The Civil War Letters of Charles Barber, Private, 104th New York Volunteer Infantry*. Torrance, Cal.: Gary E. Swinson, 1991.

Baer, Elizabeth R., ed. *Shadows on My Heart: The Civil War Diary of Lucy Rebecca Buck*. Athens: University of Georgia Press, 1997.

Basler, Roy P., ed. *The Collected Works of Abraham Lincoln*. 8 vols. New Brunswick, N.J.: Rutgers University Press, 1953–55.

Bates, Samuel P. *History of the Pennsylvania Volunteers, 1861–65*. 5 vols. Harrisburg, Penn.: B. Singerly, 1871.

———. *Martial Deeds of Pennsylvania*. Philadelphia: T. H. Davis, 1875.

Bayard, Samuel J. *The Life of George Dashiell Bayard*. New York: G. P. Putnam's Sons, 1874.

Beatie, Russel H. *The Army of the Potomac: Birth of Command, November 1860–September 1861*. Cambridge, Mass.: Da Capo Press, 2002.

———. *The Army of the Potomac: McClellan Takes Command, September 1861–February 1862*. Cambridge, Mass.: Da Capo Press, 2004.

———. *The Army of the Potomac: McClellan's First Campaign, March–May 1862*. New York: Savas Beatie, 2007.

Beaudot, William J. K., and Lance J. Herdegen, eds. *An Irishman in the Iron Brigade: The Civil War Memoirs of James P. Sullivan, Sergt., Company K, 6th Wisconsin Volunteers*. New York: Fordham University Press, 1993.

Becker, Carl, and Ritchie Thomas, eds. *Hearth and Knapsack: The Ladley Letters, 1857–1880*. Athens: Ohio University Press, 1988.

Beckett, Ian F. W. *The War Correspondents: The American Civil War*. London: Grange Books, 1993.

Benedict, G. G. *Vermont in the Civil War*. 2 vols. Burlington, Vt.: Free Press Association, 1886–88.

Beringer, Richard E., et al. *Why the South Lost the Civil War*. Athens: University of Georgia Press, 1986.

Billings, John D. *Hardtack and Coffee; or, The Unwritten Story of Army Life*. Boston: George M. Smith, 1887.

Bilotta, James D. *Race and the Rise of the Republican Party, 1848–1865*. New York: Peter Lang, 1992.

Blackford, Susan Leigh, comp. *Letters from Lee's Army; or, Memoir of Life in and out of the Army in Virginia during the War between the States*. Ed. Charles Minor Blackford III. New York: Charles Scribner's Sons, 1947.

Blair, William Alan, ed. *A Politician Goes to War: The Civil War Letters of John White Geary*. University Park: Pennsylvania State University Press, 1995.

———. *Virginia's Private War: Feeding Body and Soul in the Confederacy, 1861–1865*. New York: Oxford University Press, 1998.

Blake, Henry Nichols. *Three Years in the Army of the Potomac.* Boston: Lee and Shepard, 1865.

Blight, David W. *Beyond the Battlefield: Race, Memory, and the American Civil War.* Amherst: University of Massachusetts Press, 2002.

Blight, David W., and Brooks D. Simpson, eds. *Union and Emancipation: Essays on Politics and Race in the Civil War Era.* Kent, Ohio: Kent State University Press, 1997.

Blumin, Stuart M. *The Emergence of the Middle Class: Social Experience in the American City, 1760–1900.* New York: Cambridge University Press, 1989.

Bogue, Allan G. *The Congressman's Civil War.* New York: Cambridge University Press, 1989.

———. *The Earnest Men: Republicans of the Civil War Senate.* Ithaca, N.Y.: Cornell University Press, 1981.

Boman, Dennis K. *Lincoln and Citizens' Rights in Civil War Missouri: Balancing Freedom and Security.* Baton Rouge: Louisiana State University, 2011.

Boritt, Gabor S., ed. *Lincoln, the War President: The Gettysburg Lectures.* New York: Oxford University Press, 1992.

———, ed. *Lincoln's Generals.* New York: Oxford University Press, 1994.

———. *Why the Confederacy Lost.* New York: Oxford University Press, 1992.

Boyle, John Richards. *Soldiers True: The Story of the One Hundred and Eleventh Regiment Pennsylvania Veteran Volunteers.* New York: Eaton and Mains, 1903.

Bradley, George C, and Richard L. Dahlen. *From Conciliation to Conquest: The Sack of Athens and the Court-Martial of Colonel John B. Turchin.* Tuscaloosa: University of Alabama Press, 2006.

Brasher, Glenn David. *The Peninsula Campaign and the Necessity of Emancipation: African Americans and the Fight for Freedom.* Chapel Hill: University of North Carolina Press, 2012.

Bremner, Robert H. *The Public Good: Philanthropy and Welfare in the Civil War Era.* New York: Knopf, 1980.

Brewer, James H. *The Confederate Negro: Virginia's Craftsmen and Military Laborers, 1861–1865.* Durham, N.C.: Duke University Press, 1969.

Brown, E. R. *The Twenty-Seventh Indiana Volunteer Infantry in the War of the Rebellion.* Monticello: Privately printed, 1899.

Browning, Judkin. *Shifting Loyalties: The Union Occupation of Eastern North Carolina.* Chapel Hill: University of North Carolina Press, 2011.

———, ed. *The Southern Mind under Union Rule: The Diary of James*

*Rumley, Beaufort, North Carolina, 1862–1865*. Gainesville: University Press of Florida, 2009.

Bumbera, Marlene C., comp. *The Civil War Letters of Cpl. John H. Strathern: Eighth Pennsylvania Reserve Corps*. Apollo, Penn.: Clossen, 1994.

Burton, Brian K. *Extraordinary Circumstances: The Seven Days Battles*. Bloomington: Indiana University Press, 2001.

Burton, William L. *Melting Pot Soldiers: The Union's Ethnic Regiments*. Ames: Iowa State University Press, 1988.

Butts, Joseph Tyler, ed. *A Gallant Captain of the Civil War*. New York: F. Tennyson Neely, 1902.

Carmen, Harry J., and Reinhold H. Luthin. *Lincoln and the Patronage*. New York: Columbia University Press, 1943.

Carroon, Robert Girard. *From Freeman's Ford to Bentonville: The 61st Ohio Volunteer Infantry*. Shippensburg, Penn.: Burd Street Press, 1998.

Cashin, Joan E., ed. *The War Was You and Me: Civilians in the American Civil War*. Princeton, N.J.: Princeton University Press, 2002.

Castel, Albert. *Victors in Blue: How Union Generals Fought the Confederates, Battled Each Other, and Won the Civil War*. Lawrence: University Press of Kansas, 2011.

Chaffin, Tom. *Pathfinder: John Charles Frémont and the Course of Empire*. New York: Hill and Wang, 2002.

Charnley, Jeffrey G. "Michigan's General A. S. Williams and Civil War Historians: A Century of Neglect." *Michigan Historical Review* 12, no. 1 (Spring 1986): 1–28.

Clausewitz, Carl von. *On War*. Trans. and eds. Michael Howard and Peter Paret. Princeton, N.J.: Princeton University Press, 1976.

Cleaves, Freeman. *Meade of Gettysburg*. Norman: University of Oklahoma Press, 1960.

Cobb, Richard. *The People's Armies*. Trans. Marianne Elliott. New Haven, Conn.: Yale University Press, 1987.

Coco, Gregory A., ed. *Through Blood and Fire: The Civil War Letters of Major Charles J. Mills, 1862–1865*. Gettysburg, Penn.: Privately published, 1982.

Coffman, Edward M. *The Old Army: A Portrait of the American Army in Peacetime, 1784–1898*. New York: Oxford University Press, 1988.

Collea, Joseph D. *The First Vermont Cavalry in the Civil War: A History*. Jefferson, N.C.: McFarland, 2009.

Collmeyer, Patricia M. "Southern Sentiments: A Look at Attitudes of

Civil War Soldiers." *Cumberland County History* 7, no. 2 (Winter 1990): 68–79.

Comey, Lyman Richard, ed. *A Legacy of Valor: The Memoirs and Letters of Captain Henry Newton Comey, 2nd Massachusetts Infantry.* Knoxville: University of Tennessee Press, 2004.

Cook, Benjamin F. *History of the Twelfth Massachusetts Volunteers (Webster Regiment).* Boston: Twelfth (Webster) Regimental Association, 1882.

Cook, Robert J. *Civil War Senator: William Pitt Fessenden and the Fight to Save the American Republic.* Baton Rouge: Louisiana State University Press, 2011.

Cooling, B. Franklin. *Counter-Thrust: From the Peninsula to the Antietam.* Lincoln: University of Nebraska Press, 2008.

Cooper, William J., Jr., and John M. McCardell, eds. *In the Cause of Liberty: How the Civil War Redefined American Ideals.* Baton Rouge: Louisiana State University Press, 2009.

Copeland, Robert Morris. *Country Life: A Handbook of Agriculture, Horticulture, and Landscape Gardening.* Boston: Dinsmoor and Company, 1866. Reprint ed., Amherst: University of Massachusetts Press, 2009.

Cott, Nancy F. *The Bonds of Womanhood: "Woman's Sphere" in New England, 1780–1835.* New Haven, Conn.: Yale University Press, 1977.

Cottom, Robert I., Jr., and Mary Ellen Hayward. *Maryland in the Civil War: A House Divided.* Baltimore: Maryland Historical Society and Johns Hopkins University Press, 1994.

Cox, Jacob D. *The Second Battle of Bull Run.* Cincinnati: Peter G. Thomson, 1882.

Cozzens, Peter. *General John Pope: A Life for the Nation.* Urbana: University of Illinois Press, 2000.

———. *Shenandoah 1862: Stonewall Jackson's Valley Campaign.* Chapel Hill: University of North Carolina Press, 2008.

Craig, Gordon A. *The Politics of the Prussian Army, 1640–1945.* New York: Oxford University Press, 1955.

Cresap, Bernarr. *Appomattox Commander: The Story of General E. O. C. Ord.* San Diego: A. S. Barnes, 1981.

Crofts, Daniel W. *Reluctant Confederates: Upper South Unionists in the Secession Crisis.* Chapel Hill: University of North Carolina Press, 1989.

Crook, George. *General George Crook: His Autobiography.* Ed. Martin F. Schmitt. Norman: University of Oklahoma Press, 1960.

Crozier, Emmet. *Yankee Reporters, 1861–65.* New York: Oxford University Press, 1956.

Crumb, Herb S., and Katherine Dhalle, eds. *No Middle Ground: Thomas Ward Osborn's Letters from the Field, 1862–1864*. Hamilton, Ont.: Edmonston, 1993.

Cummins, D. Duane, and Daryl Hohweiler, eds. *An Enlisted Soldier's View of the Civil War: The Wartime Papers of Joseph Richardson Ward, Jr.* West Lafayette, Ind.: Belle Publications, 1981.

Cunningham, Horace H. *Field Medical Services at the Battles of Manassas (Bull Run)*. Athens: University of Georgia Press, 1968.

Current, Richard Nelson. *Lincoln's Loyalists: Union Soldiers from the Confederacy.* Boston: Northeastern University Press, 1992.

Curry, Richard O. *A House Divided: A Study of Statehood Politics and the Copperhead Movement in West Virginia*. Pittsburgh: University of Pittsburgh Press, 1964.

Curry, W. J., comp. *Four Years in the Saddle: History of the First Regiment, Ohio Volunteer Cavalry.* Columbus, Ohio: Champlin, 1898.

Dahlgren, John Adolphus Bernard. *Memoir of Ulric Dahlgren: By His Father, Rear-Admiral Dahlgren*. Philadelphia: J. B. Lippincott, 1872.

Daniel, Larry J. *Days of Glory: The Army of the Cumberland, 1861–1865*. Baton Rouge: Louisiana State University Press, 2004.

———. *Shiloh: The Battle That Changed the Civil War.* New York: Simon and Schuster, 1997.

Daniel, Larry J., and Lynn Bock. *Island No. 10: Struggle for the Mississippi Valley.* Tuscaloosa: University of Alabama Press, 1996.

Davis, Charles E., Jr. *Three Years in the Army: The Story of the Thirteenth Massachusetts Volunteers from July 16, 1861 to August 1, 1864*. Boston: Estes and Lauriat, 1894.

Davis, William C. *Battle at Bull Run: A History of the First Major Campaign of the Civil War.* Baton Rouge: Louisiana State University Press, 1977.

———. *Lincoln's Men: How President Lincoln Became Father to an Army and a Nation*. New York: Free Press, 1999.

Davis, William C., and James I. Robertson, Jr. *Virginia at War, 1862*. Lexington: University Press of Kentucky, 2007.

Dawes, Rufus R. *Service with the Sixth Wisconsin Volunteers*. Marietta, Ga.: E. R. Alderman, 1890.

Dean, Eric T., Jr. *Shook over Hell: Post-Traumatic Stress, Vietnam, and the Civil War.* Cambridge, Mass.: Harvard University Press, 1997.

Deane, Frank P., ed. *My Dear Wife: The Civil War Letters of David Brett, 9th Massachusetts Battery, Union Cannoneer.* Fayetteville: University of Arkansas Press, 1964.

Dell, Christopher. *Lincoln and the War Democrats: The Grand Erosion of the Conservative Tradition.* Rutherford, N.J.: Fairleigh Dickinson University Press, 1975.

Denison, Frederic. *A Chaplain's Experiences in the Union Army.* Providence: Rhode Island Soldiers and Sailors Society, 1893.

———. *Sabres and Spurs: The First Regiment Rhode Island Cavalry in the Civil War, 1861–1865.* Central Falls, R.I.: First Rhode Island Cavalry Association, 1876.

DePeyster, John Watts. *Personal and Military History of Philip Kearny, Major-General United States Volunteers.* Newark: Bliss, 1869.

Dicey, Edward. *Spectator of America.* Ed. Herbert Mitgang. Chicago: Quadrangle Books, 1971. Originally published as *Six Months in the Federal States.* 2 vols. London: Macmillan, 1863.

Donald, David H., ed. *Gone for a Soldier: The Civil War Memoirs of Private Alfred Bellard.* Boston: Little, Brown, 1975.

———, ed. *Inside Lincoln's Cabinet: The Civil War Diaries of Salmon P. Chase.* New York: Longmans Green, 1954.

Doubleday, Abner. *Reminiscences of Forts Sumter and Moultrie in 1860–'61.* New York: Harper and Brothers, 1876.

Dougherty, Kevin. *Civil War Leadership and Mexican War Experience.* Jackson: University Press of Mississippi, 2007.

Dowdey, Clifford, and Louis H. Manarin, eds. *The Wartime Papers of R. E. Lee.* Boston: Little, Brown, 1961.

Drake, J. Madison. *The History of the Ninth New Jersey Veteran Volunteers: A Record of Its Service from September 13, 1861, to July 12, 1865.* Elizabeth, N.J.: Journal Printing House, 1889.

Duncan, Louis C. *The Medical Department of the United States in the Civil War.* Washington, D.C.: Government Printing Office, n.d.

Duncan, Russell, ed. *Blue-Eyed Child of Fortune: The Civil War Letters of Colonel Robert Gould Shaw.* Athens: University of Georgia Press, 1992.

Dunn, Craig L. *Iron Men, Iron Will: The Nineteenth Indiana Regiment of the Iron Brigade.* Indianapolis: Guild Press of Indiana, 1995.

Durkin, James, and Jennifer N. Whitcomb, eds. *Civil War Letters of the National Guards, the 19th and 90th Pennsylvania Volunteers.* Glenside, Penn.: J. M. Santarelli, 1994.

Dwight, Eliza Amelia. *Life and Letters of Wilder Dwight, Lieut.-Col. Second Mass. Inf. Vols.* Boston: Ticknor and Field, 1868.

Earley, Gerald L. *The Second United States Sharpshooters in the Civil War: A History and Roster.* Jefferson, N.C.: McFarland, 2009.

Eberly, Robert E. *Bouquets from the Cannon's Mouth: Soldiering with the Eighth Regiment of the Pennsylvania Reserves*. Shippensburg, Penn.: White Mane, 2005.

Eby, Cecil D., Jr., ed. *A Virginia Yankee in the Civil War: The Diaries of David Hunter Strother.* Chapel Hill: University of North Carolina Press, 1961.

Eddy, Richard. *History of the Sixtieth Regiment New York State Volunteers*. Philadelphia: Richard Eddy, 1864.

Efford, Alison Clark. *German Immigrants, Race, and Citizenship in the Civil War Era*. New York: Cambridge University Press, 2013.

Eisenschiml, Otto. *The Celebrated Case of Fitz John Porter.* Indianapolis: Bobbs-Merrill, 1950.

Ellis, Richard N. *General Pope and U.S. Indian Policy.* Albuquerque: New Mexico University Press, 1970.

Ely, Melvin Patrick. *Israel on the Appomattox: A Southern Experiment in Black Freedom from the 1790s through the Civil War.* New York: Knopf, 2004.

Engle, Stephen D. *All the President's Statesmen: Northern Governors and the American Civil War.* Marquette, Wis.: Marquette University Press, 2006.

———. *Struggle for the Heartland: The Campaigns from Fort Henry to Corinth*. Lincoln: University of Nebraska Press, 2001.

———. *Yankee Dutchman: The Life of Franz Sigel*. Fayetteville: University of Arkansas Press, 1993.

Engs, Robert F., and Randall M. Miller, eds. *The Birth of the Grand Old Party: The Republicans' First Generation*. Philadelphia: University of Pennsylvania Press, 2002.

Epstein, Robert M. "The Creation and Evolution of the Army Corps in the American Civil War." *Journal of Military History* 55, no. 1 (January 1991): 21–46.

Escott, Paul D. *"What Shall We Do with the Negro?" Lincoln, White Racism, and Civil War America*. Charlottesville: University of Virginia Press, 2009.

Etcheson, Nicole. *Bleeding Kansas: Contested Liberty in the Civil War Era*. Lawrence: University Press of Kansas, 2004.

Fahrney, Ralph Ray. *Horace Greeley and the Tribune in the Civil War.* Cedar Rapids, Iowa: Torch Press, 1936.

Faust, Drew Gilpin. *This Republic of Suffering: Death and the American Civil War.* New York: Knopf, 2008.

Fehrenbacher, Don E., and Virginia Fehrenbacher, eds. *Recollected Words of Abraham Lincoln*. Stanford, Cal.: Stanford University Press, 1996.

Fellman, Michael. *Inside War: The Guerrilla Conflict in Missouri during the American Civil War.* New York: Oxford University Press, 1989.

Fermer, Douglas. *James Gordon Bennett and the New York Herald: A Study of Editorial Opinion in the Civil War Era, 1854–1867.* New York: St. Martin's Press, 1986.

Ferrero, Edward. *The Art of Dancing, Historically Illustrated.* New York: Edward Ferrero, 1859.

Fishel, Edwin C. *The Secret War for the Union: The Untold Story of Military Intelligence in the Civil War.* Boston: Houghton Mifflin, 1996.

Fletcher, Daniel Cooledge. *Reminiscences of California and the Civil War: By Daniel Cooledge Fletcher, Sergt. Co. H, 40th Regt., N.Y.V.* Ayer, Mass.: Press of H. S. Turner, 1894.

Fluharty, Linda Cunningham, ed. *Civil War Letters of Lt. Milton B. Campbell.* Kearney, Neb.: Morris, 2004.

Foner, Eric. *The Fiery Trial: Abraham Lincoln and American Slavery.* New York: Norton, 2010.

———. *Free Soil, Free Labor, Free Men: The Ideology of the Republican Party before the Civil War.* New York: Oxford University Press, 1970.

———, ed. *Our Lincoln: New Perspectives on Lincoln and His World.* New York: Norton, 2009.

Foote, Lorien. *The Gentlemen and the Roughs: Manhood, Honor, and Violence in the Union Army.* New York: New York University Press, 2010.

Forret, Jeff. *Race Relations at the Margins: Slaves and Poor Whites in the Antebellum Southern Countryside.* Baton Rouge: Louisiana State University Press, 2006.

Förster, Stig, and Jörg Nagler, eds. *On the Road to Total War: The American Civil War and the German Wars of Unification.* New York: Cambridge University Press, 1997.

Frank, Joseph Allen. *With Ballot and Bayonet: The Political Socialization of American Civil War Soldiers.* Athens: University of Georgia Press, 1998.

Freeman, Douglas Southall, ed. *Lee's Dispatches: Unpublished Letters of General Robert E. Lee, C.S.A. to Jefferson Davis and the War Department of the Confederate States of America, 1862–65.* Baton Rouge: Louisiana State University Press, 1994.

Freeman, Warren Hapgood, and Eugene Harrison Freeman. *Letters from Two Brothers Serving in the War to Their Family at Home in West Cambridge, Mass.* Cambridge: H. O. Houghton, 1871.

Fuller, Richard F. *Chaplain Fuller: Being a Life Sketch of a New England Clergyman and Army Chaplain.* Boston: Walker, Wise, 1863.

Gaff, Alan D. *Brave Men's Tears: The Iron Brigade at Brawner Farm.* Dayton, Ohio: Morningside, 1985.

———. *On Many a Bloody Field: Four Years in the Iron Brigade.* Bloomington: Indiana University Press, 1996.

Gallagher, Gary W., ed. *The Antietam Campaign.* Chapel Hill: University of North Carolina Press, 1999.

———. *The Richmond Campaign of 1862: The Peninsula and the Seven Days.* Chapel Hill: University of North Carolina Press, 2000.

———. *The Shenandoah Valley Campaign of 1862.* Chapel Hill: University of North Carolina Press, 2003.

———. *The Union War.* Cambridge, Mass.: Harvard University Press, 2011.

Galwey, Thomas F. *The Valiant Hours.* Harrisburg, Penn.: Stackpole, 1961.

Gates, Theodore B. *The "Ulster Guard" and the War of the Rebellion.* New York: Benjamin H. Tyrrel, 1879.

Geiger, Mark W. *Financial Fraud and Guerrilla Violence in Missouri's Civil War, 1861–1865.* New Haven, Conn.: Yale University Press, 2010.

George, Mary Karl. *Zachariah Chandler: A Political Biography.* East Lansing: Michigan State University Press, 1959.

Gerteis, Louis. *Civil War St. Louis.* Lawrence: University Press of Kansas, 2001.

Gibbon, John. *Personal Recollections of the Civil War.* New York: G. P. Putnam's Sons, 1928. Reprint ed., Dayton, Ohio: Morningside, 1978.

Gibbs, Joseph. *Three Years in the Bloody Eleventh: The Campaigns of a Pennsylvania Reserves Regiment.* University Park: Pennsylvania State University Press, 2002.

Gienapp, William E. *Abraham Lincoln and Civil War America: A Biography.* New York: Oxford University Press, 2002.

———. *The Origins of the Republican Party, 1852–1856.* New York: Oxford University Press, 1987.

Giesberg, Judith. *Army at Home: Women and the Civil War on the Northern Home Front.* Chapel Hill: University of North Carolina Press, 2009.

Giunta, Mary A., ed. *A Civil War Soldier of Christ and Country: The Selected Correspondence of John Rodgers Meigs, 1859–64.* Urbana: University of Illinois Press, 2006.

Gjerde, Jon. *The Minds of the West: Ethnocultural Evolution in the Rural Midwest, 1830–1917.* Chapel Hill: University of North Carolina Press, 1997.

Glatthaar, Joseph T. *General Lee's Army: From Victory to Collapse.* New York: Free Press, 2008.

———. *Partners in Command: The Relationships between Leaders in the Civil War.* New York: Free Press, 1994.

———. *Soldiering in the Army of Northern Virginia: A Statistical Portrait of the Troops Who Served under Robert E. Lee.* Chapel Hill: University of North Carolina Press, 2011.

Glazier, Willard. *Three Years in the Federal Cavalry.* New York: R. H. Ferguson, 1870.

Glover, Edwin A. *Bucktailed Wildcats: A Regiment of Civil War Volunteers.* New York: Yoseloff, 1960.

Goldfield, David. *America Aflame: How the Civil War Created a Nation.* New York: Bloomsbury Press, 2011.

Goodwin, Doris Kearns. *Team of Rivals: The Political Genius of Abraham Lincoln.* New York: Simon and Schuster, 2005.

Gordon, George H. *History of the Campaign of the Army of Virginia from Cedar Mt. to Alexandria.* Boston: Houghton, Osgood, 1880.

Goss, Thomas J. *The War within the Union High Command: Politics and Generalship during the Civil War.* Lawrence: University Press of Kansas, 2003.

Gould, John Mead. *The History of the First-Tenth-Twenty-Ninth Maine Regiment.* Portland, Maine: Stephen Berry, 1871.

Grimsley, Mark. *And Keep Moving On: The Virginia Campaign, May–June 1864.* Lincoln: University of Nebraska Press, 2002.

———. *The Hard Hand of War: Union Military Policy toward Southern Civilians, 1861–1865.* New York: Cambridge University Press, 1995.

Grow, Michael J. *"Liberty to the Downtrodden": Thomas L. Kane, Romantic Reformer.* New Haven, Conn.: Yale University Press, 2009.

Guelzo, Allen C. *Gettysburg: The Last Invasion.* New York: Knopf, 2013.

Hadden, Sally E. *Slave Patrols: Law and Violence in Virginia and the Carolinas.* Cambridge, Mass.: Harvard University Press, 2001.

Hadley, John V. "An Indiana Soldier in Love and War." *Indiana Magazine of History* 59, no. 3 (September 1963): 189–288.

Hagerty, Edward J. *Collis' Zouaves: The 114th Pennsylvania Volunteers in the Civil War.* Baton Rouge: Louisiana State University Press, 1997.

Hall, Isaac. *History of the Ninety-Seventh Regiment New York Volunteers.* Utica, N.Y.: L. C. Childs and Son, 1890.

Halsey, Ashley. *A Yankee Private's Civil War.* Chicago: Henry Regnery, 1961.

Halttunen, Karen. *Confidence Men and Painted Women: A Study of Middle-Class Culture in America, 1830–1870.* New Haven, Conn.: Yale University Press, 1982.

Hardin, Martin D. *History of the Twelfth Regiment, Pennsylvania Reserve Volunteer Corps.* New York: Martin D. Hardin, 1890.

Harman, George. "The Military Experience of James A. Pfeifer." *North Carolina Historical Review* 32 (1955): 385–409, 544–72.

Harrington, Fred. *Fighting Politician: Major General N. P. Banks.* Philadelphia: University of Pennsylvania Press, 1948.

Harris, Robert F., and John Niflot, comps. *Dear Sister: The Civil War Letters of the Brothers Gould.* Westport, Conn.: Praeger, 1998.

Harrison, Robert. *Washington during Civil War and Reconstruction: Race and Radicalism.* New York: Cambridge University Press, 2011.

Harrold, Stanley. *Border War: Fighting over Slavery before the Civil War.* Chapel Hill: University of North Carolina Press, 2010.

Hassler, Warren W., Jr. *Commanders of the Army of the Potomac.* Baton Rouge: Louisiana State University Press, 1962.

———. *General George B. McClellan: Shield of the Union.* Baton Rouge: Louisiana State University Press, 1957.

Hastings, William H., ed. *Letters from a Sharpshooter: The Civil War Letters of Private William B. Greene, Co. G 2nd United States Sharpshooters (Berdan's) Army of the Potomac, 1861–1865.* Belleville, Wis.: Historic Publications, 1993.

Hattaway, Herman, and Archer Jones. *How the North Won: A Military History of the Civil War.* Urbana: University of Illinois Press, 1983.

Hearn, Chester G. *Lincoln, the Cabinet, and the Generals.* Baton Rouge: Louisiana State University Press, 2010.

Hebert, Walter H. *Fighting Joe Hooker.* Lincoln: University of Nebraska Press, 1999.

Hedrick, Burton J. *Lincoln's War Cabinet.* Boston: Little, Brown, 1946.

Hennessy, John J., ed. *Fighting with the Eighteenth Massachusetts: The Civil War Memoir of Thomas H. Mann.* Baton Rouge: Louisiana State University Press, 2000.

———. *Return to Bull Run: The Campaign and Battle of Second Manassas.* New York: Simon and Schuster, 1993.

Herdegen, Lance J., and Sherry Murphy, eds. *Four Years with the Iron Brigade: The Civil War Journal of William Ray, Company F, Seventh Wisconsin Volunteers.* Cambridge, Mass.: Da Capo Press, 2002.

———. *The Men Stood Like Iron: How the Iron Brigade Won Its Name.* Bloomington: Indiana University Press, 1997.

Herr, Pamela, and Mary Lee Spence, eds. *The Letters of Jessie Benton Frémont.* Urbana: University of Illinois Press, 1993.

Hill, A. F. *Our Boys: The Personal Experiences of a Soldier in the Army of the Potomac*. Philadelphia: John E. Potter, 1864.

Hinkley, Julian Wisner. *A Narrative of Service with the Third Wisconsin Infantry*. Madison: Wisconsin History Commission, 1912.

Hoffer, Williamjames Hull. *The Caning of Charles Sumner: Honor, Idealism, and the Origins of the Civil War*. Baltimore: Johns Hopkins University Press, 2010.

Hollandsworth, James G. *Pretense of Glory: The Life of General Nathaniel P. Banks*. Baton Rouge: Louisiana State University Press, 1998.

Honeck, Mischa. *We Are the Revolutionists: German-Speaking Immigrants and American Abolitionists after 1848*. Athens: University of Georgia Press, 2011.

Hough, Franklin B. *History of Duryee's Brigade, during the Campaign in Virginia under Gen. Pope*. Albany: J. Munsell, 1864.

Howard, Oliver Otis. *Autobiography of Oliver Otis Howard, Major General United States Army*. 2 vols. New York: Baker and Taylor, 1908.

Howard, Victor B. *Religion and the Radical Republican Movement, 1860–1870*. Lexington: University Press of Kentucky, 1990.

Hsieh, Wayne Wei-Siang. *West Pointers and the Civil War: The Old Army in War and Peace*. Chapel Hill: University of North Carolina Press, 2009.

Hughes, William E., ed. *The Civil War Papers of Lt. Colonel Newton T. Colby, New York Infantry*. Jefferson, N.C.: McFarland, 2003.

Hurst, Samuel H. *Journal History of the Seventy-Third Ohio Volunteer Infantry*. Chillicothe: Privately published, 1866.

Hurt, R. Douglas. *The Ohio Frontier: Crucible of the Old Northwest, 1720–1830*. Bloomington: Indiana University Press, 1996.

Hyde, Thomas W. *Following the Greek Cross; or, Memories of the Sixth Army Corps*. Boston: Houghton Mifflin, 1894.

Hyman, Harold M. *Era of the Oath: Northern Loyalty Tests during the Civil War and Reconstruction*. Philadelphia: University of Pennsylvania Press, 1954.

Inscoe, John C., and Robert C. Kenzer, eds. *Enemies of the Country: New Perspectives on Unionists in the Civil War South*. Athens: University of Georgia Press, 2001.

Irons, Charles F. *The Origins of Proslavery Christianity: White and Black Evangelicals in Colonial and Antebellum Virginia*. Chapel Hill: University of North Carolina Press, 2008.

Jackson, Mary Anna. *Life and Letters of General Thomas J. Jackson*. New York: Harper and Brothers, 1892.

Jackson, Samuel M. *Diary of General S. M. Jackson for the Year 1862*. Apollo: Privately published, 1925.

Jackson, William J. *New Jerseyans in the Civil War: For Union and Liberty.* New Brunswick, N.J.: Rutgers University Press, 2000.

Jermann, Donald R. *Fitz-John Porter, Scapegoat of Second Manassas: The Rise, Fall and Rise of the General Accused of Disobedience.* Jefferson, N.C.: McFarland, 2008.

Jimerson, Randall C. *The Private Civil War: Popular Thought during the Sectional Conflict.* Baton Rouge: Louisiana State University Press, 1988.

Johnson, Timothy D. *A Gallant Little Army: The Mexico City Campaign.* Lawrence: University Press of Kansas, 2007.

Jones, Archer. *Civil War Command and Strategy: The Process of Victory and Defeat.* New York: Free Press, 1992.

Jones, R. Steven. *The Right Hand of Command: Use and Disuse of Personal Staffs in the American Civil War.* Mechanicsburg, Penn.: Stackpole, 2000.

Jones, Wilbur D. *Giants in the Cornfield: The 27th Indiana Infantry.* Shippensburg, Penn.: White Mane, 1997.

Jordan, David M. *"Happiness Is Not My Companion": The Life of General G. K. Warren.* Bloomington: Indiana University Press, 2001.

Jordan, Ervin L. *Black Confederates and Afro-Yankees in Civil War Virginia.* Charlottesville: University of Virginia Press, 1995.

Jordan, William B., Jr., ed. *The Civil War Journals of John Mead Gould, 1861–1866.* Baltimore: Butternut and Blue, 1997.

Joyner, Fred B. "Robert Cumming Schenck: First Citizen and Statesman of the Miami Valley." *Ohio Archaeological and Historical Quarterly* 58, no. 3 (1949): 245–59.

Julian, George W. *Speeches on Political Questions, 1850–1868.* New York: Hurd and Houghton, 1872.

Kajencki, Francis C. *Star on Many a Battlefield: Brevet Brigadier General Joseph Kargé in the American Civil War.* Rutherford, N.J.: Fairleigh Dickinson University Press, 1989.

Kallgren, Beverly Hayes, and James L. Crouthamel, eds. *"Dear Friend Anna": The Civil War Letters of a Common Soldier from Maine.* Orono: University of Maine Press, 1992.

Kalyvas, Stathis N. *The Logic of Violence in Civil War.* New York: Cambridge University Press, 2006.

Kamphoefner, Walter D., and Wolfgang Helbich, eds. *Germans in the Civil War: The Letters They Wrote Home.* Trans. Susan Carter Vogel. Chapel Hill: University of North Carolina, 2006.

Kaufmann, Wilhelm. *The Germans in the American Civil War. Trans. Steven Rowan.* Carlisle, Penn.: John Kallmann, 1999.

Keegan, John. *The American Civil War: A Military History.* New York: Knopf, 2009.

Keifer, Joseph Warren. *Slavery and Four Years of War: A Political History of Slavery in the United States, Together with a Narrative of the Campaigns and Battles of the Civil War in Which the Author Took Part: 1861–1865.* 2 vols. New York: G. P. Putnam's Sons, 1900.

Keller, Christian B. *Chancellorsville and the Germans: Nativism, Ethnicity, and Civil War Memory.* New York: Fordham University Press, 2010.

Kempfer, Lester L. *The Salem Light Guard, Company G, 36th Ohio Volunteer Infantry, Marietta, Ohio, 1861–1865.* Chicago: Adams, 1973.

Kendall, Amos. *Letters Exposing the Mismanagement of Public Affairs by Abraham Lincoln.* Washington, D.C.: Constitutional Union Office, 1864.

Keneally, Thomas. *American Scoundrel: The Life of Notorious Civil War General Dan Sickles.* New York: Doubleday, 2002.

Kenly, John Reese. *Memoirs of a Maryland Volunteer.* Philadelphia: J. B. Lippincott, 1873.

Kent, Arthur A., ed. *Three Years with Company K: Sergt. Austin C. Stearns, Company K, 13th Mass. Infantry.* Rutherford, N.J.: Fairleigh Dickinson University Press, 1976.

Kester, Donald E. *Cavalryman in Blue: Colonel John Wood Kester of the First New Jersey Cavalry.* Hightstown, N.J.: Longstreet House, 1997.

Kreiser, Lawrence A., Jr. *Defeating Lee: A History of the Second Corps Army of the Potomac.* Bloomington: Indiana University Press, 2011.

Krick, Robert K. *Conquering the Valley: Stonewall Jackson at Port Republic.* New York: Morrow, 1996.

———. *Stonewall Jackson at Cedar Mountain.* Chapel Hill: University of North Carolina Press, 1990.

Lang, Theodore F. *Loyal West Virginia from 1861 to 1865.* Huntington, W.V.: Blue Acorn, 1998.

Lavery, Dennis S., and Mark H. Jordan. *Iron Brigade General: John Gibbon, A Rebel in Blue.* Westport, Conn.: Greenwood Press, 1993.

Lee, Wayne E. *Barbarians and Brothers: Anglo-American Warfare, 1500–1865.* New York: Oxford University Press, 2011.

Leech, Margaret. *Reveille in Washington: 1860–1865.* New York: Harper and Brothers, 1941.

Locke, William Henry. *The Story of the Regiment.* Philadelphia: J. B. Lippincott, 1868.

Longacre, Edward G. *General John Buford.* Conshohocken, Penn.: Combined Books, 1995.

———. *The Man behind the Guns: A Biography of General Henry Jackson Hunt, Chief of Artillery, Army of the Potomac.* South Brunswick, N.J.: A. S. Barnes, 1977.

Lonn, Ella. *Foreigners in the Union Army and Navy.* Baton Rouge: Louisiana State University Press, 1951.

Loving, Jerome, ed. *Civil War Letters of George Washington Whitman.* Durham, N.C.: Duke University Press, 1975.

Lowery, Roland. *The Story of Battery I, First Regiment, Ohio Volunteer Light Artillery, 1861–1865.* Cincinnati: R. Lowery, 1972.

Lowry, Thomas P. *Curmudgeons, Drunkards, and Outright Fools: Courts-Martial of Civil War Union Colonels.* Lincoln: University of Nebraska Press, 2003.

Luebke, Frederich, ed. *Ethnic Voters and the Election of Lincoln.* Lincoln: University of Nebraska Press, 1971.

Lusk, William Thompson. *War Letters of William Thompson Lusk: Captain, Assistant Adjutant-General, United States Volunteers, 1861–1863.* New York: Privately printed, 1911.

Lyle, Rev. W. W. *Lights and Shadows of Army Life; or, Pen Pictures from the Battlefield, the Camp, and the Hospital.* 2nd ed. Cincinnati: R. W. Carroll, 1865.

Lynn, John A. *The Bayonets of the Republic, Motivation and Tactics in the Army of Revolutionary France, 1791–94.* Urbana: University of Illinois Press, 1984.

Lyon, James S. *War Sketches: From Cedar Mountain to Bull Run.* Buffalo: Young, Lockwood, 1882.

Mackall, Mary L., Stevan F. Meserve, and Anne Mackall Sasscer, eds. *In the Shadow of the Enemy: The Civil War Journal of Ida Powell Dulany.* Knoxville: University of Tennessee Press, 2009.

Mackey, Robert R. *The Uncivil War: Irregular Warfare in the Upper South, 1861–1865.* Norman: University of Oklahoma Press, 2004.

Magid, Paul. *George Crook: From the Redwoods to Appomattox.* Norman: University of Oklahoma Press, 2011.

Mahin, Dean B. *The Blessed Place of Freedom: Europeans in Civil War America.* Herndon, Va.: Brassey's, 2002.

Mahon, Michael G. *The Shenandoah Valley, 1861–1865: The Destruction of the Granary of the Confederacy.* Harrisburg, Penn.: Stackpole, 1999.

Mahood, Wayne. *General Wadsworth: The Life and Times of Brevet Major General James S. Wadsworth.* Cambridge, Mass.: Da Capo Press, 2003.

Manning, Chandra. *What This Cruel War Was Over: Soldiers, Slavery, and the Civil War.* New York: Knopf, 2007.

Mannis, Jedediah, and Galen R. Wilson, eds. *Bound to Be a Soldier: The Letters of Private James T. Miller, 111th Pennsylvania Infantry, 1861–1864*. Knoxville: University of Tennessee Press, 2001.

Marcus, Edward, ed. *A New Canaan Private in the Civil War: Letters of Justus M. Silliman, 17th Connecticut Volunteers*. New Canaan, Conn.: New Canaan Historical Society, 1984.

Margraff, William F. *A Civil War Soldier's Last Letters*. New York: Vantage, 1975.

Marks, Bayly Ellen, and Mark Norton Schatz, eds. *Between North and South: A Maryland Journalist Views the Civil War: The Narrative of William Wilkins Glenn, 1861–1869*. Rutherford, N.J.: Fairleigh Dickinson University Press, 1976.

Marshall, Jeffrey D, ed. *A War of the People: Vermont Civil War Letters*. Hanover, N.H.: University Press of New England, 1999.

Marszalek, John F. *Commander of All Lincoln's Armies: A Life of General Henry W. Halleck*. Cambridge, Mass.: Belknap Press of Harvard University Press, 2004.

Martin, David G. *The Second Bull Run Campaign: July–August 1862*. Conshohocken, Penn.: Combined Books, 1997.

Martin, Samuel J. *"Kill-Cavalry," Sherman's Merchant of Terror: The Life of Union General Hugh Judson Kilpatrick*. Madison, N.J.: Fairleigh Dickinson University Press, 1996.

Marvel, William. *Burnside*. Chapel Hill: University of North Carolina Press, 1991.

Marvin, Edwin E. *The Fifth Regiment Connecticut Volunteers: A History*. Hartford: Wiley, Waterman and Eaton, 1889.

Mason, Jack C. *Until Antietam: The Life and Letters of Major General Israel B. Richardson, U.S. Army*. Carbondale: Southern Illinois University Press, 2009.

Matsui, John H. "War in Earnest: The Army of Virginia and the Radicalization of the Union War Effort, 1862." *Civil War History* 58, no. 2 (June 2012): 180–223.

McClellan, George B. *European Cavalry*. Philadelphia: J. B. Lippincott, 1861.

———. *Regulations and Instructions for the Field Service of the United States Cavalry in Time of War*. Philadelphia: J. B. Lippincott, 1861.

McClenthen, Charles S. *A Sketch of the Campaign in Virginia and Maryland of Towers' Brigade, Ricketts' Division, from Cedar Mountain to Antietam*. Syracuse, N.Y.: Masters and Lee, 1862.

McClure, James P., Peg A. Lamphier, and Erika M. Kreger, eds. *"Spur up Your Pegasus": Family Letters of Salmon, Kate, and Nettie Chase, 1844–*

*1873*. Kent, Ohio: Kent State University Press, 2009.

McConnell, William F. *Remember Reno: A Biography of Major General Jesse Lee Reno*. Shippensburg, Penn.: White Mane, 1996.

McCurry, Stephanie. *Confederate Reckoning: Power and Politics in the Civil War South*. Cambridge, Mass.: Harvard University Press, 2010.

McMurry, Richard M. *Two Great Rebel Armies: An Essay in Confederate Military History*. Chapel Hill: University of North Carolina Press, 1989.

McDonald, JoAnna M. *"We Shall Meet Again": The First Battle of Manassas (Bull Run), July 18–21, 1861*. New York: Oxford University Press, 2000.

McPherson, James M. *Abraham Lincoln and the Second American Revolution*. New York: Oxford University Press, 1991.

———. *Battle Cry of Freedom: The Civil War Era*. New York: Oxford University Press, 1988.

———. *Crossroads of Freedom: Antietam*. New York: Oxford University Press, 2002.

———. *Drawn with the Sword: Reflections on the Civil War*. New York: Oxford University Press, 1996.

———. *For Cause and Comrades: Why Men Fought in the Civil War*. New York: Oxford University Press, 1997.

———. *The Struggle for Equality: Abolitionists and the Negro in the Civil War and Reconstruction*. Princeton, N.J.: Princeton University Press, 1964.

———. *Tried by War: Abraham Lincoln as Commander in Chief*. New York: Penguin, 2008.

McWhiney, Grady, ed. *Grant, Lee, Lincoln and the Radicals*. Evanston, Ill.: Northwestern University Press, 1964.

Meier, Kathryn Shively. *Nature's Civil War: Common Soldiers and the Environment in 1862 Virginia*. Chapel Hill: University of North Carolina Press, 2013.

Merchant, Thomas Edward. *Eighty-Fourth Regiment, Pennsylvania Volunteers*. Philadelphia: Sherman, 1889.

Merritt, Edwin Atkins. *Recollections, 1828–1911*. Albany: J. B. Lyon, 1911.

Messent, Peter, and Steve Courtney, eds. *The Civil War Letters of Joseph Hopkins Twichell: A Chaplain's Story*. Athens: University of Georgia Press, 2006.

Milano, Anthony J. "Letters from the Harvard Regiments. Part Two: The Second Massachusetts Regiment—From the Outbreak of War through Cedar Mountain." *Civil War: The Magazine of the Civil War Society* 13 (June 1988): 15–73.

Miller, David W. *Second Only to Grant: Quartermaster General Montgomery C. Meigs*. Shippensburg, Penn.: White Mane, 2001.

Miller, Edward A., Jr. *Lincoln's Abolitionist General: The Biography of David Hunter.* Columbia: University of South Carolina Press, 1997.

Miller, William Lee. *Arguing about Slavery: The Great Battle in the United States Congress.* New York: Knopf, 1996.

Mills, J. Harrison. *Chronicles of the Twenty-First Regiment New York State Volunteers.* Buffalo: 21st Regiment Veteran Association of Buffalo, 1887.

Mitchell, Charles W., ed. *Maryland Voices of the Civil War.* Baltimore: Johns Hopkins University Press, 2007.

Mitchell, Reid. *The Vacant Chair: The Northern Soldier Leaves Home.* New York: Oxford University Press, 1993.

Moe, Richard. *The Last Full Measure: The Life and Death of the First Minnesota Volunteers.* New York: Holt, 1993.

Moore, Rogan H., ed. *The Civil War Memoirs of Sergeant George W. Darby, 1861–1865.* Bowie, Md.: Heritage, 1999.

Morell, Craig A., ed. *Seymour Dexter, Union Army: Journal and Letters of Civil War Service in Company K, 23rd New York Volunteer Regiment of Elmira, with Illustrations.* Jefferson, N.C.: McFarland, 1996.

Morse, Charles F. *Letters Written during the Civil War, 1861–1865.* Boston: Privately printed, 1898.

Mountcastle, Clay. *Punitive War: Confederate Guerrillas and Union Reprisals.* Lawrence: University Press of Kansas, 2009.

Mullin, Robert Bruce. *Episcopal Vision/American Reality: High Church Theology and Social Thought in Evangelical America.* New Haven, Conn.: Yale University Press, 1986.

Nagle, Theodore M. *Reminiscences of the Civil War.* Erie, Penn.: Privately printed, 1923.

Najar, Monica. *Evangelizing the South: A Social History of Church and State in Early America.* New York: Oxford University Press, 2008.

Nash, Howard P. *Stormy Petrel: The Life and Times of General Benjamin F. Butler, 1818–1893.* Rutherford, N.J.: Fairleigh Dickinson University Press, 1969.

Neely, Mark E., Jr. *The Civil War and the Limits of Destruction.* Cambridge, Mass.: Harvard University Press, 2007.

———. *The Fate of Liberty: Abraham Lincoln and Civil Liberties.* New York: Oxford University Press, 1991.

———. *The Union Divided: Party Conflict in the Civil War North.* Cambridge, Mass.: Harvard University Press, 2002.

Neff, Stephen C. *Justice in Blue and Gray: A Legal History of the Civil War.* Cambridge, Mass.: Harvard University Press, 2010.

Nelson, Scott Reynolds, and Carol Sheriff. *A People at War: Civilians and Soldiers in America's Civil War, 1854–1877.* New York: Oxford University Press, 2007.

Nevins, Allan, ed. *A Diary of Battle: The Personal Journals of Colonel Charles S. Wainwright, 1861–1865.* New York: Harcourt, 1962.

———. *Ordeal of the Union.* 8 vols. New York: Scribner, 1947–71.

Nichols, Edward J. *Toward Gettysburg: A Biography of General John F. Reynolds.* University Park: Pennsylvania State University Press, 1958.

Niven, John. *Connecticut for the Union: The Role of the State in the Civil War.* New Haven, Conn.: Yale University Press, 1965.

———. *Salmon P. Chase: A Biography.* New York: Oxford University Press, 1995.

Nolan, Alan T., and Sharon Eggleston Vipond, eds. *Giants in Their Tall Black Hats: Essays on the Iron Brigade.* Bloomington: Indiana University Press, 2001.

———. *The Iron Brigade: A Military History.* Bloomington: Indiana University Press, 1994.

———. *Lee Considered: General Lee and Civil War History.* Chapel Hill: University of North Carolina Press, 1991.

Noyalas, Jonathan A. *"My Will Is Absolute Law": A Biography of Union General Robert H. Milroy.* Jefferson, N.C.: McFarland, 2006.

Noyes, George Freeman. *The Bivouac and the Battle-Field; or, Campaign Sketches in Virginia and Maryland.* New York: Harper and Brothers, 1863.

Oakey, Daniel. *History of the Second Massachusetts Regiment of Infantry.* Boston: George H. Ellis, 1884.

Oates, Stephen B. *A Woman of Valor: Clara Barton and the Civil War.* New York: Free Press, 1994.

Ofele, Martin W. *True Sons of the Republic: European Immigrants in the Union Army.* Westport, Conn.: Praeger, 2008.

Osborn, Hartwell. *Trials and Triumph: The Record of the Fifty-Fifth Ohio Volunteer Infantry.* Chicago: A. C. McClurg, 1904.

Osborne, Seward R., ed. *The Civil War Diaries of Col. Theodore B. Gates, 20th New York State Militia.* Hightstown, N.J.: Longstreet House, 1991.

Paret, Peter. "The New Military History." *Parameters: The Journal of the Army War College* 21, no. 3 (Autumn 1991): 10–18.

Parker, Thomas H. *History of the 51st Regiment P.V. and V.V.* Philadelphia: King and Baird, 1869.

Paulus, Margaret B., comp. *Papers of General Robert Huston Milroy.* 4 vols. N.p.: N.p., 1966.

Perdue, Charles L., et al, eds. *Weevils in the Wheat: Interviews with Virginia Ex-Slaves.* Charlottesville: University Press of Virginia, 1976.

Pfanz, Harry W. *Gettysburg: The First Day.* Chapel Hill: University of North Carolina Press, 2000.

Pickerill, William N. *History of the Third Indiana Cavalry.* Indianapolis: Aetna, 1906.

Pierce, Edward L., ed. *Memoir and Letters of Charles Sumner.* 4 vols. Boston: Roberts Brothers, 1877–93.

Powell, William H. *The Fifth Army Corps: A Record of Operations during the Civil War in the United States of America, 1861–1865.* New York: G. P. Putnam, 1896.

Priest, John Michael. *Antietam: The Soldier's Battle.* New York: Oxford University Press, 1994.

———, ed. *From New Bern to Fredericksburg: Captain James Wren's Diary, B Company, 48th Pennsylvania Volunteers, February 20, 1862–December 17, 1862.* Shippensburg, Penn.: White Mane, 1990.

Prokopowicz, Gerald J. *All for the Regiment: The Army of the Ohio, 1861–1862.* Chapel Hill: University of North Carolina Press, 2001.

Pryor, Elizabeth Brown. *Clara Barton, Professional Angel.* Philadelphia: University of Pennsylvania Press, 1987.

Pula, James S. *The History of a German-Polish Civil War Brigade.* San Francisco: R. and E. Research Associates, 1976.

———, ed. *The Memoirs of Wladimir Krzyzanowski.* Trans. Stanley J. Pula. San Francisco: R and E. Research Associates, 1978.

Pyne, Henry R. *Ride to War: The History of the First New Jersey Cavalry.* Ed. Earl Schenck Miers. New Brunswick, N.J.: Rutgers University Press, 1961.

Quaife, Milo M., ed. *From the Cannon's Mouth: The Civil War Letters of General Alpheus S. Williams.* Detroit: Wayne State University Press, 1959.

Quint, Alonzo H. *The Potomac and the Rapidan: Army Notes from the Failure at Winchester to the Reenforcement of Rosecrans, 1861–3.* Boston: Crosby and Nichols, 1864.

Raab, Steven S., ed. *With the 3rd Wisconsin Badgers: The Living Experience of the Civil War through the Journals of Van R. Willard.* Harrisburg, Penn.: Stackpole, 1999.

Rable, George C. *Civil Wars: Women and the Crisis of Southern Nationalism.* Urbana: University of Illinois Press, 1989.

———. *Fredericksburg! Fredericksburg!* Chapel Hill: University of North Carolina Press, 2001.

———. *God's Almost Chosen Peoples: A Religious History of the American Civil War.* Chapel Hill: University of North Carolina Press, 2010.

Rafuse, Ethan S. *McClellan's War: The Failure of Moderation in the Struggle for the Union.* Bloomington: Indiana University Press, 2005.

Ramage, James A. *Gray Ghost: The Life of Col. John Singleton Mosby.* Lexington: University Press of Kentucky, 1999.

Ramold, Steven J. *Baring the Iron Hand: Discipline in the Union Army.* DeKalb: Northern Illinois University Press, 2010.

Randall, James G., and Theodore C. Pease, eds. *The Diary of Orville Hickman Browning.* 2 vols. Springfield: Illinois State Library, 1925.

Raphelson, Alfred C. "Alexander Schimmelfennig: A German-American Campaigner in the Civil War." *Pennsylvania Magazine of History and Biography* 87 (April 1963): 156–81.

Raus, Edmund J., Jr. *Banners South: A Northern Community at War.* Kent, Ohio: Kent State University Press, 2005.

Rawling, Charles J. *History of the First Regiment [West] Virginia Infantry.* Philadelphia: J. B. Lippincott, 1887.

Rea, Lilian, ed. *War Record and Personal Experiences of Walter Raleigh Robbins, from April 22, 1861, to August 4, 1865.* Chicago: N.p. 1923.

Reader, Francis S. *History of the Fifth West Virginia Cavalry, Formerly the Second (West) Virginia Infantry.* New Brighton, W.V.: F. S. Reader, 1890.

Reardon, Carol. *With a Sword in One Hand and Jomini in the Other: The Problem of Military Thought in the Civil War North.* Chapel Hill: University of North Carolina Press, 2012.

Reese, Timothy J. *Sykes' Regular Infantry Division, 1861–1864: A History of Regular United States Infantry Operations in the Civil War's Eastern Theater.* Jefferson, N.C.: McFarland, 1990.

Reid-Green, Marcia, ed. *Letters Home: Henry Matrau of the Iron Brigade.* Lincoln: University of Nebraska Press, 1993.

Remini, Robert V. *The House: The History of the House of Representatives.* Washington, D.C.: Smithsonian, 2006.

*Report of the Joint Committee on the Conduct of the War: In Three Parts.* Washington, D.C.: Government Printing Office, 1863.

Republican Congressional Committee. *Leave Pope to Get Out of His Scrape: McClellan's Dispatches.* Washington, D.C.: McGill and Witherow, 1864.

Rhodes, Charles D. *History of the Cavalry of the Army of the Potomac, Including That of the Army of Virginia.* Kansas City: Hudson-Kimberly, 1900.

Rhodes, James Ford. "Newspapers as Historical Sources." *Atlantic Monthly* 103 (1909): 650–57.

Richards, George W. *Lives of Generals Halleck and Pope.* Philadelphia: J. Magee, 1862.

Robinson, Charles M., III. *General Crook and the Western Frontier.* Norman: University of Oklahoma Press, 2001.

Rogers, D. Laurence. *Apostles of Equality: The Birneys, the Republicans, and the Civil War.* East Lansing: Michigan State University Press, 2011.

Rolfs, David. *No Peace for the Wicked: Northern Protestant Soldiers and the American Civil War.* Knoxville: University of Tennessee Press, 2009.

Ropes, John Codman. *The Army under Pope.* New York: Charles Scribner's Sons, 1881.

Ross, Sam. *The Empty Sleeve: A Biography of Lucius Fairchild.* Madison: State Historical Society of Wisconsin, 1964.

Rothenberg, Gunther E. *The Art of Warfare in the Age of Napoleon.* Bloomington: Indiana University Press, 1978.

Rowland, Thomas J. *George B. McClellan and Civil War History.* Kent, Ohio: Kent State University Press, 1998.

Royster, Charles. *The Destructive War: William Tecumseh Sherman, Stonewall Jackson, and the Americans.* New York: Knopf, 1991.

Ruffner, Kevin Conley. *Maryland's Blue and Gray: A Border State's Union and Confederate Junior Officer Corps.* Baton Rouge: Louisiana State University Press, 1997.

Rusling, James F. *Men and Things I Saw in Civil War Days.* New York: Eaton and Mains, 1899.

Russell, William Howard. *My Diary North and South.* 2 vols. London: Bradbury and Evans, 1863.

Ryan, Mary P. *Civic Wars: Democracy and Public Life in the American City during the Nineteenth Century.* Berkeley: University of California Press, 1997.

———. *Women in Public: Between Banners and Ballots, 1825–1880.* Baltimore: Johns Hopkins University Press, 1990.

Sachsman, David B., S. Kittrell Rushing, and Roy Morris, Jr., eds. *Words at War: The Civil War and American Journalism.* West Lafayette, Ind.: Purdue University Press, 2008.

Samito, Christian G. *Becoming American under Fire: Irish Americans, African Americans, and the Politics of Citizenship during the Civil War*

*Era*. Ithaca, N.Y.: Cornell University Press, 2009.

Sanger, George P., ed. *The Statutes at Large, Treaties, and Proclamations of the United States of America*. Vol. 12. Boston: Little, Brown, 1863.

Schuckers, J. W. *The Life and Public Services of Salmon Portland Chase*. New York: D. Appleton, 1874.

Schultz, Jane E. *Women at the Front: Hospital Workers in Civil War America*. Chapel Hill: University of North Carolina Press, 2004.

Schurz, Carl. *Reminiscences of Carl Schurz*. 3 vols. New York: McClure, 1907–8.

Schutz, Wallace J., and Walter N. Trenerry. *Abandoned by Lincoln: A Military Biography of General John Pope*. Urbana: University of Illinois Press, 1990.

———. "John Pope: The Professional Soldier as Unwilling Servant of Party Politics, 1861–1865." Paper presented at the Fourth Annual Illinois History Conference, Springfield, December 2–3, 1983.

Scott, Robert Garth, ed. *Forgotten Valor: The Memoirs, Journals, and Civil War Letters of Orlando B. Willcox*. Kent, Ohio: Kent State University Press, 1999.

Sears, Stephen W, ed. *The Civil War Papers of George B. McClellan: Selected Correspondence, 1860–1865*. New York: Ticknor and Fields, 1989.

———. *Controversies and Commanders: Dispatches from the Army of the Potomac*. Boston: Houghton Mifflin Harcourt, 1999.

———, ed. *For Country, Cause, and Leader: The Civil War Journal of Charles B. Haydon*. New York: Ticknor and Fields, 1993.

———, ed. *On Campaign with the Army of the Potomac: The Civil War Journal of Theodore Ayrault Dodge*. New York: Cooper Square Press, 2001.

———. *To the Gates of Richmond: The Peninsula Campaign*. Boston: Houghton Mifflin, 1992.

SeCheverell, J. Hamp. *Journal History of the Twenty-Ninth Ohio Veteran Volunteers, 1861–1865, Its Victories and Its Reverses*. Cleveland: J. Hamp SeCheverell, 1883.

Shaffer, Duane E. *Men of Granite: New Hampshire's Soldiers in the Civil War*. Columbia: University of South Carolina Press, 2008.

Shanks, John Peter Cleaver. *Vindication of Major General John C. Frémont, against the Attacks of the Slave Power and Its Allies*. Washington, D.C.: Scammell, 1862.

Shannon, Fred A. *The Organization and Administration of the Union Army, 1861–1865*. 2 vols. Cleveland: Arthur H. Clark, 1928.

Shattuck, Gardiner H., Jr. *A Shield and Hiding Place: The Religious Life of the Civil War Armies*. Macon, Ga.: Mercer University Press, 1987.

Sheehan-Dean, Aaron, ed. *The View from the Ground: Experiences of Civil War Soldiers*. Lexington: University Press of Kentucky, 2007.

———. *Why Confederates Fought: Family and Nation in Civil War Virginia*. Chapel Hill: University of North Carolina Press, 2007.

Shreve, William Price. *The Story of the Third Army Corps Union*. Boston: N.p., 1910.

Siddali, Silvana R. *From Property to Person: Slavery and the Confiscation Acts, 1861–1862*. Baton Rouge: Louisiana State University Press, 2005.

Silber, Nina. *Daughters of the Union: Northern Women Fight the Civil War.* Cambridge, Mass.: Harvard University Press, 2005.

Silber, Nina, and Mary Beth Sievens, eds. *Yankee Correspondence: Civil War Letters between New England Soldiers and the Home Front*. Charlottesville: University Press of Virginia, 1996.

Silbey, Joel H. *The American Political Nation, 1838–1893*. Stanford, Cal.: Stanford University Press, 1991.

———. *A Respectable Minority: The Democratic Party in the Civil War Era, 1860–1868*. New York: Norton, 1977.

Simpson, Brooks D. *Let Us Have Peace: Ulysses S. Grant and the Politics of War and Reconstruction, 1861–1868*. Chapel Hill: University of North Carolina Press, 1991.

Skelton, William B. *An American Profession of Arms: The Army Officer Corps, 1784–1861*. Lawrence: University Press of Kansas, 1992.

Slotkin, Richard. *The Long Road to Antietam: How the Civil War Became a Revolution*. New York: Liveright, 2012.

Smalley, George W. *Anglo-American Memories*. New York: G. P. Putnam's Sons, 1911.

———. "Chapters in Journalism." *Harper's New Monthly Magazine*, August 1894, 426–27.

Smith, Abram P. *History of the Seventy-Sixth Regiment New York Volunteers*. Cortland, N.Y.: Truair, Smith and Miles, 1867.

Sneden, Robert Knox. *Eye of the Storm: A Civil War Odyssey.* Ed. Charles F. Bryan, Jr., and Nelson D. Lankford. New York: Free Press, 2000.

Snell, Mark A. *From First to Last: The Life of Major General William B. Franklin*. New York: Fordham University Press, 2002.

Sparks, David S., ed. *Inside Lincoln's Army: The Diary of General Marsena Rudolph Patrick*. New York: Thomas Yoseloff, 1964.

Sperber, Jonathan. *Rhineland Radicals: The Democratic Movement and the Revolution of 1848–1849*. Princeton, N.J.: Princeton University Press, 1991.

Stackpole, Edward J. *From Cedar Mountain to Antietam.* Mechanicsburg, Penn.: Stackpole, 1993.

Starr, Louis M. *Bohemian Brigade: Civil War Newsmen in Action.* New York: Knopf, 1954. Reprint ed. Madison: University of Wisconsin Press, 1987.

Starr, Stephen Z. *The Union Cavalry in the American Civil War.* 3 vols. Baton Rouge: Louisiana State University Press, 1979–85.

Stevens, Hazard. *The Life of Isaac Ingalls Stevens.* 2 vols. Boston: Houghton Mifflin, 1900.

Stevens, Michael E., ed. *As If It Were Glory: Robert Beecham's Civil War from the Iron Brigade to the Black Regiments.* Madison, Wis.: Madison House, 1997.

Stoker, Donald. *The Grand Design: Strategy and the U.S. Civil War.* New York: Oxford University Press, 2010.

Stone, James Madison. *Personal Recollections of the Civil War.* Boston: N.p., 1918.

Stout, Harry S. *Upon the Altar of the Nation: A Moral History of the Civil War.* New York: Viking, 2006.

Stutler, Boyd B. *West Virginia in the Civil War.* Charleston, W.V.: Education Foundation, 1966.

Sutherland, Daniel E. "Abraham Lincoln, John Pope, and the Origins of Total War." *Journal of Military History* 56 (October 1992): 567–86.

———, ed. *Guerrillas, Unionists and Violence on the Confederate Homefront.* Fayetteville: University of Arkansas Press, 1999.

———. *A Savage Conflict: The Decisive Role of Guerrillas in the American Civil War.* Chapel Hill: University of North Carolina Press, 2009.

———. *Seasons of War: The Ordeal of a Confederate Community, 1861–1865.* New York: Free Press, 1995.

Swanberg, W. A. *Sickles the Incredible: A Biography of Daniel Edgar Sickles.* New York: Scribner, 1956.

Swiger, Elizabeth Davis, ed. *Civil War Letters and Diary of Joshua Winters: A Private in the Union Army Company G, First Western Virginia Volunteer Infantry.* Parsons, W.V.: McClain, 1991.

Sypher, J. R. *History of the Pennsylvania Reserve Corps.* Lancaster, Penn.: Elias Barr, 1865.

Taaffe, Stephen R. *Commanding the Army of the Potomac.* Lawrence: University Press of Kansas, 2006.

Tap, Bruce. *Over Lincoln's Shoulder: The Committee on the Conduct of the War.* Lawrence: University Press of Kansas, 1998.

Taylor, Brian D. *Politics and the Russian Army: Civil-Military Relations,*

*1689–2000.* New York: Cambridge University Press, 2003.

Taylor, Paul. *Glory Was Not Their Companion: The Twenty-Sixth New York Volunteer Infantry in the Civil War.* Jefferson, N.C.: McFarland, 2005.

Thackery, David T. *A Light and Uncertain Hold: A History of the Sixty-Sixth Ohio Volunteer Infantry.* Kent, Ohio: Kent State University Press, 1999.

Thomas, Benjamin P., and Harold M. Hyman. *Stanton: The Life and Times of Lincoln's Secretary of War.* New York: Knopf, 1962.

Thomas, Mary W., and Richard A. Sauers, eds. *The Civil War Letters of First Lieutenant James B. Thomas, Adjutant, 107th Pennsylvania Volunteers.* Baltimore: Butternut and Blue, 1995.

Thompson, Jerry. *Civil War to the Bloody End: The Life and Times of Major General Samuel P. Heintzelman.* College Station: Texas A&M University Press, 2006.

Thomson, Orville. *From Philippi to Appomattox: Narratives of the Service of the Seventh Indiana Infantry in the War for the Union.* N.p.: N.p., n.d.

Thomson, Osmund, and William H. Rausch. *History of the "Bucktails," Kane Rifle Regiment of the Pennsylvania Reserve Corps.* Philadelphia: Electric Printing Company, 1906. Reprint ed., Dayton, Ohio: Morningside, 1988.

Thornbrough, Emma Lou. *Indiana in the Civil War Era, 1850–1880.* Indianapolis: Indiana Historical Bureau, 1965.

Throne, Mildred. *Cyrus Clay Carpenter and Iowa Politics, 1854–1898.* Iowa City: State Historical Society of Iowa, 1974.

Tidball, Eugene C. *"No Disgrace to My Country": The Life of John C. Tidball.* Kent, Ohio: Kent State University Press, 2002.

Tobie, Edward P. *History of the First Maine Cavalry, 1861–1865.* Boston: Emery and Hughes, 1887.

Todd, William. *The Seventy-Ninth Highlanders: New York Volunteers in the War of Rebellion, 1861–1865.* Albany: Brandow, Barton, 1886.

Townsend, George Alfred. "Campaigning with General Pope." *Cornhill Magazine,* December 1862, 765–824.

———. *Campaigns of a Non-Combatant.* New York: Blelock and Company, 1866. Reprinted as *Rustics in Rebellion: A Yankee Reporter on the Road to Richmond, 1861–65.* Chapel Hill: University of North Carolina Press, 1950.

Trefousse, Hans L. *Benjamin Franklin Wade: Radical Republican from Ohio.* New York: Twayne, 1963.

———. *Carl Schurz: A Biography.* Knoxville: University of Tennessee Press, 1982.

———. *"First Among Equals": Abraham Lincoln's Reputation during His Administration.* New York: Fordham University Press, 2005.

———. *The Radical Republicans: Lincoln's Vanguard for Racial Justice.* New York: Knopf, 1969.

———. *Thaddeus Stevens: Nineteenth-Century Egalitarian.* Chapel Hill: University of North Carolina Press, 1997.

Tripp, Wendell, ed. *Through "Poverty's Vale": A Hardscrabble Boyhood in Upstate New York, 1832–1862.* Syracuse, N.Y.: Syracuse University Press, 1974.

Truxall, Aida Craig, ed. *"Respects to All": Letters of Two Pennsylvania Boys in the War of the Rebellion.* Pittsburgh: University of Pittsburgh Press, 1962.

Tuck, Stephen. *We Ain't What We Ought to Be: The Black Freedom Struggle from Emancipation to Obama.* Cambridge, Mass.: Belknap Press of Harvard University Press, 2010.

Turner, George Edgar. *Victory Rode the Rails: The Strategic Place of the Railroads in the Civil War.* Indianapolis: Bobbs-Merrill, 1953.

Ural, Susannah J., ed. *Civil War Citizens: Race, Ethnicity, and Identity in America's Bloodiest Conflict.* New York: New York University Press, 2010.

Urban, John W. *Battle Field and Prison Pen; or, Through the War, and Thrice a Prisoner in Rebel Dungeons.* Philadelphia: Hubbard Brothers, 1882.

———. *My Experience Mid Shot and Shell and in Rebel Den: A Graphic Recital of Personal Experiences Throughout the Entire Civil War.* Lancaster: N.p., 1882.

Valuska, David L., and Christian B. Keller, eds. *Damn Dutch: Pennsylvania Germans at Gettysburg.* Mechanicsburg, Penn.: Stackpole, 2004.

Viola, Herman J., ed. *The Memoirs of Charles Henry Veil: A Soldier's Recollections of the Civil War and the Arizona Territory.* New York: Orion Books, 1993.

Walcutt, Charles F. *History of the Twenty-First Regiment Massachusetts Volunteers.* Boston: Houghton, Mifflin, 1882.

Walker, Francis A. *History of the Second Army Corps in the Army of the Potomac.* New York: C. Scribner's Sons, 1886.

Wallace, Frederic A. *Framingham's Civil War Hero: The Life of General George H. Gordon.* Charleston: History Press, 2011.

Wallace, Frederick S. *The Sixty-First Ohio Volunteers, 1861–1865.* Marysville, Ohio: T. Mullen, 1902.

Wallenstein, Peter, and Bertram Wyatt-Brown, eds. *Virginia's Civil War.* Charlottesville: University of Virginia Press, 2005.

Ward, Andrew. *The Slaves' War: The Civil War in the Words of Former Slaves.* Boston: Houghton Mifflin, 2008.

Warden, Robert R. *An Account of the Private and Public Services of Salmon Portland Chase.* Cincinnati: Wilstak, Baldwin, 1874.

Warner, Ezra J. *Generals in Blue: Lives of the Union Commanders.* Baton Rouge: Louisiana State University Press, 1964.

*War of the Rebellion: A Compilation of the Official Records of the Union and Confederate Armies.* 70 vols. in 128 serials. Washington, D.C.: Government Printing Office, 1880–1901.

Waugh, Joan, and Gary W. Gallagher, eds. *Wars within a War: Controversy and Conflict over the American Civil War.* Chapel Hill: University of North Carolina Press, 2009.

Wayland, Francis F., ed. "Fremont's Pursuit of Jackson in the Shenandoah Valley: The Journal of Colonel Albert Tracy, March–July 1862." *Virginia Magazine of History and Biography* 70, no. 2 (April 1962): 165–94.

———. "Fremont's Pursuit of Jackson in the Shenandoah Valley . . . (cont.)." *Virginia Magazine of History and Biography* 70, no. 3 (July 1962): 332–54.

Weber, Jennifer L. *Copperheads: The Rise and Fall of Lincoln's Opponents in the North.* New York: Oxford University Press, 2006.

Weigley, Russell F. *A Great Civil War: A Military and Political History.* Bloomington: Indiana University Press, 2000.

———. *Towards an American Army: American Military Thought from Washington to Marshall.* New York: Columbia University Press, 1962.

Weisberger, Bernard A. *Reporters for the Union.* Westport, Conn.: Greenwood Press, 1977.

Weld, Stephen Minot. *War Diary and Letters of Stephen Minot Weld, 1861–1865.* Boston: Massachusetts Historical Society, 1979.

Welles, Gideon. *Diary of Gideon Welles.* 3 vols. Boston: Houghton Mifflin, 1911.

Welton, J. Michael, ed. *"My Heart Is So Rebellious": The Caldwell Letters, 1861–1865.* Warrenton, Va.: Bell Gale Chevigny, 1991.

Werstein, Irving. *Kearny, the Magnificent: The Story of General Philip Kearny, 1815–1862.* New York: John Day, 1962.

Wert, Jeffrey D. *The Sword of Lincoln: The Army of the Potomac.* New York: Simon and Schuster, 2005.

White, Russell D., ed. *The Civil War Diary of Wyman S. White, First Sergeant of Company "F" of the 2nd United States Sharpshooters.* Hemet, Cal.: Russell D. White, 1979.

Whitehouse, Hugh L., ed. *Letters from the Iron Brigade: George Washington Partridge, Jr., 1839–1863, Civil War Letters to His Sister.* Indianapolis: Guild Press of Indiana, 1994.

Wiley, Bell Irvin. *The Life of Billy Yank: The Common Soldier of the Union.* Baton Rouge: Louisiana State University Press, 1952.

Wilkes, George. *McClellan: From Ball's Bluff to Antietam.* New York: Sinclair Tousey, 1863.

Williams, T. Harry. "The Attack upon West Point during the Civil War." *Mississippi Valley Historical Review* 25 (1939): 491–504.

———. *Hayes of the Twenty-Third: The Civil War Volunteer Officer.* New York: Knopf, 1965.

———. *Lincoln and His Generals.* New York: Knopf, 1952.

———. *Lincoln and the Radicals.* Madison: University of Wisconsin Press, 1960.

Wilson, Lawrence. *Itinerary of the Seventh Ohio Volunteer Infantry, 1861–1864: With Roster, Portraits, and Biographies.* New York: Neale, 1907.

Wingerd, Mary L. *North Country: The Making of Minnesota.* Minneapolis: University of Minnesota Press, 2010.

Witt, John Fabian. *Lincoln's Code: The Laws of War in American History.* New York: Free Press, 2013.

Woodbury, Augustus. *Major General Ambrose E. Burnside and the Ninth Army Corps.* Providence: Sidney S. Rider and Brother, 1867.

Woodward, Colin Edward. *Marching Masters: Slavery, Race, and the Confederate Army during the Civil War.* Charlottesville: University of Virginia Press, 2014.

Woodward, E[van] M[orrison]. *History of the Third Pennsylvania Reserve: Being a Complete Record of the Regiment.* Trenton: MacCrellish and Quigley, 1883.

———. *Our Campaigns: The Second Regiment Pennsylvania Reserve Volunteers.* Shippensburg, Penn.: Burd Street Press, 1995.

Woodworth, Steven E., ed. *Davis and Lee at War.* Lawrence: University Press of Kansas, 1995.

———. *Nothing but Victory: The Army of the Tennessee, 1861–1865.* New York: Knopf, 2005.

Work, David. *Lincoln's Political Generals.* Urbana: University of Illinois Press, 2009.

Yates, Richard, and Catherine Yates Pickering. *Richard Yates: Civil War Governor.* Ed. John K. Krenkel. Danville, Ill.: Interstate, 1966.

Zon, Calvin Goddard, ed. *The Good Fight That Didn't End: Henry P. Goddard's Account of Civil War and Peace.* Columbia: University of South Carolina Press, 2008.

# Index

## Recent Books in the Series
## A Nation Divided: Studies in the Civil War Era

*Civil War Petersburg: Confederate City in the Crucible of War*
**A. Wilson Greene**

*Take Care of the Living: Reconstructing Confederate Veteran Families in Virginia*
**Jeffrey W. McClurken**

*The Big House after Slavery: Virginia Plantation Families and Their Postbellum Experiment*
**Amy Feely Morsman**

*The Enemy Within: Fears of Corruption in the Civil War North*
**Michael Thomas Smith**

*Civil War Talks: Further Reminiscences of George S. Bernard and His Fellow Veterans*
**Hampton Newsome, John Horn, and John G. Selby, editors**

*Worth a Dozen Men: Women and Nursing in the Civil War South*
**Libra R. Hilde**

*Reconstructing the Campus: Higher Education and the American Civil War*
**Michael David Cohen**

*Frederick Douglass: A Life in Documents*
**L. Diane Barnes, editor**

*Confederate Visions: Nationalism, Symbolism, and the Imagined South in the Civil War*
**Ian Binnington**

*Marching Masters: Slavery, Race, and the Confederate Army during the Civil War*
**Colin Edward Woodward**

*Slavery and War in the Americas: Race, Citizenship, and State Building in the United States and Brazil, 1861–1870*
**Vitor Izecksohn**

*Lincoln's Dilemma: Blair, Sumner, and the Republican Struggle over Racism and Equality in the Civil War Era*
**Paul D. Escott**

*Intimate Reconstructions: Children in Postemancipation Virginia*
**Catherine A. Jones**

*Daydreams and Nightmares: A Virginia Family Faces Secession and War*
**Brent Tarter**

*Gold and Freedom: The Political Economy of Reconstruction*
**Nicolas Barreyre (translated by Arthur Goldhammer)**

*"War upon Our Border": Two Ohio Valley Communities Navigate the Civil War*
**Stephen I. Rockenbach**

*The First Republican Army: The Army of Virginia and the Radicalization of the Civil War*
**John H. Matsui**